FIND ME AT THE JAFFA GATE

Micaela Sahhar is an Australian–Palestinian writer and educator living on unceded Wurundjeri Country. Her essays, poetry and commentary have appeared in *Cordite*, *Meanjin*, *Overland*, *Rabbit* and *Sydney Review of Books*, among others. She is a Wheeler Centre Next Chapter Fellow (2021), a grant recipient from the Neilma Sidney Literary Travel Fund (2022), which enabled a trip to Jerusalem in the latter stages of writing this book, and was commended for the Peter Blazey Fellowship (2024).

'Micaela Sahhar's *Find Me at the Jaffa Gate* is one of the most inventive, thought-provoking and captivating chronicles of Palestinian diasporic life I've had the pleasure of reading. It is a memoir written by a poet, poetry written by a novelist, literature written by an academic – it is all these things at once, insisting with a gentle yet unwavering confidence in the power of its unique, brilliantly evocative and genre-defying voice. Sahhar's love for her family, homeland, the details and intimacies of everyday life; for language, history, archives, photographs and the treasured ephemera of a life in diaspora, shine through every line. The result is a book in which every word is deliberate, each line commands attention, each chapter is a world within a world.'

Randa Abdel-Fattah, academic and writer, author of *11 Words for Love*

'Micaela Sahhar's family history has everything that makes any Palestinian family history worth telling and reading about. On the one hand, a rich culture that ranges from distinctive culinary practices to a distinctive sense of humour, and on the other hand, a tragic settler-colonial history of dispossession and oppression leading to a transnational diasporic existence, and that makes for a characteristic sense of space and place. But this is not any book about Palestine. Sahhar is a superior storyteller with a knack for highlighting evocative details. Storytelling, like any craft, embodies in different degrees the labour of the many people who have told stories about one's subject matter in the past. The more a writer is well-read the more this shows in the historical density and the social complexity of their storytelling. Sahhar's book is definitely dense and socially complex in this way. This could make for 'heavy' reading if it wasn't for Sahhar's superior writing skills. Indeed, I would say that more than anything else, this is a book for people who enjoy good writing, regardless of what the story is about. But of course, it matters what this story is about. This is a book about Palestine and Palestinians, and in the way the book is grounded in both the Palestinian tragedy and the Palestinian unlimited capacity to affirm life, the spirit of anti-colonial resistance animates every one of its pages. Sahhar finishes the book saying that like Mahmoud Darwish's father she hopes that one day she will be able to go to Palestine, to the streets where her family originates from, and shout *I am I. And I am here*. But in a way, by writing this book, she already does that, if not from Palestine at least from the position she occupies within the transnational space of western colonialism.'

Ghassan Hage, professor of anthropology at the University of Melbourne and author of *The Diasporic Condition: Ethnographic Explorations of the Lebanese in the World*

'*Find Me at the Jaffa Gate* is an aching and tender study of diaspora, grief, memory and history. Sahhar has a masterful voice, playing subtly with tense and form to give agency to a beautifully layered narrative, interwoven with fragments, records and intimate moments of lives permanently changed by Nakba. *Find Me at the Jaffa Gate* tells an unmissable story of Palestinian survival and resistance across space and time.'

Evelyn Araluen, Bundjalung poet and author of *Dropbear*

'Sahhar chronicles the essential truths of Palestine with intricacy and finesse and in doing so, has crafted a mighty text that demands unbroken attention. *Find Me at the Jaffa Gate* is a book that will be read, re-read, dog-eared, underlined and recited.'

Hasib Hourani, author of *rock flight*

'*Find Me at the Jaffa Gate* opens with a recollection of the five-year-old Micaela bobbing off to preparatory school with pigtails, glasses and missing teeth. As she enters the classroom, her sense of self is shattered – in a nation that is home but not home, when a teacher butchers her family name and is visibly appalled when told the name is Palestinian. As the child of diaspora, born on the unceded lands of Australia, Micaela is ever conscious of the tension between being in exile on homelands now occupied; and living, working and writing on the occupied lands of Naarm – in colonial Australia – a site of invasion, and genocide.

Find Me at the Jaffa Gate writes of and to dispossession, displacement, trauma, loss, resilience and is testimony to the power of intergenerational story and memory that survives, and lives on so that all those who remain, and their children and children's children remember. In this polyphonic narrative, we hear many voices – some still living, others passed, now scattered across nations and continents, yet still connected through home – Palestine.'

Jeanine Leane, Wiradjuri writer, critic, poet and author of *Gawimarra: Gathering*

'At a time when Israel is literally trying to wipe Palestinians off the map, this book lands with a powerful thud of fury, beauty and resistance. Weaving personal stories with history in all its unvarnished details, Micaela Sahhar delivers a deeply affecting story that articulates one of the great outrages of our time.'

Antony Loewenstein, independent journalist, film-maker and author of *The Palestine Laboratory*

FIND ME AT THE JAFFA GATE

An encyclopaedia of a Palestinian family

MICAELA SAHHAR

NEWSOUTH

UNSW Press acknowledges the Bedegal people, the Traditional Owners of the unceded territory on which the Randwick and Kensington campuses of UNSW are situated, and recognises the continuing connection to Country and culture. We pay our respects to Bedegal Elders past and present.

A NewSouth book

Published by
NewSouth Publishing
University of New South Wales Press Ltd
University of New South Wales
Sydney NSW 2052
AUSTRALIA
https://unsw.press/

Our authorised representative in the EU for product safety is Mare Nostrum Group B.V., Doelen 72, 4831 GR Breda, The Netherlands (gpsr@mare-nostrum.co.uk).

First published 2025
Reprinted with updates 2026

A catalogue record for this book is available from the National Library of Australia

ISBN 9781761170287 (paperback)
9781761179181 (ebook)
9781761178313 (ePDF)

Internal design Josephine Pajor-Markus
Cover design Mika Tabata
Cover image Detail from a stereoview titled, 'The Jaffa Gate – from outside – Jerusalem, Palestine'. Underwood & Underwood, c. 1899.
Printer Griffin Press

This book is printed on paper using fibre supplied from plantation or sustainably managed forests.

For Palestinians everywhere.
Especially my dear Dad.

CONTENTS

UNDER PIGEONS: A MELBOURNE PROLOGUE

There had already been enough trouble from those pigeons. Andoni hoists himself up through the manhole when no-one can bear the sound of scaly clawed feet scratching about in the roof any longer, night on night, disturbing their sleep. From the loungeroom beneath, Joey and Irene and Sylvie and Vera are shouting out instructions as they hear their brother and the pigeon circling one another in the dark above. They can hear Andoni's careful tread punctuated by the erratic taps of a hunted pigeon. Then everything is still. In the roof above, Andoni launches himself at the intruder, leaving the safety of the support beams and lunging across the tongue-and-groove ceiling boards to capture the bird when the ceiling gives way. His legs break through the ceiling and dangle uselessly into the room. Gripping the pigeon, his body is stuck between the joists. The littlest children nearly die of laughter as if some divine intercession has presented them with this spectacular farce of brother legs and pigeon legs suspended in the air. And when Andoni shouts out instructions it only has the effect of renewing their peals of uproarious laughter. Finally Juju and their mother Ellen regain sufficient composure to move a table and then a chair on top of the table to relieve the worn-out boards in the ceiling from the weight of a man and a pigeon. Such was the great gaping hole it left in the middle of the lounge room that many more pigeons followed the first, to lodge in the roof, before Pa assembled the materials to patch up the son-shaped chasm above them.

Although everyone knows who is responsible for the loft massacre, there is nothing to be done. Dad can't quite explain how it happened, but the survivors formed some unspoken consensus and migrated overnight into the kitchen roof.

It was fortunate that the roof was slanted and that the kitchen was otherwise detached from the old weatherboard house that stood on a quiet corner of 1950s Newport, until it was replaced by a brick one some fifteen years later. Though it was under a deep but silent sufferance that Ellen watched the survivors take up residence in the space between the rafters.

'What sort of pigeons did you have, Dad?' I ask him on the phone. Dad's voice is as iridescent now as if he were still young Joey answering this question: he describes the Blue Bars with their long beaks and the three sergeant stripes on their wings, the red and white Feather Foots with their comical legs, and the short-beaked Tumblers.

In the roof of the external kitchen, the pigeons resumed their lives, as if Mr Marsters' cats were not to blame for the slaughter of their brethren. An uneasy truce between Joey's flock and the usual kitchen inhabitants was forged: Taata shelling broad beans or Anasta moulding ma'amoul at Greek Easter or Ellen blanching the smallest, most delicate grape leaves for stuffing. In fruiting season such tensions intensified. Ellen ran Joey ragged, sending him back and forth between the granary on Melbourne Road near the railway line, and the kitchen at Mirls Street, to keep his pigeons in wheat. This they shared with Ellen's chooks, whose diets also included pollard and food scraps (though what scraps there were to be had after thirteen children and five adults had eaten must have been paltry indeed).

Along the fence of lilacs and among the wild mint, the chooks ran free range, and in the back right-hand corner my resourceful Pa constructed a second chicken-wire framed coop with extra reinforcements. Joey and Irene, Ellen's youngest, were charged with collecting the eggs and taking carefully wrapped parcels to customers in Anderson Street and Wood Street and Ford Street for six shillings and sixpence a dozen, which their mother recorded neatly into a ledger of accounts against the outgoing expenses. Though Dad loved his pigeons, there was no room in this house for the middle-class tenderness of naming. When Ellen bought new laying hens, her supplier would throw in a few three-day-old male chicks as a bonus for eventual boiling when they grew a bit larger. There was no lifetime of feed for a chicken that couldn't lay.

It was another stroke of luck that Pa and Ellen's first-born son was already a medical student when the white chooks Ellen bought in Yarraville developed abscesses on their feet. Andoni drained each growth over the gully trap, Irene the nurse assisting, and injected the birds with out-of-date penicillin he somehow got his hands on, wrapping their feet in one-inch-wide gauze bandages. Over the wild mint a week later the bandages came loose. Ellen went out through the back of the house one morning to find the chickens trailing lengths of muddy bandages behind them, a derelict stucco installation transforming a suburban yard in Newport. 'The treatment worked', Dad crows now, pride in his voice for the ingenuity of these people who laboured against the tide.

Ellen had a flair for small business, and she looked on with approval when Joey formed an alliance with a Russian gentleman a few streets over. Each week he would sell him a pair of his loveliest pigeons (though Dad later discovered the man was eating them). It was at her suggestion when the primary school fundraiser rolled around that Joey walked up and down Mirls Street asking for egg donations, which he placed in a container only questionably fit for purpose. He broke a good deal of them on his way home. It was with a certain pride in his acumen that Ellen refused her youngest son's proposition: she could keep all the broken eggs if she replaced them with whole ones.

Tumblers, a young Joey thought, as my dear dad says now, 'were the best sort of pigeon a boy could have'. They would break out of their lines of flight to perform cartwheels in the sky, and their soaring and tumbling lifted a young boy's heart to see it. The Tumbler was the most Palestinian of all the pigeons.

'I suppose', Dad says, 'this was some great evolutionary genius that the Tumbler might be chased by eagles or hawks and yet they would always evade their predator'.

'It's a bit like southpaw for pigeons', I remark. He says they are even more unpredictable than that, and I think he can see the Tumblers whenever we speak of them.

I find it difficult to reconcile these scenes of my grandparents: two small people who shrank as they aged so that reports of a driverless car were legendary on the roads near the Williamstown Gospel Mission on Electra Street. Or of Yousef, more often Joey, a boy with big knees and ears like the *Mad* comic's mascot, who is an old man now, though he has never lost his earnestness nor simple knack for insight. Nor his brother Andoni, nor sisters Juju, Salma, Vera and Irene, all of whom lived with the names of 'here' and 'not there'.

Not one of these loved gentle people, the aunts and uncles and cousins who coloured my childhood, raises in me – nor my memories of Ellen and Pa's last home, so far from the first – any inkling of the horror which 'Palestine' evoked for my preparatory school music teacher. This was the first time, bobbing off in pigtails and round-faced glasses and missing baby teeth to the first days of my schooling, that I learnt of the breach between who my family was and who we were perceived to be.

For our last period, we sat in a circle on the floor in the portable music classroom, a room furnished with drums, triangles, a piano and the ubiquitous Mercator projection on the wall. Our bent knees dripped with sweat in the late February heat. Mrs Collins read our names off the roll, which she kept in an impressively official-looking folder, pausing over my surname, which she butchered as she rolled it around her mouth.

'Where', she asked, 'does a name like that come from?', and like my dad, earnest girl that I was, I took delight in this curiosity and replied with enthusiasm, 'Palestine!'.

Mrs Collins was visibly appalled. She swallowed hard and fixed me in a long stare, and I looked down at her swollen blueish feet in tooled tan-leather sandals, before she finished, 'I would think that is *very unlikely*'.

I was so pained to be called a liar in front of my peers, maligned by a teacher who seemed to know more about me than I did, that I ambushed my father from the back of the car that afternoon.

'Our name's from Palestine, right Dad?' I said, worried, and Dad looked at me in the rear-view mirror of his dark brown Torana and said, 'Of course it is', and Mum said, 'Why do you ask, darl?', and I told them about how Mrs Collins had embarrassed me in front of the class. Mum reflected, 'I suppose you could say Middle Eastern if you wanted to be less confrontational'. And Dad sighed through the windscreen at the idea that saying where you are from should ever be construed by a stranger as confrontational.

Dad doesn't know when the pigeons left, and we talk instead about the fig tree on the back fence. This was a tree of my childhood, and one that Joey and Irene would sit in to overlook the Western Suburban Football League ground behind their block on game day. The street was no stranger to football legends. Once Skinny Martyn even pushed Pa's failing Austin Mini Van to turn over the engine, and Pa instructed everyone to jump in from a running start. Dad says it might even have been the year Skinny won the Syd Barker Best & Fairest medal at the North Melbourne Football Club. In 1957, he was just as nice off the field as he was adjudicated to be on it.

This was a fig that was never planted, but grew from the cut branches Pa tossed down the back of the yard, remnants of the first fig tree that had leant against the internal porch. But this was cleared for a renovation, after everyone but Irene and Joey had moved away – Juju first, then Andoni, Sylvie and Vera – all of them long married.

He didn't live long enough for me to ask, but I like to think my Pa would have admired that second fig tree with its wide low branches, sticky broad leaves and fat ripe fruit, too many to eat. It was this unintended fig that his children swung into, propelling his grandchildren, defying gravity, and growing year on year, without encouragement, to flourish against his boundary fence.

1. ORIGIN

Who has a plot: a rhetorical question. We all have one. Your family is already a story before you are born. Do you ask the question – do you live inside this plot or step outside of it? Is it possible to step out of a plot when you are a plot point arriving?

One day, when I am an unremarkable bald baby and my Pa is a remarkable old bald man, he hands me his greatest love while I am sitting on the shoulders of my father. This is captured in a photograph, you can see how he passes it to me with his eyes and exhorts me to tend it for him in his inevitable absence. My own dear dad, Joey, will help me with this. He has heard each word of my story and told me his own, my life through, and on the phone while I wrote this, and while we searched for the story of a diaspora uniquely our own.

The loss of a homeland is no small thing. It is a yawning chasm and each of us is delivered to its precipice, struggling against the crumbling edge, against being swallowed whole. What does it mean to be exiled and how do we take our revenge? What intimacies lie in these wreckages and may we lay our burdens down? If we were different people, to write down these words might be to leave them behind us. But words are our artifacts, and I am seeding a trail for the journey, home.

We are far from home here. But we are long past started. Already the story-holders are mostly gone; I know their luminous names, but I have known too few of them. I am never so happy as when my young cousin says to me in the saloon bar of the

Stag's Head in Dublin, 'You really do look like Ellen', and it is the second time I am honoured in this way after dear Najla has said the same thing at her home in Phoenix, Arizona ten years earlier. The story-holders are slim as reeds in their childhood, and dark-eyed as adults with small but definite noses and close-lipped smiles, so it is clear to anyone how they were cut from the very same family.

If not knowing is a problem of time and of space then a restitution of sorts is an invitation. That these loved names and the bodies they described might dwell here together on my page. These are the reunions a Palestinian might spend their life dreaming about but never living. Do I believe that words can effect such a meeting?

As I stitch the fragments together, I must try.

Juju asks, 'Whose story are you writing?'. And in truth it is a story that is not mine nor hers; I am searching for the shape of what is *ours*. We are the amber beads of a broken wedding necklace, a diaspora who fight at the precipice and who are lost to our home and if we are not careful, lost twice.

Most of all I must fight against errors, and I will correct them if I can. This was an early lesson in my first published poem, when I swapped one location for another and the aunts called my father, my father called me, his quiet disappointment palpable – wicking up the joy of a first poem published. I see after twenty years that errors are errors and that no story is better than the truth of it. I understand that the truth, then as now, was more beautiful than my error. Why did I make it?

Because truth stabs painfully, glitteringly, a fluid on the surface that forms and re-forms in liquid pools. Sometimes truth is too big to bear; it is happening to us, happening still, happening now, was happening to me and to you before we were born. It is not an explanation, but at least if you cannot understand it, then try to feel it.

In a psychoanalytic sense, I have read that wounds are impossible to heal when the wounds remains unacknowledged. Here they are in plain sight, terrible and ignored. So much psychic wounding, is there room to also be whole?

Except this is not a story about wounds but about the preservation of something all its own. We are not artifacts or fables, not inventions or ideas. We are sumud and survivance and life life life is among us and we are not a duality, a binary, a dichotomy, but a story of our own.

What is the task but to find my way back to the unfragmentation of the world as we knew it; to collect the uncollected, to make the unmade? To refuse victimhood even when annihilation seems to insist on it. To make a thing out of nothing, to make a diaspora into something, real enough to share.

This is a true story though it is madc of things I do not know alongside those I do. It begins with two true words. Poetry is an uncontested word that is true and through which one might feel a truth they do not understand anew. Palestine is a true word too, but it is contested. About both these words, I assure you, I am not in error.

How the light will bend about me I do not know, but I will always try to show you.

2. PATRIARCHS

Take four brothers. Four brothers are a plot. Four brothers make a story that contains three continents and two islands. I must take care not to spill all the brothers at once. The brothers are like a torrent rushing onto the page.

Take four brothers. Three on a document of title. One left (although all dead). Five wives between them.

Four brothers are a riddle. The Salvation Army looks for one in Australia – the children who answer the door are pressed away by the adults. My father is one of those children, and since he remembers, I remember too.

The children never learn the story, but they know there is a story. Take a milk bar, and a missing man – with wine and a small bowl of giardiniera behind the counter that my father remembers was pronounced by his uncle 'garden-era'. The children work there. Recently, Vera tells my father she is still owed two weeks of wages from the milk bar. 'He was a terrible employer', she says. My father remembers a popsicle flavoured with banana and cream. My father remembers the wine (white) and the pickles. My father has no truck with wine, but he is always ready for pickles.

Take a headstone, where we learn who died first, and of dates and ordering. The lawn cemetery knows a good deal, presenting remarkable news in its unremarkable flat rows.

When a woman I never met living dies, my father sings a song I have never heard before or since, driving between the church and the wake down Ferguson Street in Williamstown. The nieces sit in the pews weeping, some in their sixties, some in their seventies, Vera with her short grey hair brushed beautifully, looking from behind like my grandmother, Ellen, looking from the side like a small child, wiping away her tears like she was five only yesterday.

When we arrive at a narrow house, turned on its side to fit on the narrow block, the nephews and nieces are reminded of their uncle's greed. An uncle who has lain in the lawn cemetery now for twenty-five years. There is a daughter my father mistakes for his cousin, twenty years older, and relatives muttering stories, as small as ourselves and as big as our home, by the graveside. And then there is only a narrow house in Williamstown that remains of the love and the grief one person tracks through the lives of others, which is the thing I cannot get out of my mind.

There is something about this narrow house that reminds me of a folk tale. A story of a spinning house that speeds up and slows down but not when you want it to. It is hard to get in or out so of course it is all about timing. What is the story of the spinning house? I don't really know. But I do know the spinning house is an exercise in patience (it's obvious thinking about it now), and patience takes its lessons in Palestine.

Of some other brothers, connected to these ones in ways we cannot quite recall, there was a book my Pa once ordered for viewing, out of the vaults of the State Library. Sometimes we remember the name, recommence the search, to find, again, no trace of it. There is something crucial in that book if we could find it. Something beyond the edge of our living memories but a memory nevertheless. Irene thinks it might have something to say about patriarchs but the size of the P remains a speculative question. We invest our hope in a book, of which there is no trace, that such a book might explain us to ourselves. *My Little House in Kent*. It sounds unlikely, don't you think? Did it explain something about an inheritance, a title deed, Cyprus? Was it the origin story of our name, to replace the one we all half know that I have heard recounted in New Jersey and in Doha and from relatives whose words I have only read but never met in Western Europe? Why do I write about brothers? It is easier to follow their line.

How do you tell a story you are reaching to understand? One word in front of the other. A story is still a story; this will be the story if I cannot find the story I am searching for.

3. AUNTS

My youngest aunt suspects that a Cyrillic name is connected to ours. Maybe a sacked cabinet minister in Russia, or maybe a Nobel Prize winner. It's hard to follow half-trains of thought.

My eldest aunt, Juju, carries a name in her pocket, a name she refuses to remember. A name she has the foresight to remember that she will want to discuss in the course of a day's conversation, before she promptly forgets it again. She is a wise woman who does not hold onto a name of grief; she externalises it – outsourced to this note in her pocket.

Two years ago I heard a story about Alice and her father. I heard it during some dark nights of the soul in Los Angeles, a place that seems like a terminal. In this terminal people with hair plugs and new teeth wait to be discovered and I keep my head down. I buy bottles of water from service stations and pay big bank notes for toast with a slice of smoked salmon. I feel outraged that people here believe they are living the dream. My Uber is plastered with home-made notes that say *close the door quietly*. I am relieved to close the door (quietly) and return to the airport.

Alice is pronounced like Elise. My middle name that wounded my grandmother – 'Why not Ellen?' she asked. I can see her smile and gentle laugh – the hallmark of her waiting when she was too direct for comfort. I am not so precocious that I remember it (I am not some demonic baby invented by Günter Grass) – but I see it, as I paste the fragments I have with the fragments I don't have, recreating this digression which plays out in my mind when I call the bank or the electoral commission and they ask me to state my full name.

Alice – who finished her days in the citrus state of California, who looked like my aunt Vera, one of Ellen's own daughters – is Ellen's sister. A sister who maintained the fiction that Ellen was very tall, though she was shorter than my 5′2″, though she spent the last decades of her life growing smaller. This belief is based on a studio portrait from 1932 – after Fouad was born, but I assume before Ellen married. A portrait that captures in time the first passing out of the family just as the youngest arrives to it. Nine children arranged in order of height, and as it would happen also eldest to youngest.

In Los Angeles I learn more of the sisters and I learn more of Ellen. After 1952 they saw her one more time. Those who are left were children then; some in Damascus still. None in Jerusalem, nor Amman, where they saw out the final bitter years of the 1940s.

It wakes me one morning, how Ellen was so very far from her family. When I asked her about this in 2002, she told me instead about the orientation of Newport in the 1950s, about a cancer she had in her mouth, about my Pa's heart. (Why was it? Too painful. Why was it? You don't get the stories you ask for, just the ones you are given.) Vera drives to Adelaide Airport to collect me when I am there, sometime after the American visit. She says as we wind through the multi-story carpark, 'Mum missed out'. How a seventy-something-year-old woman still feels it keenly. And I think that she too has missed out, in a way I see now, in Adelaide, when her own family remained in Melbourne. In her voice I hear her mother's youth. I hear the missing which

I learnt only recently. A missing I already had a name for but one I now feel. Luminous and terrible:

Nakba.

In 1948, Alice was unmarried and still in Palestine. One evening, bullets tore through their house near the old city walls of Jerusalem. Alice lay with her father Hanna, face-down on the floor. When she slept in this position it must have seemed to her that she had died, or if she had not, that she would die in the night. In the morning, true story, she was born again.

4. FREEMASONS

A photograph I have never seen is of Hanna dressed as a Freemason. He is pictured, apparently, in full regalia. I am told it is somewhere in storage with the son of his youngest daughter, Rose.

As a young woman, it is said that Rose resembled Elizabeth Taylor. Her sister, Najla, has pictures displayed on an untuned piano, some framed and others curling, unframed, on the narrow lid of the spinet. The resemblance is quite striking – though *National Velvet* comes to mind ahead of *Cleopatra*, by which point Rose and Taylor had diverged in the course of their career as doppelgangers.

I speak to Rose once on the phone, I at a Japanese restaurant in New Jersey, she in a home in California. Her voice sounds like my grandmother's. The cousin who places the call, Tony Issa, says I look like my grandmother when I listen to Rose on the phone. Rose asks when I am coming to visit her. I want to go in that instant, but I never do visit.

I am told by Najla that Rose didn't take care of herself. That even at over eighty, this was a young death in a family who felt each aunt might defy their age and carry on indefinitely. Who when Najla, the last sister, died, were astonished by this misfortune (which surely it was, untimely) at ninety-seven.

Yet families who have children seem to prevail. Age-defying, seeding their stories into generations that succeed them. You see, the secret of youth is not among individuals.

Hanna was reportedly an important Jerusalemite Freemason. The youngest, Fouad, might know. Fouad is now eighty-eight (now eighty-nine, now ninety, this book a slow thing to bring heaving into the world), though younger when I met him, once. Fouad has a sense of justice and asks my father why his brother didn't buy Ellen better clothes. In 2015, he tells my father that he was disgusted by a mid-calf dress with brown swirls my grandmother was wearing on her visit, nearly fifty years ago.

Hanna, the Sedo of whom so little was said in Australia, lived with Fouad, I am told, in the time after Palestine, and lived until relatively recently compared to the Tetas, or Taata Barbara's husband, Andoni, who had died long before the end of the Mandate. But though a headstone would have more to say, where it is placed is now impossible to discover.

Fouad appreciates a Steinway piano – he has a teak-coloured grand in the front room of a house positioned on the edge of a golf course in Santa Barbara. When I visit him I play the opening bars of Grieg's windy disquieting concerto and he shoots like a bullet down the hall. His daughter asks me what my secret is to make her father move like that, in a way she hasn't seen in many years.

Hanna lives with Fouad for a long time, between Palestine and the end of his life. There is a Christmas picture, from the 1970s I suppose, with Hanna among George's family, and I hear later he lived with them also, passing between sons and states. At this time he may have been living with Ellen's gentle brother George, or perhaps he was just visiting when this Christmas portrait was taken. Photographs give a kind of permanence to things that may not have been (permanent).

Here is the one thing I knew about Hanna from Australia:

that my grandmother was not a violent woman. That nothing was ever said about her father excepting one time. On one single occasion my Pa made a comment about his father-in-law to his wife. The children do not recall what it was. What the children recall is this – that the remark was made in the kitchen. That the remark was made while Ellen and Pa chopped ingredients finely for tabbouleh. Then, like magic, the knife in my grandmother's hand left its task and was hurled in the direction of Pa. The story does not recall if he ducked or how accurate she was as a shot.

How does a man who lives with his son behind a golf course in Santa Barbara head up the Freemasons in Jerusalem once? When a man is the image of his country, I guess.

When Hanna dies there is an obituary in a local American paper which gives you the sense that somewhere he had once been a someone, and that even in his obscurity on Turtle Island, he was deserving of a column to mark his passing.

5. PALESTINE RESTAURANTS

My father tells me that Hanna ran a café in Bethlehem, and later a restaurant in Jerusalem. The fact of his restaurant is preserved in contemporary newspapers. But Hanna did not serve the food he liked to eat. Hanna liked burnt food and conspired to burn the food he ate – while his wife Ajia was cooking he turned up the gas when she wasn't looking.

My eldest aunt, Juju, thinks she remembers the restaurant – upstairs in the Old City of Jerusalem near the Jaffa Gate, where the clock tower had already been dismantled but where a crush of little tourist offices had stood and still did – a beautiful airy room with full-length windows and a breeze. She does not remember the food. Just the afternoon between meal services when her sedo was tired and he let her climb on him and play with his hair. She thinks she must have gone there many times, but her memories have flattened out into just this one.

The Palestine Restaurants are an initiative of the British Mandate. March 9, 1944, an advertisement in *The Palestine Post*: *Opening Today!* There are two restaurants under this banner – Sahhar's Central Café (Hanna) and another, Students Mensa on Mordechai Ben Hillel Street. There is a formal opening at both venues and it is much anticipated.

A clipping from December 16, 1943, reports delays: *HOPE DEFERRED – what's happening to the promised 'Palestine Restaurants'? The enticing preliminary publicity whetted the appetite of diners – but only to be disappointed at least for some time.*

Here is the concept as reported on October 22, 1943: *Shilling Restaurants for Palestine to be run on cafeteria principle*, first Jerusalem, then all over the country (if successful).

And again on November 10: *the committee appointed to advise the Food Controller on the Restaurants consists of* [list of names].

Jerusalemite social historian, George Hintlian, recalls that Hanna's restaurant, which he confirms was situated above the Jaffa Gate, was called Abou Petro Restaurant. Ellen's eldest brother is after all Peter, and his eldest Hanna, as is intergenerationally correct between men, so this is what the Palestinians must call it, though it may not have been the name on the awning. Hintlian does not describe this restaurant as one known for excellent hummus or a good kebab. But he offers the following details:

> It was also known as utility for the British during the war, subsidized meals for the public (meat x rice) for 7.5 Kirsh. Abou Petro was described as a short, fat, mustached person with Chinese eyes. He had a garden where you could have Nargileh and a space for 100 persons ('An attempt to reconstruct the pre-48 Arab commercial center of Jerusalem', 2004, p. 28).

The photos I have of Hanna do not confirm this account of his eyes, but this is the most complete account I will likely obtain of his restaurant. And I am pleased that though he was long gone from Jerusalem and perhaps also long dead, the old Jerusalemites who knew Hanna as children remembered these details for Hintlian's oral history. And perhaps middle-aged men are always oddly described as they are dredged up from the memories of children, especially children who grew old in Jerusalem and saw more than most do in a lifetime.

I have previously tried to learn more of the brief Mandate enterprise that Hanna's restaurant took part in. For example, who is the Food Controller? From *Men of Capital*:

> The Conservation of Resources and Provision of Essential Needs section was the largest and included the food controller. Geoffrey Walsh, formerly the economic advisor, took on the new position and replaced Heron at the helm of austerity management. With its headquarters in Jerusalem and offices in each of Palestine's six districts, Food Control was an unwieldy venture ... (Seikaly, 2015, p. 86).

The Palestine Restaurants follow the modern science of nutrition. The League of Nations sets a base requirement for calculating calorific intake, and sets also a reduced Palestinian level. It will not be the last time that external parties impose diets on Palestinians.

In footnote 14, Seikaly gives a crucial biographic detail of the Food Controller, Geoffrey Walsh: *killed in the Irgun bombing of the King David Hotel.*

The audacious experiment of the Palestine Restaurants is dogged (July 19, 1945): *Government is to stop financing Palestine Restaurants. Arrangements are being made for the liquidation of accounts with existing establishments.* This is the last entry I have; *The Palestine Post* seems to lose interest in a scheme that once enticed them. Between the cracks of the pages I attribute the policy change to a failing Mandate, which slips to its ignominious end after the Second World War.

It will be twelve more months before Walsh is murdered on July 22, 1946, at the hands of the *Irgun*.

The superlative Arab cultural idiom is hospitality. I read that the great Khalil Sakakini is captured because his guest insists on the preparation of kosher food. This will always be linked in my mind to the gloss Coleridge will eventually write to accompany *The Rime of the Ancient Mariner*. At line 79: *The ancient Mariner inhospitably killeth the pious bird of good omen*. Sakakini's capture is not materially related to his death, though it is the origin of his exile from Jerusalem.

6. BETHLEHEM

The Palestine Restaurants teach us that it is not later than 1943 when Hanna returns to Jerusalem. His children, all nine, are born in Bethlehem, where he has a café somewhere near the Church of the Nativity. His daughter, Najla, entreats me to visit it, and my aunt Juju also. But I cannot reconcile their directions with the Bethlehem I find in the twenty-first century. And it is left only for me to say, 'I will visit it', and to say not a word about what I find when I get there: the café disappeared, perhaps beneath the new Bethlehem Peace Centre, diagonal to the famously low entrance of the church that dominates the square.

There are two Palestinian staff who work where I'm staying, and they conspire to find my Jerusalemite relatives, a gift to this diasporic Palestinian woman coming home to no fanfare. The gardener also translates the news for me over coffee each morning. It is 2015 and there is speculation in English about a third intifada. The actual news is worse than what makes the English news according to Sami. One morning, for instance, he tells me that a refugee camp in Jerusalem, Shuafat – also excised from Jerusalem, much like the peculiar legal fiction Australia pursued in its own Migration Act – has been sealed up in an act of collective punishment. It is several days later that the receptionist comes into the library where I am working and says there's a man on the phone for me, handing me also a carefully transcribed number. This is the first Sahhar I will meet whose family remained, despite Nakba.

I walk past the security guards at the District Court on Salah Ad-Din Street, and turn onto Al-Zahra Street at the WF Albright Institute of Archaeological Research. Here, I will meet my cousin, and see for the first and only time a once well-known bookshop (now closed) that my cousin's father opened, named simply after the presence of our family in Jerusalem, Maktub Sahhar. My cousin closes his shop for the day and we have warm falafel sandwiches for breakfast. And he is proud that his number plates will give us no trouble, driving to Bethlehem. He confirms I have remembered my passport.

On the road I think of a short film made by a friend that documents the drive through the West Bank on Palestinian roads. Hadeel's film is wordless but for a caption, used twice. As she weaves through the hills, lingering on the slant of the light and on olive groves, a dog enters the scene: kalb! (flashes up on the screen). And then a checkpoint does (kalb, again).

My cousin parks a long way from the main square and as we walk through the radial streets of Bethlehem I am reminded of the streets that slope down towards the campo in Siena, fanned out in nine sections to represent the Noveschi, who governed there in the late thirteenth to mid-fourteenth century. We are not sure what we are looking for. I have come recently from Najla's house in Arizona where she has dusky purple-red rockeries in both her front and back gardens. We are searching for Hanna's café on Najla's instructions (she has given me two), and her childhood home. 'You can see the café from the Church of the Nativity', she assures me, 'and from there take a downward slope to the house', marked out (she insists on its permanence) by a fruit-laden mulberry tree (but we don't see any).

We make enquiries at each of the cafés from which the Church of the Nativity can be seen. I am told that even after

Hanna returned to Jerusalem a photo of him remained on the wall of his café, and it makes Najla smile to think of her father still remembered there in the place she was born, in the place they are from. We buy many little coffees (ahweh in finjans), speaking with each proprietor as we go. I say 'mazboot', just the right amount of sugar. I say 'mazboot', hoping for just the right amount of information. At the fifth tiny cup, my hand grows less steady, the caffeine and sugar a gauge of the dwindling possibilities, and looming probability that there is no-one now left who knew Hanna.

We walk along Star Street where they still carve nativities, and I regret not buying a donkey, but the carvers are reluctant to part with a single piece: 'Why not a set?' they ask, kindly. We visit the church, bowing our heads, a gesture of humility though I think of the six tiny sisters hardly grazing five feet. I am awed by the worn stone steps at each door as we walk through walls between the Orthodox, Armenian and Catholic sections. The Catholics have a courtyard with carefully pruned squares of green and citrus trees, an enclosed but airy relief, as it must have been for the men who endured the Siege of the Church of the Nativity.

Our pupils dilate and it is then, in the light again, that I see a row of old shops. Furthest from the church is a man selling found objects from old Palestine (dreams). He consults with a man in the business next door, and with the help of his assistant they locate a nearby street vendor. In his eighties at least, this old man recounts an animated story to my cousin and me and the Bethlehemite salesmen. He remembers Hanna; he widens his eyes at me and I hold each gesture close.

The street vendor bows and smiles with all his gums and then his story is over. The antique dealer says, 'But your family is from Jerusalem, how long were they here, a hundred years?'. Then the winding shot, 'What are you doing here anyway? Chasing dreams'. I am ashamed to say my eyes fill with tears. He pulls out a drawer from beneath the counter of pendants, and I choose two small Jerusalem crosses, which since that day are at my neck always, and a medallion of Mary, which I wrap in tissue paper and post to Najla in Arizona.

About a year later Hadeel is here in winter. We agree that in Bethlehem you have to find your own way, and she debunks the genius of the walking through walls thesis. 'It's just another example of racist binaries that imply the culture is all on their side', she says, huddled under the bedclothes as she balances the phone. Hadeel says the maps are technical drawings that capture a definitive colonial arrogance. Maps, we agree, open out a chasm between the documentation and reality of Palestine.

We meet my cousin's neighbour on the side of the road between Bethlehem and Jerusalem and drive him back to the Damascus Gate, where he has some business to attend. My cousin boasts about my doctorate; his neighbour states that even after great separation this news is consistent with what he knows of the family. This familial knowledge is common among Palestinians, the old families still know what they know.

But I am delighted when it happens, just once, in an un-air-conditioned room in a humid Melbourne September. I am sitting in a writing workshop where we experiment with one provocation then another, and we read out the snippets and we sweat until our bare thighs stick to the old vinyl chairs. And another student asks me if I am related to the Sahhars of Willie High. She says she grew up hearing about each and every one of them from her mother. 'All brilliant', her mother has taught her. My dad beams with awkward pride when I tell him this.

7. ABANDONED

We are walking at night between the King David Hotel and Qatamon when it so happens that stacked on a low stone wall we find a few discarded volumes of a Hebrew encyclopaedia. I am with my lover, if I'm honest, although that story is brief and I like to think unimportant (though at the time my mother is horrified, forbidding too late my own little *West Side Story*). It spans hardly the stretch of a hand, from a Jerusalem October to the twelfth stroke of the next new year, in Puerta del Sol, Madrid. I remember missing for a long time the way that love felt, walking Jerusalem that unseasonably warm autumn, returning under the perfume of jasmine to the opening line of *Eureka Street*, Robert McLiam Wilson's masterpiece: *All stories are love stories.* It was surprising to find then that the inky weighted text of the typewriter which replicates this line in the Northern Ireland screen adaptation, and which I watched and rewatched countless times on a VHS tape sixteen years earlier, should have stamped itself into the blueprint of my soul.

Of the encyclopaedias there is an index and a few other volumes, I do not think the complete set. They are dated 1963. My companion asks if I would like him to read me an entry (and he will translate one important thing before we're done) but I don't even know what to ask for, from this fragmentary time capsule of when Jordan held the West Bank and Egypt Gaza. What does a Hebrew encyclopaedia have to say, for instance, on the subject of what they maintain is a divided Jerusalem at that time? But their perspective is no secret now, and the nature of good things turned bad was never my question.

We leave the encyclopaedias stacked up again on the low stone wall, where for all I know they might be stacked still.

It is this night I think of three years later when I arrive in Jerusalem a second time to find, around bedtime, I am locked out of the imposing doors of my institution. I circle around the front and the back and ring all the bells fruitlessly, before leaving the premises and pacing the Nablus Road and Salah Ad-Din Street, wondering where I will go for the night. I feel at once quiet and alarmed – it is hard to explain it – walking the streets of my Pa and of Ellen, my mind straying over the roof-tops and as the crow flies to our own dear home in the Occupied West of this city, where I imagine these dear dead souls receiving me.

There is nothing to do but return to the grand old Jerusalem Hotel, where I have taken dinner and where, though closing, they admit me, bemused, and offer a complimentary drink to the weary traveller. Tired though I am I notice the raised eyebrows between them, the receptionist and the night porter, when I ask for a gin. But consummately gracious, they present it so very elegantly on an evening tray with juice and some pretzels. And I am never before or after so pleased to see the small travel toothbrush in the bathroom. I sit at a desk and write on the hotel notepaper. Then I carefully take off all my clothes, hanging them on the railing, before I conceal my entire body under the sheets because even in winter I fear the mosquitos, leaving only a small tunnel to breathe through. (I do not quickly forget the steroids in Damascus and the week of prescription sunglasses which hardly fit over the swollen bridge of my bitten nose.)

In the morning I am ushered into a basement room with a window close to the ceiling for breakfast and my own pot of coffee. I have seen this room one other time, I am certain, in a Palestinian film where two men, drinking heavily, vie for a woman's attention.

When I return to the institute all the doors are wide open. The Palestinian staff are furious with me for vanishing and we have an argument about the dysfunctional lock on the door and they make me practise the use of it. And I think of them as if of my family, at once enraged and relieved to see me again, these two self-appointed guardians of a returning Palestinian.

It is difficult to discover the chief work of the institute, itself a Mandate relic. The library has a staggering collection of diverse texts (catalogued), and rooms of documents that though long held remain uncatalogued. The day before, at the border, a young guard who spends four hours interrogating me keeps asking, 'Could anyone stay there?', when I give her my anticipated address in Jerusalem. 'Any scholar', I say.

I am startled by her insistence, even as she polices my entrance with a remarkable stamina to harangue until I misspell my father's full name, dehydrated and exhausted. She, above all, must never be forbidden an entry she has set her mind to. What can she do but punish me for it.

8. JERUSALEM RAILWAY STATION

Maybe you know the High Line Park in New York, its stilted relief from dense city blocks that make *metropolis* really mean something. Most beautiful I think is where the tracks have been preserved, and vegetation grows through with a haphazard look that alleviates if only briefly the looming claustrophobia I find unavoidable in that city. I ask because I do not think you will know the Train Track Park, built around the same time, in Jerusalem. It is opened in sections over several years, wooden walkways fitted into the rail irons that once ran from Jerusalem to Jaffa (a train to the sea!), following the ancient donkey's trail, opened in the late nineteenth century.

I hear this story about the opening of the first section of the track around Qatamon, which, now West Jerusalem, is an old Palestinian neighbourhood in what we once called the New Jerusalem until the arbitrary regions of a compass split the city in two. It is advertised on flyers that are plastered on public noticeboards and walls and placed in cafés. A friend, who is in Jerusalem at the time, goes to the opening. All the old Palestinians go to the opening. My friend tells me this is the most disappointing opening one could imagine: the flyers say, *grand re-opening of train track!* The Palestinians arrive with their memories of Jaffa, seafood, the beach and the clock tower. The Palestinians find wooden planks boarding over the tracks and a conceptual light show depicting the historic and now imaginary route of this grand old line. It is hard to overstate the effect of this anticlimax. Although anticlimaxes mark a change from unwelcome ones.

Sary and I have a project in mind, to write about Ottoman buildings in Mandate Palestine, and I am visiting the train station to make a start on our plan. I walk through the Old City, entering at the Damascus Gate, and past the tourists who crowd the forecourt of the Church of the Holy Sepulchre. I stop by a store displaying Palestinian filigree. A small, neat proprietor offers me tea, and we talk about Bethlehem wedding hats, which are worth thousands, he tells me (giving me his card, in case I find one). I can tell when I get to the Jewish part, because the crowds thin and the energy of the city peters out (an anaemic anticlimax). Here I am at the Prophet David Gate (you might know it as *Zion*) already. As I exit into West Jerusalem, I have a few plans on my mind.

I am looking for the Mamillah Pool on my way to the station. But this is what happens. A large man detains me. I am wearing an olive tree around my neck, its silver curls beaten by a woman in Bethlehem, but it is covered by a scarf. He asks where I'm going and my heart is in my throat, beating against the necklace. The man mistakes me for a young Jewish woman on a birthright tour (half-right, I think wryly). My cousin has said to me only the night before I must watch how I go; he fears the Palestinians will not recognise how I am Palestinian, and it is owing to his concern that I am wearing this symbol of the olive tree. Now the man asks if he can walk with me and takes my silence as an assent, so he walks with me, fat and out of breath, saying, 'You could learn Hebrew with *Ulpan* then you would really enjoy yourself here'. Now we are on clear footing (the olive tree at my throat is searing a brand into my neck) and here's what he does. I forget about the Mamillah Pool and we chart a course for the station, and as we do, he points out a surveillance drone. We are on Hebron Road and I remember this because he points out the *Menachem Begin Heritage Centre*. There is barbed wire and a string of small flags, blue and white, stars of David rippling in the wind. He smiles and he says, 'It makes you really feel welcome here' (true story, no jokes about him).

This short walk to the station gapes out as the longest walk of my life until we arrive at the complex, now renamed *The First Station*, full of cafés, shops and outdoor stages. The man is proud to tell me it is also the site of Israeli cultural festivals. All along the railway platform are placards with pictures and photographs, bilingual explanations in Hebrew and English, although I am told the English does not always say what the Hebrew tells you. I take a lot of photographs of these placards, on a phone that gives me much trouble, a prepaid I have bought a month before in America. At the border, they insist on knowing this phone's number, and I say, 'It's useless here, it's locked to an American network', but then I accede and pull out handfuls and handfuls of scraps of paper searching for the number, which though innocent they find deeply suspicious. A woman about my height with a long pony tail calls the number when I find it. We watch together (I am muttering Hail Marys and willing a miracle), this inert object sitting between us, and finally she says, 'Yeah, so, it's dead', and then she says it again into the radio she pulls out of her belt. My interrogation continues.

The man who has insisted on following me announces that he is bored by me taking the pictures I have come here to take and by which I am trying to salvage this unfortunate encounter. He wants to tell me his story, though I don't want to hear it, and I am reminded of another story I am not disposed to hearing though I'm glad that I do. I am visiting Melbourne's Holocaust

Museum in Elsternwick and a dear old survivor in his eighties says, 'If you have time I would like to tell you my story', as I race through the exhibit looking for painted gum leaves and William Cooper's petition, which I hear are both housed there, for an article that is later published on Israel's appropriation of Indigeneity. Joe is his name, which he offers and by which I am instantly endeared since my father shares it. And I cannot refuse him his story, since I well know the reciprocity of listening (you get what you're given). Joe, I have never forgotten, is from the Netherlands, and spent a harrowing time in the 1940s in somebody's basement, but the real story, I think, is that suffering, I suppose, from survivor's guilt, Joe is galvanised to tend to the plight of all refugees for the rest of his life. Joe is as good as I hope and better than I expect him to be, and I wish for Joe that he might always tell museum-goers the story he gifted to me.

So I feel obstructed and vaguely menaced by a man at *The First Station* who has trailed after me for hours, and who wants to tell me his story, which I know he must. But, along with his name, I forget it now (because, like my aunt, I refuse to carry the burden of names that spike my heart rate). And while I am waiting for him to finish I invent an urgent pretext, and we start at a cracking pace back to the Old City, though not fast enough to be free of this burdensome escort.

Here we are in the park we first met in and he says I look stressed and that he is a physiotherapist. He is puffing a lot and says he needs to sit down and recover his breath. He asks me to sit down beside him from where he starts massaging my shoulders. 'Oh no', he says, 'you'll need to take off your jacket and scarf for this'. And terrified that my olive tree will identify me, and terrified also that what is happening is an assault in a public park in broad daylight, I jump up at once, and with no better excuse I say over my shoulder, 'I must get on!'. He looks sad (or pathetic even, on which I will shortly elaborate), like in his mind the Old City is a boundary he won't cross. 'Watch out', he says, 'I don't like it in there, full of thieves'. He writes his name and his email address on a map I am clutching before I dash off.

In the Old City I breathe in the scent (or the colour) of pomegranates being crushed for juice and the Jerusalemite cake that I have only ever seen here excepting my own family's kitchens. I buy a pepper grinder and some discounted spices, the vendor's wife a lost relative of mine, and once I am back out the Damascus Gate, on Salah Ad-Din Street, I find a public bin where I discard the map, which is spoiled with the contact details of my assailant. I buy a few kilos of coffee, my order half dark, half light, with hel, I buy a bag of nuts, and return to the institute's library. 'The only thief is a man who has stolen my time', I will say to Ahmad, later. On this visit I never do see the Mamillah Pool. On this visit I never do call by the address of the house my grandpa built.

9. BEST CAKE (HILBE)

This cake is named for the little seeds of fenugreek that you make into a tea. You add the seeds to the dough. Later you add the tea. If you boil the seeds for too long, they turn bitter. When you do not boil the seeds for long enough, they remain hard. This is my grandmother Ellen's cake. I think it is her speciality and now it is my speciality but she does not teach me to make it. In California they tell me that this is her sister Badia's speciality but by then she is dead so I cannot compare it (I can say that more than one person is entitled to own it). My father and I reconstruct this cake in the years after Ellen's death, which are piling up now, more and more, and in a few years I will have been in the world without her longer than I was in the world with her.

So I have said I will not share the recipe with you, but Mum says my father shares the recipe with anyone who asks for it. Much good it will do you. There is something mysterious about this cake and people report that it won't come together when they try to create it. I will give you this clue: the correct dimensions are those of a lamington tin. It is perhaps a chance thing, this Australian dimension of a Jerusalemite recipe, a small unsung resilience of Ellen's invention that I don't notice until I am making it often. Best is an exacting process; the same ingredients combined in the wrong order will produce a wet, thready paste and you will have to start again.

The key ingredient is semolina. There are some other semolina cakes you will find in the cake shops: Namoora (Lebanese) and Basboosa (Egyptian). They look the same, a split almond baked onto the top of each piece, each drenched in sugar syrup, but are not very like it. Nader says there is also a Cypriot cake (not sure if this is Greek or Turkish and in truth it could be either), which is called 'A good thing'. Nader reports that on account of regional variations this cake is well named since it is surely a good thing but not Best, and this is an appropriate place to tell you about coincidence.

Best Cake, my aunt Vera will tell you, was named by her son as a small boy; hard to pin down the date of that, maybe the 1960s. It is called Best Cake by him with no article, such a superlative bestowed that it does not describe Ellen's cake (the best) but rather renames it (Best). It is not a boastful cake (not like the Cypriots', from whichever side they are making it). It has this plain little name in most places, Hilbe, and is ubiquitous in Jerusalem though I have rarely seen it elsewhere. Even so, Best has a reputation in Melbourne, and when I post a picture of it for a fundraiser all my friends buy it, enticed by the scarcity of Best, which has a life of its own.

I conduct ethnographies of Best Cake (*Hilbe, please*) in the Old City. I buy a piece from every tray I see. It is all very nice, little squares handed to me on thin oily paper. But as I say to Ahmad on his balcony in the third circle of Amman some nights later, my grandmother's recipe is superlative and it is only right and true that everyone should call it Best. 'You're a snob', he says. We are eating tart green olives from Palestine and he does his very own special snicker that rains down on me with the warmth of his loving eyes (I miss that sound).

I leave a lot of things in a drawer under Ahmad's bed when I go to the border of Palestine. And out of these things he picks a pen, from the Institute of Palestine Studies, a lovely purple and gold, and says he will use it until I return. I hope he is using it still and that it makes him happy. And though I bring him souvenirs, a brass pendant with a laser-cut word, Al Quds (we say Uds), in it, I am ashamed to bring him anything from a city that belongs to all Palestinians but which he cannot visit.

My bus is delayed, waiting to return to Ahmad, and I sit with an off-duty young Israeli Jew (no interrogation, easier to leave than to enter). She has called the shuttle, she says, laughing at me for boarding the crowded Palestinian bus with the wrong papers. Last time I was sitting here I had Taybeh beer for Ahmad's brother, Amro, who looks a lot like him, and the Jordanians kept a bottle for themselves. She opens a bag of peanut-flavoured snacks and offers me some. 'From Australia?' she asks, and to pass the time I tell her I miss the sound of the birds, the cascading magpie warble so often the opening grammar of a Melbourne morning. Then my bus comes, and she hands me the snacks and they sit in my bag until I get to Ahmad's flat. And I tell him about the sad disavowal I am forced to make of myself there at the crossing, and to lift my spirits he grabs the snacks out of my backpack, and we punch them into the bin.

10. EAST/WEST

It is three years earlier when Amro drives me to the border between Jordan and the Occupied Territories. Ahmad's brother come to rescue me in Ahmad's absence, the both of them carefully shepherding this Palestinian with no Arabic as far as they can with their bountiful hospitality. Amro comes into the terminal to sit with me on the Jordanian side, and thinking he is my husband, the Jordanians allow it. An American woman is sitting there with us, and though we have no wish to speak with her, she tells us she is studying Middle Eastern politics and the Arabic language. I remember this detail because I find it odd when I overhear her tell the official she will visit her American boyfriend in a settlement, *Ariel*. And I remember her because I find it stranger still when Amro tells me, later, that she gives him her number.

On the drive, Amro regales me with border stories, which if not comforting, are stories that prepare me for the deep dry mouth and cold sweat of what I will experience. For instance, he tells me he is made to wait at the checkpoint by a Jewish-Israeli woman who works there and wants to go on a date with him. And he sits there for some seven hours until the end of her shift, when he says he is married and opens his wallet to reveal miniature portraits of his son. This ordinary coercion is the awkward price of being a handsome Palestinian man who wants to cross from one side to the other again.

We drive down beneath sea level and my ears start ringing and Amro says two things I remember. He says he will teach his son how to use a gun, and he says, 'Just wait till you see the wall, it's pathetic'. I think of Amro now when I see the wall and when I see pictures of it. I think of this adjective when I am sitting on a bus at Qalandia checkpoint, between Ramallah and Jerusalem, and two soldiers get on with their rifles slung casually behind them, slapping their calves. I think of this when the Palestinian men get back on the bus, holding plastic shopping bags and folding their papers back into their wallets and their wallets into their back pockets. The Palestinian men are more dignified than soldiers with rifles. The soldiers in their pairs are pathetic. The checkpoint, also pathetic. See: wall (*pathetic*).

Here is the question you need to ask yourself about East and West: East of what? West of what? The West Bank is in the east part of old Palestine. And if you ask west of what, you will see it is the bank of the Jordan River on a map. It is just one reason why disjointed dispatches in media reports are often misunderstood and always misleading. So I have already mentioned the New Jerusalem, where the old Palestinian neighbourhoods are built and where wealthy Israelis now profit from the wealth of our labour. Here is the thing about Jerusalem – there is no wall there. East and West exists in Jerusalem most of all as a psychological barrier. The people who colonise the New Jerusalem are a barrier too, true. It is too simple to say that one side is well paved or that one side is teeming with bakery carts that lift a dust haze permanently into the atmosphere, since if that is true, it is merely a reflection of the discriminatory municipal funding of occupation. But there is surely a zone of liminal transition palpable at the Al-Ayed restaurant, where the babel of diners combine to form an incomprehensible politics, perched on a so-called 'east-west axis road' at the perimeter of this divide.

I have mistakenly walked to the East Jerusalem Central Bus Station, from where you can visit Hebron or Ramallah, Bethlehem or Nablus, all to the east of Jerusalem, all designated West Bank. And what I am looking for, though now I'm ashamed to confess it, is a service that a friend tells me can be caught from the west side of Jerusalem, west of West Bank. But though I find the square she directs me to, the service is no longer there. This will be easy to fix, I think, because like you, I have seen all the movies where Israelis speak beautiful English and where Palestinians speak with thick accents, wear dowdy clothes, are trapped by their too-big families. In the movies, Israelis are relatably cosmopolitan, Palestinians impenetrably parochial.

One year at the Australian Palestinian Film Festival we sit down for a documentary that traces an imponderable romance, between a Palestinian man and an Israeli woman, and over the opening credits a narrator informs us 'every Palestinian man is in love with an Israeli woman' while the camera rolls over the inaccessible but Palestinian sea. Sary and Ahmad and I never do learn what becomes of these star-crossed lovers, our patience exhausted by a scene in a Tel Aviv lawyer's office where the lawyer laughs to the lady, 'You wouldn't credit it, this legal system is just like something out of Kafka's universe'. Broken by arch literary references, we walk out.

So, like anyone who has watched these movies I assume that all the Israelis have well-heeled English and I wander around in the west and ask for directions. I meet some friendly American Jews on *Israel Our Home* tours, with beautiful native English but no local knowledge, and I meet some Israelis who say they learnt English at school but can't really speak it. And I drag myself through the streets with my ill-advised luggage, emboldened to speak to anyone who knows where I'm going (but no-one does) until I walk through the glass doors of a fancy hotel and a man from Eastern Europe has all the answers.

Directions of East and West, my lover points out, make no sense. We are in a bus, somewhere near Guernica, the town, which we don't actually visit. He is writing the introduction to a book that is not, to my knowledge, ever published. We discuss the conceptual terrain of East and West, old and new, and he writes about our Palestinian neighbourhoods. I give him an example, because although he is trying to see, it is hard to see what you have been taught to ignore, the way young Australian children are taught about Gallipoli but know nothing of the Frontier Wars. When I am first planning to visit Jerusalem, I find an apartment available on Pa's street, which boasts *Arab style fittings*. I tell him that quite obviously this apartment is not 'Arab style', but 'Arab in fact'.

The introduction to his book describes our suburbs as *ghost suburbs*, a poetic device to broach occupation. I tell him Occupation is bigger than he can imagine. And if I am chasing dreams then I can say they are no less real than the dreams a young Shimon Peres once made manifest. I am reminded of an interview with Netanyahu in a film by Oliver Stone. A bureaucrat passes Netanyahu a note. He stops the interview when he reads it.

'We've had a bombing', Netanyahu says.

'What's out there, a settlement?' Stone asks.

'No, everything's a settlement', (Netanyahu again).

He indicates with his thumb out the window. 'This is a settlement called Jerusalem', he says.

11. WEDDING (1932)

What I know is that Ellen loves love stories. She avidly follows the adaptation of *Pride and Prejudice* when we wait a whole week for each episode and incessantly rewatch the VHS tapes Dad makes of the earlier ones while we do. This is the version that leads to such a cult following (Colin Firth so unexpectedly but universally loved by the young and the old, the unreplicable heart of the formula) that the ABC is inundated with requests and rescreens the series only months after first airing it. My father tells Ellen one day that I have fallen in love in Italy, and he drives me straight from the airport because above all, these are the stories Ellen most wants to share in. Always gracious, also a great lover of stories, Ellen waits patiently, and then less patiently after lunch is cleared away from the heavy plastic she keeps folded over the chrome and laminate table at Mirls Street. She says, with her characteristic smile, 'So tell me about Omar!' (little laugh in her voice) and she listens with the look of a dream on her face as the torrent of my story envelops us both in her kitchen.

Her daughter recalls this too. Juju's is a very romantic story, you can see how her face melts to the girl of sixteen, in a white graduation dress Badia stitched, when she speaks of him. She says there were so many children in the house that when her future husband was once invited for tea it was served for just him in her bedroom. A relative dobbed her in to my Pa, in hospital at that precise moment, lamenting the steep descent of family morals since he'd been on the ward. But Ellen went into the bedroom (that smile, I can see it) and asks what it's like to have tendrils of love encircle your heart.

What do I know about Ellen's wedding to Pa? I know she is only nineteen, and I know he is less young but also not old (younger than unmarried me). When they leave Jerusalem sixteen years later they carry with them armfuls of photographs, which I have never grown tired of examining for this or that vital clue about who we all were before Nakba. There are our photographs, there are Najla's, Badia's, Alice's, probably also Lily's. There might be Rose's, Butros's, George's, Fouad's. Were there Nicola's (less certain), Emile's and Issa's? Certainly there are Yousra's, several hundred of them, pictured with her sons, her husband, with Taata her mother, and an uncounted number of miscellaneous figures (about whom I cannot say if they are related, but if not to me then to someone at least is certain).

But despite all these photographs, which may number in their thousands, the studio portraits, the costumes, the snow fights, what there is not is Ellen in bridal costume. Did she wear the Bethlehem wedding hat, tall and conical, stitched with Ottoman piastres, or something thoroughly modern? Did Pa look as fine in a suit as he does in a fez by his first new car?

There must have been photos. I ask Juju. 'There were', she says, 'but not from the day'.

Ellen is very ill on the eve of the wedding, and she is still distraught the next day. She is a bride too disconsolate for wedding portraiture but sometime later, a year even, after the arrival of Pa's dearest firstborn (so he addresses Juju in the letters he writes her, in a neat Arabic hand), they recreate the day. Do they treat this like costume portraiture the way many

Jerusalemites think it great fun to pose at the photographers' studios with earthenware jugs in traditional stitching? Like Ellen will do one similar day, with her mother Ajia and sister-in-law Yousra, creating a rare glimpse of my Ellen as a woman not yet exhausted by exile.

I hear at a pier in Los Angeles or somewhere in a car on the superhighways of that great constellation of suburbs and counties they humour themselves is a city, a story about what Ellen did on the eve of her wedding. I do not learn this story from her and what I can say is some stories are painful and better left secrets. What I also learn is that Ellen enters her father's soul (*my dearest firstborn*). Whatever the merits of my Pa, and they are surely many, Hanna will arrange no more marriages. Each of the five other daughters marries for love, and Badia so late there is no need for children.

It is hard to reconcile the sadness of a young Ellen with the image of two tiny people barely visible over the dash of an Austin Mini Van, who drive very slowly from Newport to East Malvern looking for wayfinders like the hashabate (which my father recalls as planks of wood and which Irene says was in truth a white picket fence), which guided them down Queens Road, and is one day removed to no end of confusion. And who, when they pass the Queen Vic market, cannot pass by without stopping for a string bag of oranges; two peas in a pod, reassuring one another there is time to do everything.

This tender woman (who is not violent, I have said this already and I say it one more time to preface this story) is promised to a man almost twice her age and without her knowing it. Ellen, the eldest, and a brilliant student. Ellen, whose dream is as big (and as small) as the scholarship she is awarded to the American University of Beirut.

In 2003 at a picnic on Williamstown Beach, Ellen tells me about this turning point in her quiet direct way, while we wait for my dad to bring the car closer. It had been her reasonable enough belief, since Hanna has sent her away to a boarding school in Ramallah, attended by all manner of important girls from the region, that her father tended to the same dream as her, a career launched by a university degree. (I never do think to ask Ellen what she thinks of Ramallah. But my mother, who enters this Palestinian family six weeks before my parents are married, when she lives with Ellen and writes down her recipes, does ask. And later she tells me, 'She thought it was *bee-yout-tiful*', and I can hear Ellen say it, in that mock-turtle way she drew out her vowels in approval.)

When Ellen leaves her Ramallah school one last time, she is welcomed home to a glittering party and she is flushed with the future she sees laid out before her. A brother approaches (not the baby Fouad, of that we can be certain), but Butros perhaps or sweet George, the George wearing ladies' boots in the picture, left on the right foot etcetera. He approaches his eldest sister and says, 'Congratulations on your engagement, Ellen!'.

She pauses to look at the sea as dusk falls in Williamstown, us bent in together on a bench, fourteen years since Pa's death. And I sense Ellen can hardly see me while she conjures a scene from seventy years ago. There's a little laugh in her voice now when she says, 'I was so angry and I punched him', and her young brother flew, so astonishing was Ellen's response to this epithet, colliding with a drinks table upon his descent. Though the engagement guests, and I imagine the groom, must have been stunned, this episode had no impact on the arrangements. And I know it is the first time, but not the last, that Ellen would grieve for the loss of a life she was promised.

I do not know how Pa felt about this same wedding or these ancillary events (not so defining of a man's life, that much it is safe to say). I do know that Pa was a great documenter of things, and to this day his papers remain carefully collected along with the ledger of births and deaths he notated in the family bible. His wedding ring is inscribed with the year of this occurrence and their initials, *E & A*, sweetly sentimental and almost worn off.

Years later, in a bedroom in Newport, my aunt finds a hundred dark amber beads wrapped into a monogrammed handkerchief. Ellen says this is from a wedding necklace Pa gave her. In the absence of photographs (photographs of a re-enactment, recalling the devastating start of an otherwise excellent pairing), I cannot imagine how so many beads were worn together on the day of their marriage, or when the necklace broke, or why she saved them.

12. FRIENDS GIRLS' SCHOOL

At thirty I sit eating breakfast alone in a ballroom on the first floor of the Rocky Hotel in Ramallah. It is in Ramallah, but not in its heart, and an online review states: *nice views of Jerusalem*, though in truth the two are not far apart (although they can be very far depending on who you are). This is where I pass the very first night I ever do pass in Palestine.

In the lobby the owner returns me my passport. 'You're a Sahhar', he says (*yes*, I agree). 'Why didn't you say! You said Sahhar but then I saw Sah-haar! One of ours!'. He invites me to take coffee with him and two friends. One in a suit, the other a cable-knit jumper. They formulate an ad hoc council to find my family (*I am not looking for the living*, I say. *We are still here*, they say).

They drink coffee and flick the ends of their cigarettes into crystal ashtrays, one each, laid out on a central table. 'I recall a Sahhar', the one in the suit now says, 'but you just missed him'. He makes some calls: 'He emigrated to Canada, less than a year ago, yes, just recently'. The cable-knit jumper says, 'But you're from Jerusalem! There's a Sahhar there I think', and he makes some calls, 'at a German institute!'. And he writes out its name in the back of my notebook. Then he instructs me, 'So here's what you do – you go there (when you go there) and you say, *I'm family and I want to meet you!*'.

'I'm looking for the Friends Girls' School', I say, and the man in the jumper takes me, he's driving that way. The owner of the Rocky is delighted for me. 'He's the town engineer', he says, proudly.

In a greenish-blue box, part rust and part still enamel, there is a portrait of Badia as a young student. I've seen it once, a photograph with a cardboard frame glued around the bust of her, slightly incongruous for a schoolgirl, shaped like a love heart, the sort of shape a young Badia might have selected herself for her portrait. Both Ellen and Badia complete their schooling there (Alice, between them, is spared for Ajia). Though the school has graduation photos, neither Ellen nor Badia are in them, and I have to guess what years they matriculate. Ellen I suspect in the spring of 1932, in the months before her wedding, and Badia maybe two maybe three years later (and the dates on her gravestone would sharpen the point of it). Two sisters attend the school and there is just this one picture between them. This in itself is not shocking, since though we have armfuls of photographs, there are photographs with no arms to carry them. When we find Badia's portrait in the box, Juju laments, 'None of Mum', shaking her head, again.

Records of girls matriculating from the school are incomplete, though they surface from time to time. An image from 1931 is too early, 1940 too late, and I wonder where Najla and Lily and Rose go, but not here, as far as I know. Classes of seven or eight young women are common in these years, most often arranged in two rows for the picture. Some years later, the Friends Girls' School publishes a centennial collection that comprises tens of portraits of matriculating women. In 1932 there are only five people. In 1931, seven; in 1933, eight. If you are thinking what I'm thinking, it's that the number of girls in 1932 is not enough. It's that Ellen is missing. When I am a child fifty years later and children are missing on portrait days, they note our names with a cryptic abbreviation (they record our existence despite our absence). In 1932, there are only five women, or girls hanging on the precipice of adulthood, and only two with Palestinian first names (but all Palestinian last names). The others are named for queens like Victoria, or goddesses (Aphrodite). If these were Ellen's friends, I never did hear of them. I wish that Ellen and I had spoken of this time, the graduand portrait between us, because it is not that I didn't know her, I see now, but that I asked the wrong questions.

The town engineer has set me out at the end of the street where I will find the Friends Girls' School, a Quaker-run outfit, twinned by a Friends Boys' School, which is, unusually, four decades younger than its counterpart. The pictures show it was really a beautiful school. When Ellen is there it has just had some major endowments: a tennis court one year, a library the next. It is hard to imagine the body of Ellen, lithe on a court with a racket, when it is a tiny arthritic woman I see in my mind.

The gates are sealed up for school holidays, and what I see on this visit, I see from the street. There is a fence, partly stone, partly iron railings, and through these I glimpse the gorgeous arched building that Ellen must have studied her teenaged years through in. I imagine her sitting here now, on one side of the fence, and me on the other. I see her long dark pigtails and smooth lips, almost certainly reading literature and quite certainly not contemplating me as she reads it. She is slim and straight-backed, charged with the electricity that ideas fill young people with. And I touch the fence and the little snap of an electric shock runs through me.

Then I walk down Jaffa Street, weaving my way to the Mahmood Darwish Museum and Memorial, a garden with lavender and water, and they are closing but they let me enter.

I sit by the reflection pool breathing in dusk and the heady scent of that unseasonably warm autumn. Ellen would have liked it here, I know, not particularly because we spoke in her life about Darwish, but because there isn't a Palestinian alive (or dead even) who doesn't like Darwish, nor gardens or lavender either.

Sometimes I think I will write to the school to ask for the records of Badia and Ellen. Each time I think to do so, I do not do so. There are two reasons for this. Why search for information when you already have it? And why search for information that might negate what you know? There is a delicate balance between information and knowing and there is a delicate art between confirmation and negation. And all of these things are things that Palestinians know.

13. INTIFADA

The insurrection we've been waiting for. I am trawling through my memory for Pa. If Pa is there, then this is the intifada.

Why trawl through my memories like this? For scraps of a wedding, for a grandfather who once sat in a suburban kitchen, four decades since? This story is the same as a box of confetti I collect as a three-year-old at a family wedding, a box I will discover at bedtime is filled mostly with grass, and not the precious shimmering paper I believe I have saved. I grant you, a diaspora is not an epic. But a diaspora is something and the thing I know best. A diaspora is something, real enough to share.

So, we are in the kitchen. Everyone has an anodised aluminium cup. Mine is always the purple one unless Uncle Tony is there, who takes the purple himself and gives me the green one. The purple cup marks my place, next to Dad, and opposite Ellen – three etched lines close to the brim. They're good cups, coloured inside and out with slight silvering around the base, especially the purple one. Out of these cups we drink flat sweet lemon Mirinda and orange Sunkist.

The evening meal has finished and the table is still laden with twenty or thirty different dishes on it. I can see the green Tupperware salad bowl – when we arrive the vegetables are already placed in this but not yet cut up (they don't look like much). I can see the CorningWare and the tanjarahs, on their stand, stacked small to big, descending. While Dad plunges on with the dishes, Ellen takes out a glass jar of Turkish Style Bushells and arranges almonds onto a plate.

I am tired and it is very hard to sit up straight in my seat as the table is cleared. But then I do, because there has been some *big news* and Ellen or Pa lay out the greenish-blue box and beside it they start to arrange the stacks of papers it holds on the table.

Something else that lives in the box is the key to our house in Jerusalem; the box lives under the place where Pa sleeps, in the bedroom facing out onto Mirls Street. When Pa is agitated he retrieves this key and waves it around (*the Israelis are on my back* – key cuts the air; *who despised Balfour more than me!* – key draws the shape of his punctuation).

This is the night I learn of the records that substantiate our family's dreams of restoration. There is a large Mandate scroll in Arabic and English that states twice, once in each language, that the above named is the owner of a plot at Asa Street (more later).

I spend my childhood reading stories about people enforcing their origins to find reward, discovery, riches (Nesbitt, Baum and Lewis). I cannot think of a single children's story that describes what happens to Ellen or Pa, to Juju, to Dad or to Vera. Does it happen to me? I can say I grow up with it, saving whatever it is my family of scattered Palestinians, who raise me and who know no other story, can spare.

There are rates notices in this pile, bank ledgers and character references. There are two vaunted portraits of Pa, as a staggeringly beautiful young man in a fez, and beside his first new car. There are letterheads from a business, and postcards from clients. There are documents covered in stamps from a house still standing in a long-gone place.

In the kitchen that night there's a nervous crackle in the

laughter and a tremble in the smiles. Something on the news has done this. Return seems imminent.

Later, as a doctoral student, I cannot reconcile my memory of that night in the Mirls Street kitchen with a thing that Yitzak Rabin says for which he is not, but should be, remembered:

> We will fight with all our power against any element that tries by violence to upset our full control over Judea, Samaria and the Gaza Strip ... I know the descriptions of what is going on in the territories, the way it is interpreted in the media, is not helping the image of Israel in the world ... But I am convinced that above and beyond the temporary problem of an image, the supreme responsibility of our Government is to fight the violence in the territories and to use all the means at our disposal to do that ... We will do that, and we will succeed (quoted in Kifner, *New York Times*, December 24, 1987).

And after this quote, I will write in my doctorate what I say here again:

> It is argued that the First Intifada demonstrated to the world the legitimate national sentiments of the Palestinian people. However, the 'peace process' that was to follow, sequestering Palestinian aspirations into the problematic terms which Israel stipulated for two-states, eroded much of this recognition, solidarity, social organisation and momentum over the following twenty years.

Pa is born under the Ottomans and dies in the light of what might have been a real revolution. He has waited nearly forty years for this sign, always ready with title deeds and the key to our beloved Jerusalem home. Pa parses words carefully, talking about Jerusalem, but nor does he lay waste to half a life lived in Australia ('and we are very happy to be here', he says to the tape that's recording him, key slicing the air into quarters).

I remember he sits on a beige vinyl couch, with a tear, books upside-down and back to front beside him, English spines mixed with the Arabic ones. He tells us that no-one drowns in the Dead Sea, 'I floated', he crows, waving his key. He says, given the choice, his dream is to be buried in the soil that tended his soul for a lifetime, where a father was laid some long time before they were forced to leave him – alone, but happy in his unknowing – in Jerusalem. It is difficult to find my memories of Pa, here in the 1980s; he dies when I have just turned seven and my memory is not so audacious.

Pa lives into the dawn of a promising era, and from a kitchen table in Newport, we lived in the fantasy of it too, for as long as anyone could dare to live in it.

In Syria my taxi from the airport is a Peugeot 404. They drive for literally ever. The glass of the window is sealed shut with gaffer tape.

14. CARS

I will start with the very last car that Abdullah owned in Jerusalem. I grew up with a picture of this one, the black Chevrolet, and I can hear Pa rolling the sound, shevro-lett, in the ear of my mind when I think of it. The picture I have is of Dad in Amman, maybe 1949 to look at the size of him, standing in front of the back of the car in a hand-me-down dress, maybe Sylvie's or Vera's. I hear the price of this car is what buys a whole family of berths on *The Roma*, which arrives to a Melbourne dock three years later.

The very first car does not belong to Pa. When the Mandate conquers Jerusalem, which is how Jerusalemites still speak of the British, Pa gets a job in the Public Works Department as a mechanic. He says, 'I learnt how to drive. I became a driver. I drove for the government of the city, his name Mister ... [impossible to make out on the tape]. I used to drive one of those old Fords and the petrol tank is under the steering'.

So Pa and I are ineluctably similar; he begins his life story like this: 'I remember I was not the firstborn', and you might ask how an unborn child remembers, but I am the living proof that we do. 'My first Christian name is Abdullah, which is the name of my grandfather. As usual they name the first son the name of his grandfather.' Abdullah is not the firstborn, but he becomes the eldest, quite unluckily, when a sister, Salha, dies in early childhood, followed by a brother, Solomon, who does not live long. Little can be known of these children, but they leave an absence behind them, and Pa says only of these small, loved lives, 'I didn't see how they died'.

Pa tells the story of his life in Jerusalem and of Jerusalem too, folding in both the Mandate and Jesus, and he walks up the re-imagined streets of his youth where he tarries beneath the arches of his story. Abdullah was just as proud of his cars when he had them as my Pa is when he remembers them.

When Abdullah first learns to drive, you had to crank the car by hand to get it started, and to manage this inconvenience he reports that it was his practice to park on a hill like the old Jericho Road. The old Jericho Road, Pa says, is Roman, and he remarks, as he goes, on a biblical drought that lasted three years and six months in the annals of the Old Testament. Then Pa cuts himself short: 'I don't mean to tell these stories' (oh but you do, Pa, tell me more stories!).

It is during this time that Abdullah commences a practice he will keep with him all of his life – he buys three cars, a job lot, for forty-five pounds, and he uses all three for parts, though where he is storing three cars used for parts at that time is not something he mentions. He notes there are no petrol stations, and then he cuts himself off again, saying, 'Now I'm too old to remember, so when I remember something I'll come back with it as I'm doing now' (and as I am too young to remember, I will do as Pa does, I will do that too).

So there are no petrol stations but there are plenty of British soldiers, all issued by the Mandate with cans of petrol. Pa says that they didn't have cars but they did have a powerful thirst, and they would call out, 'George, you want some petrol?', and Abdullah would say, 'Yes', and one pound would go to the proprietor of a licensed bar, and the can of petrol into Abdullah's car. And neither Pa nor Abdullah remark on why the Mandate soldiers address Palestinian men who want petrol as 'George'.

My copy of Steimatzky's *Arabic for a Shilling*, prepared for His Majesty's Forces and printed in Palestine, has some useful insights on this subject. On page eleven is the entry *Siyyaraat Taxi*. Abdullah describes the plates of the first taxi in Jerusalem, JM 12, remarking on the capitals of the notation (the transcript does not clearly state if this was his car or just a car he admired). Steimatzky gets off to a civil start:

Drive me to—, Wait here, How much is that?

The entry goes on:

You ask too much, I don't understand this, You are wrong, I shall call a policeman!

At page fifty (there's a little rosette of mould in the binding) some remarks on unforeseen vehicular issues conclude *addesh laazem antazer* (how long shall I have to wait)?

A prophetic question, Steimatzky!

Abdullah is waiting a very long time, and if only he had been waiting at the side of the road for a motor repair, we would not be waiting as we are now, waiting still.

In 1921, Abdullah purchases a Dodge from the company offices under the Grand New Hotel at the Jaffa Gate, a car he says little about on the tape, but which my father affirms that he loved. There are two photographs of Abdullah with his Dodge. In one of these, Abdullah is pictured with three friends. He is leaning on the left-hand wheel, so he is on the right-hand side of the image. All four of the young men are fashionably dressed in collarless shirts and tarbooshes (fez) but no-one now knows the names of these friends. In the other, Abdullah is draped on the bonnet, like any young man taking a picture with his new car, a hundred years ago or today.

Abdullah buys the Dodge one year before the British Mandate officially starts – though there is not a person in Jerusalem who doesn't know what's on its way – and three years after the First World War ends, which I will tell you is a tumultuous time for Abdullah. But what Abdullah, the most beautiful man I have never seen, could not have known on the day when these portraits are taken is where he would finish his life, or what would happen between this day and his last. What is a life defined by? The word that would define his (by the time he became my Pa) was unknown to him when this photograph was taken.

In Australia, Pa is known as Albert; he changes his name and some of the children's. No-one forces him to (no gun to his head, that much is true) but the Whiteness of White Australia is unmissable. He lives with this anglicisation well enough, in the absence of everything else, including the name Taata gave him.

I recall Pa on the couch; Pa listening to Arabic tapes; Pa reading the Bible, which is how, my father tells me, Pa taught himself English; Pa kissing my cheeks when I swarmed into the lounge to be kissed on the cheeks by him. Pa, fascinated by this small child, and me, fascinated by Pa (who dies too young in my life and quite incidentally from an ill-advised medical procedure). In a photograph where Dad is as handsome and almost as young as Abdullah by his Dodge, he is holding me on his shoulders. And as I have told you before, Pa looks adoringly up at me, unremarkable bald baby though I am. And I am convinced, as you know, that this is the moment when a remarkable old bald man (in a photograph that shows me at the start of my life and Pa near the end of his), invests in me the thing he loves most, in sight of the camera. He is making sure, with all the power of our surname's meaning – *magician* – that this baby will grow up Palestinian.

Each year on May 15, I honour my Pa, and I say the name of the word that tore through the middle of his life. Each year on May 15 I dwell in a day and a year that was still two decades away for Abdullah. Nakba. And I think of my Pa with his key to our house on the Newport couch, and I think of him saying, as I also now say, *we carry Palestine in our hearts and Israel on our backs.* On Nakba, our key punctuates this statement with a magnificent and fortifying flourish.

15. THE ABC WOMEN

Abdullah, as you know, knows cars, and sometime after 1921 when he purchases the Dodge, but before he is married, he leaves the Mandate's employment and turns his attention to an expanding industry in Jerusalem. He begins this career as a sub-contractor for the Thomas Cook & Son agency, which everyone knows is to be found inside the Jaffa Gate of the Old City. Pa says that the agency would send notes to his mother to tell him not to book his car with other operators. Pa says, 'I used to learn and keep it in my head', and quite soon Abdullah had kept enough in his head to open a business, which he advertises widely in English: Sahhar Bros. Tours and Motor Service.

Pa says, 'I became sort of very well known by people that I took around, they used to recommend me'. Pa says, 'Sometimes they have competition and they take my people so I used to give them a sign, I'll be carrying a white hanky in my hand or putting it on my shoulder, come and see me'. Dad tells me later that the hanky was held in Abdullah's left hand, since the scheme became commonplace and open to abuse by unscrupulous holders of hankies, in and around the tourist hubs of Jerusalem.

Abdullah saves his money until he has plenty, and then he buys another car. He teaches his brothers, Issa and then Nicola, to drive the new one, and Pa lists the places the brothers took tourists: 'Petra, Transjordania, the sea of Galilee, Nazareth, Lebanon, and one time I took passengers over to Baghdad – we showed them all these places and they were very happy'. In its infancy, the business can be located *c/o the American Colony Stores inside the Jaffa Gate, under the Grand New Hotel.* The store, which was long known by two names wedged together – Fr. Vester & Co., The American Colony Store (how this came to happen is intriguing but elusive) – was perpendicular to the Dodge Brothers dealership. And though I only hear of one, I like to imagine Abdullah admiring the new models beneath the wide-windowed balconies of the Grand New Hotel. Later, the brothers opened an office at 94 Mamillah Road, and Abdullah crosses out the original location on his business pamphlet, printed by Jerusalem's Commercial Press to highlight sites of interest, and replaces it with the new particulars (Telephone 1397, PO Box 541, and this office is shared with a second Sahhar Bros. business for which they are still quite known among the old Palestinians). Abdullah and his brothers all spell Mamillah with an h, a thing that makes sense in view of the contraction it effects of Ma'aman Allah (the 'h' standing in for the Lord), and though it is not commonly spelt with an h nowadays, I will do as my Pa does, I will do that too. At its peak the Sahhar Bros. Tours and Motor Service had, in total, seven cars, one truck and one pickup.

I assume it is at the end of the winter months in 1928, when Ellen is enjoying the new library facility at the Friends Girls' School in Ramallah and still years away from her marriage, that the ABC women arrive in Palestine, and meet by recommendation, or by chance, with Abdullah.

'Why do you refer to them like that?' Dad asks, and quite simply this is not my own invention but the self-made economy of the ABC women, set out in the crowded hand of the one who writes to Abdullah for what I make out as a year after their meeting.

There are two surviving photographs of Abdullah with the women. One of these is easy to place – they are pictured beneath a great stone lion's head, which is sometimes described as a gargoyle and which is, to this day, still encrusted on a wall of the Temple of Jupiter at Baalbek. I am twenty-nine when I visit Baalbek, reserving a room at the grand old Palmyra Hotel, which was popular at one time with the French Surrealists, and there is a sketch above my bed, gifted by Jean Cocteau to the proprietor. And I imagine that this is where Abdullah and the ABC women once stayed, a short walk to the legendary ruins, which are visible from the Palmyra's first-floor balcony where guests can take in the night air.

The ABC women comprise, to my eye, a surprising collection: they look to be women of three different decades. The one who is writing (the B) is just past young; she is slim and elegant in dresses for dancing and long thin strands of beads that look like jet in the pictures. Two is more matronly, short hair with a fringe, and she wears a large cross at her neck. The third of these ladies is frankly an old one, bright white hair, fashionably coiffed, which blurs in the black and white gradient of a photograph with the scarf she is wearing on the day they have their picture taken, in a garden with four members of the King's Guard at Tatoi in Athens.

In total, Pa saves four pieces of correspondence from the ABC women. Abdullah must have liked these women. There is also a photograph, dated April 1, 1928, just the three of them, and beside their names they have written for him 'At the Jordan' and then their origins: A is from Detroit, Michigan; B from Newark, Ohio; and C as for B above. Why does he save these records of a gone life, a life already gone before Palestine is?

In Athens the women are still full of Palestine and in a card dated May 5, they are pictured beneath the caryatid sculptures that hold up the Erechtheion. The image is wisely composed, three ladies in hats, dwarfed by three caryatids – the caryatid they appear directly beneath is in fact the one Elgin stole. For a long time this was apparent in the substitution of a crude pillar, notwithstanding that the Earl of Guilford arranged for an artificial stone cast to be sent. And later, Elgin sent a second, though neither cast was ever installed. One supposes because there is no particular compulsion for the authors of culture to accept a poor approximation, offered up by thieves who to this day maintain their claim to the sculpture is best (though I'm not sure who but themselves they're convincing). On the reverse side of this card, the women give themselves their name (A-B-C crowd at the Acropolis). Miss Sena Bowman writes to Abdullah:

> *We have missed you every mile of the way, and all of us wish you were here with the Lodge* [this word is a vital clue I cannot decipher] *to show us the sights. We hope many other Americans who visit Palestine will be fortunate enough to have you as Courier. You certainly made our ten day trip doubly enjoyable and we all want to thank you once more for your kindness and courtesy. Most Sincerely*
>
> *Sena S. Bowman*
> *Hallie S. Caine*
> *Sillian F. Armstrong*

Why Miss Sena Bowman underlines these three words I don't know, least of all what the Lodge is, though I have wondered if the A-B-C crowd are part of a religious cult, some small dreary strand of messianic madness. Did they believe themselves the chosen people of an imaginary kingdom, or of our own ordinary home, both named Jerusalem?

From the Acropolis, Abdullah's clients are next heard of at Piazza San Marco, Venezia on September 15, where they send him a strikingly composed image. A is holding C's hand in the foreground, and B with another companion stands on the base of an obelisk, her shoes a dazzling white point of the image. Dozens of pigeons throng around them. At the side of the shot I can see the porticos of the Piazza, which houses some of Europe's oldest cafés – and I imagine they visit (as I have visited) Caffè Lavena, whose central chandelier and matching sconces comprise tens of glass-blown teste di moro (although the full red lips depicted on each of the heads seem to draw on the iconography of minstrelsy).

Miss B, it is clear, has taken a shine to Abdullah; she writes:

> *Please send me another of your new cards. They are fine – I gave the one you sent to some American ladies who expect to be in Jerusalem in February – and told them to be sure to get your car if they could. See, I am advertising for your new Business and wish you much success – Sena S. B –*

Her playful post-script:

> *We don't have our pictures so often in America. So this is the last you will get of the A-B-C crowd.*

But Miss Bowman tells a lie, as I have promised you four, and since I have spoken of two, there are still two more. The ABC women are on a Grand Tour, the kind that takes in Italy, Greece and Jerusalem, a tradition preserved in such classics as Forster's *A Room with a View*. They return last of all to Greece, where they send Abdullah the picture of Tatoi I started with, which reads on the reverse side:

> *Abdullah, See who are taking care of us now! ... Our pictures are the worst ever. I have my eyes shut. But you know we are a good looking crowd.*

Does Abdullah meet the women referred by Miss Bowman, escorting them through his home town, or Petra, Transjordania, Nazareth? Are the A-B-C crowd the tourists he once took to Baghdad?

Among Abdullah's papers is a picture Miss Sena Bowman sends of her next birthday (months before the collapse of Wall Street), writing: *My Birthday! In California* and then, *Mrs. A is on this side of me but sat back and did not get into the picture*. It is a glimpse of their ordinary life before they recede in Abdullah's rear-view; how many tourists can one man remember in the twenty years he works as a Jerusalemite tour operator?

Are the A-B-C crowd Abdullah's first clients; do they launch his new business for which he is grateful? In the last picture Pa saves we see them all by the car at the side of the road, in winter coats and heavy hats, Abdullah in a suit and a white cravat. It is impossible to say where this picture is taken, the anywhere of a road between a *there* and a *somewhere*. Yet even that road is a long way from exile, where Pa will show Jerusalem to each of his grandchildren (though this Jerusalem can be a linguistic apparition only), skilfully carved out of words.

16. *THE ROMA*

Why do they come to Australia? Quite simply, this is to do with Abdullah's age, as many years as the century, and by the time of the Nakba not a very young age to be. Put simply, Australia wants immigrants more than America, the British Isles or Canada. Put simply, in 1949, an Arab is White enough to satisfy the demands of White Australia.

Form No. 40: Application for Admission of Relative or Friend to Australia, pursuant to Commonwealth of Australia, *Immigration Act 1901–1949.* One Mr. Nicholas (Nicola) *desires permission to introduce to Australia the following person who is of Hashemite Kingdom of Jordan nationality and ~~is~~/is not Jewish* (the document is concealing and also erasing one Mr A Andoni SAHHAR's refugee status). The application states that Mr A is Mr N's brother and that his present occupation is: *Carpenter.* Given what I have so far said about tourism, you can see that if this is true, it is not the whole picture. Abdullah is a man of diverse talents and also a man with an eye to necessity. For instance, Pa recounts that in Jordan he is in the employ of UNRWA, using his black shevro-lett for the purpose. He states further that the carpentry machines are now gone (more later).

When the document is completed, there is no Irene. It states the place of Mr A's birth (correctly) along with a date that makes him younger. Ellen is recorded as *Helen* (who is several months older than Ellen, and born arbitrarily just two days after the date on which we commemorate Nakba). Juju is not listed at all, perhaps too old for a parental application for immigration. There is Sylvia (niece, an anglicised Salma), Boubarra (the same, this is Vera), Andoni A (first son with as usual the grandfather's name) along with their birthdates (I cannot confirm these are accurate). Occupation states: *School* (as above, as above). There is also my dad, Master Joseph A (though my father maintains he has no middle name); everything otherwise accurate, occupation (since he is a baby) listed as: *None*.

Of Mr A Andoni SAHHAR it states he intends to work in Carpentry and Joinery and will be *engaged in business on his own account, in house building & general carpentry work*. The particulars of the nominee are reduced to the following essential features: height – *Five feet six & half Inches* (illustrating, if nothing else, that capitalisations are neither here nor there when your first language is Arabic); colour of eyes – *brown*; colour of hair – *brown and grey*; any special peculiarities – *none*. The document is stamped with the following: *the nominee has not previously been in Australia*. The document entreats, *please turn over* – but I am working from a photocopy and what is said on this reverse side is not recorded for me.

It is my belief, though I do not have the corresponding forms filled out by other hands, that applications were made both to the heart of the empire and also to its colonial peripheries, and we should pause here to consider that as one great colonial tragedy unfolds, the Palestinians apply to both its architect and their dominions, in the hopes of being saved.

Tourist guides from Mandate Palestine anticipate a range of traveller's needs, like souvenirs and antiquities, like tobacco and tailors, and it is not uncommon to see advertisements there for Italian-operated liner companies (though it is not anticipated that a Mandate-era tourist guide like Abdullah will require such a liner, or that such a passage would entrench his refugee status). *The Roma* is built in 1941 by Americans and sold to the Flotta Lauro company in 1949, when Mr A Andoni is still in Amman.

In 1951, *The Roma* commences service between Italy and Australia. Mr A will meet it in Port Said the following year, accompanied by (H)Ellen and several dependants. They have travelled from Beirut on a boat Vera recalls, even now, as horrific, and she remembers sailing through the Suez Canal and that they expected to, but ultimately did not, stop at the Port of Aden. Columbo is substituted before they arrive in Fremantle where, in a park, they have their picture taken. (I have located no further facts among Pa's miscellany of tickets but since Vera's knowledge contradicts the ports printed on an indicative passenger service, which also states *subject to changes without notice*, a document may offer no further clarification on the route of their passage.)

I have a photograph of *The Roma*, pictured on the high seas. The image is black and white with yellowing bevelled edges, bigger than a postage stamp and smaller than the palm of my hand.

Ellen is sick, day and night, each and every twenty-four hours, and mostly confined to her narrow bunk in a cabin where she lies sick as a dog (but not a sea dog) for as many months as *The Roma* rides the waves of 1952, away from her home and towards the Great Sad Lands of Australia. I see that if Ellen was seasick, this sickness was just a symptom of the great heart-sickness she would never not carry about with her until the day she enjoyed an ice-cream the nurses gave her, and surrounded by all her children, quietly died in her gracious way, in hospital on my birthday.

The Immigration Museum at the Old Customs House (grim irony of a location) collates an exhibition on the subject of Station Pier and stories of arrival for refugees. Though *The Roma* does not arrive there, Juju, undaunted by the small matter of piers, seizes the opportunity to enlist her siblings to collate memories of their Nakba journey. It is (you might imagine) an unfinished story, beginning some years earlier in the place they are from, nor ending when they arrive to Victoria Dock in a city they will never leave.

Sylvie (now Salma again) recalls a hymn about a little fallen sparrow (or a hungry one, but there are too many hymns about sparrows to know which one, and sparrows and people can be either and for that matter are often both together). She is animated by the lyrics, which Juju recounts that she sings, and then after the hymn she says that she does not remember another thing.

Of Abdullah's brothers, there is already Nicola in Australia and Emile will arrive with his children. Too young to recall this sequence, when I ask my father, he says he thinks Emile's family came later, but it is as if those cousins are always there in his memories of Mirls Street. There is a photograph of two tired families not long after, thirteen children between them, my father looking just as my brother will look in the future, and my Pa looking just as my father looks now. Taata is with them, a crooked grimace at her mouth and in her posture, a head shorter than her own two sons behind her. Irene is hard to see, but she is old enough to stand, tucked in beside Joey.

Of Ellen's siblings there are none in Australia, and besides two brothers so far as I know, none of the rest of them – not one beloved sister – ever does visit. When Najla expresses a wish to live here with Ellen, Ellen gets her letter off quickly: *don't come! It's bad enough one of us is here suffering* (about which Juju will echo her sentiments in a poem marking the Pacific Solution that begins *Refugees! Stay where you are*).

There is a photograph of Pa, of Ellen and Badia standing in front of a ship that will take Ellen out, in three parts, to Australia. There is something on Badia's face (although I have never seen this picture, but I know what it is). On Badia's face is written, quite simply, *Nakba*, because, as Patrick Wolfe will say many years later, Nakba is not an event, but a structure. Because Nakba happens to Badia again at this separation. Because Nakba describes the separation that begins when Ellen steps onto the ship, pictured behind her, and will go on happening (and happening) for the rest of her life.

Sad to say, this is a thing that I know but will not grasp until some eleven years after Ellen dies, when I am visiting America, too late to meet Badia but when I meet Najla. And Najla confides in me that because Ellen lived in Australia, her death was indistinguishable from long separation, and Najla continued to live as if Ellen was as far away as she had been through their lives, until the day that we meet. And I hope this remained true until the day Najla died, four years later.

17. NAJLA

When anyone travelled away from Ellen, she would say in the great rich depths of her Arabic-to-English accent, 'Safety journey', looking small where we left her standing there, smiling wistfully into the middle distance. 'Safety journey', she said, a direct translation from the Arabic and one which conveys to me so much more than anything else that could be said about how you might fare as you journeyed away from where you were to wherever you went.

She is standing on the wide, plain porch of her brick veneer where she saw us off (always welcomed to the back door and farewelled through the front) into our white Peugeot with scratchy woollen upholstery, to cross the Westgate Bridge. And in spring she picked jasmine that grew in profusion there, tucking a sprig in my hair, a scent which is infused for me with Ellen and the brick house at Mirls Street (and later the alleys of Fitzroy and later again, Jerusalem).

This is the phrase that Najla says too, Najla of whom I heard so little until the year that my father and I flew to the United States of America together, and then onto Phoenix, where Najla lived until really quite recently. Dad and I queue at the Los Angeles Airport, Dad looking small with his black Crumpler backpack and baseball cap, holding the print-out of our tickets in the wrong order. And I am filled with such rage at the impatience of the flight attendant who is waiting for Dad to present the correct details, yet pauses to clap the American veterans and wave them through the gate (as is the tribal custom of that nation). On the plane we are not seated together and short flight though it is, Dad makes a few trips up and down the aisle and stands by my seat to give me an anxious smile and a wave, held down low near his waist. And I am irritated like the flight attendant then, because I am desperately trying to finish a conference paper in the narrowing window of hours I have, between family in Orange County and family in Phoenix.

Rhema and I have written back and forth for a month, planning our days together, and Dad has met Najla and her daughter many times as a baby in Amman, and once before as a man, but at the airport he turns to me and says, 'How will I know them?', brim of the baseball cap bobbing around in nervous excitement. It is the one thing I was relying on him to know and he is worrying now that he can't remember the sight of them. I text Rhema, *how will we recognise you at the airport?* And she writes, *oh, you will! Najla is the spunky ninety-year-old in a leopard-print shirt, but she won't admit to a day over seventy.*

Najla comes into view at last and she is ninety-three and she is wielding a two-tiered silver trolley around the baggage carousel to help with our luggage, and this first impression of her tenacity is for me a lasting one. Najla is undaunted by age, wearing a dark brown hairpiece and dyeing the hair she has left, and although she is the sort of evangelist who does not believe in cosmetics, she declares that since it was black from the beginning, 'There's nothing wrong or unnatural about that!'.

It is here that I first see Najla, and here again, four days later, that I will say goodbye to her, and what I can say is that the time I have spent with Najla fills a place in my memory much bigger than the linear size of it, and that it wasn't enough, and that it is all the time I ever will get with her, at least on this side of life.

On Najla's coffee table she keeps a Bible, set entirely in mother-of-pearl, and at the centre a wheel, inside which is the Star of Bethlehem. Yet this is no heirloom, strange to say, but a thing eagle-eyed Najla finds for four dollars at a garage sale. And in Phoenix at a used bookstore the next day, I will find a piece of Palestine also, *19 Varietes of Gazelle* by a poet I never have heard of, Naomi Shihab Nye, a Palestinian–American writer (of whom I will hear more later). When members of the family are invited for dinner that night, one guest asks, 'Who's this?'. To which Najla replies, 'Who do you think!', and she is sprightly up the hall to her bedroom, where from the dresser she takes down the portrait of Ellen in Bedouin garb and feels, as do I, that Ellen is with us, and maybe that in me there is Ellen, come to visit her this last time.

Dad and I both stay at Najla's house, me in a small half-bed in a room with a wardrobe bursting with Najla's stitching: scarves and pot-holders and crocheted roses (ward in Arabic); and also traditional clothes, heavy black fabrics that glitter with gold braid and silver threads. Maybe there is even a Bethlehem wedding hat stored in this cupboard (although I never do see it). When we are arriving, she wipes down the wheels of our suitcases in her garage, and we line our shoes up neatly before we enter the house. When I am leaving, Najla pulls out her handiwork and garlands it over the bed, 'See, here is one kind of scarf and here is another, and my god! I don't even know what that is' – she clicks her tongue – '*that* was a *com-pletely different i-de-a*'. I select a scarf in gold and olive green, and she pins a ward to the lapel of my jacket. I play her upright piano with a lid like a mid-century desk, pressing its two metal handles back into a recess. It is desperately out of tune (disguising how I am desperately out of practice). A few days later I am brave enough to pick out the opening bars of Schubert's *Impromptu in G flat*, on the Musical Instrument Museum's public-use Steinway, which Rhema records and sends back to me (subject line: *Beautiful Pianist*).

It is at Najla's that I will see for the first time the picture with all nine siblings, a copy of which sits with me now in a paper Italian frame, green with gold edging, that I buy with my very last birthday fifty from Ellen. Najla is the one in the white dress, in the middle of the line ordered by height and by age. She is taller (and older) than Lily, although she tells me that their papers get mixed up, and in America she is the fifth sister although fourth born in Bethlehem. She looks no more than seven and very sulky. She tells me that just before the picture was taken she had a fight with Lily about a necklace, which Lily is pictured wearing. This is how families work, I suppose, that Najla maintains that she was obliged to concede the dispute as the elder child, and Lily maintained until the day that she died that whether the necklace was hers, it was certainly not Najla's. And this slight proprietorial dispute still amuses us, despite so much else lost, and the truth of it lies far from the particulars of a necklace in a black and white photograph.

My father leaves Phoenix the day before I do, and we line up on Najla's drive to take pictures, and I clasp Najla's wrist gently before Rhema drives him back to the airport. Najla and I both worry about my dad, travelling alone to Orange County looking small in his long-brimmed cap, and she advises him, 'You know, if it's overwhelming, just tell them you need a wheelchair and they'll wheel you onto the plane! Come on! You can do it!'. After he leaves, and I have wept for hours as I try to collate images for a slide show I will deliver in Denver, Najla puts her arm in mine and says, 'He's a baby-heart', with the sound of her love in the stretched vowels of her American accent. And she is the last living aunt to spoil my father, to care who he is, to have known his parents, to make a fuss of him with favourite meals (no need to do dishes!), and Dad celebrates every small thing about Najla, the way any small boy loves the people who notice him.

That night, as I am instructed to crush tablets for Najla to lower her blood pressure, the tears start again in her kitchen, a terrible sobbing that I can scarcely conceal, and Najla cries too before asking me to show her how I arrange my scarves 'so fashionably!'. She pulls every last scarf out of her cupboard and we practise putting them all on, the different shapes, her mimicking me, and she says, 'Yeah! I *like* that!', after each one. And after I've refolded the squares, rectangles and triangles, and stacked them neatly according to her preference, I go to bed and cry again because I know in my heart that this is the first and only time I will see Najla (a thing she knows too, a thing that is not said between us).

Najla is up early before my departure, conveying an enormous watermelon with all of her body from the fridge to the counter, where she chops it into pieces for my journey and arranges the pieces in a takeaway box, with a neatly folded square of paper towelling on top. 'Choosing watermelons', Dad says, 'is a man's job in Palestine, but ask her how she chooses them', and Najla smiles with secretive glee and says she chooses watermelons better than anyone (and you can ask, literally, anyone for confirmation of that fact). Even early in the morning she is beautifully dressed (Najla says, 'I like to dress well because it makes me feel young!' smiling, not ironically, after she says this). The alarm rings and Najla takes out of her oven dozens of za'atar and other mankoushe and she places their faces together to wrap them in foil and then plastic. 'So you won't have to eat the plane food, darling', she says. 'It's appalling! And you are too thin!'

Four years later, Di writes, *Micaela, Aunty Najla is dying*, and later when she has, Alice's son writes, *like her husband, she took a left-turn to heaven*. I don't make it in time to say goodbye to Najla or attend her mourning.

But perhaps this is as it should be, since this earlier parting is the parting uppermost in my mind. On a November morning, Najla drives me with Rhema to the airport, wraps her arms around my waist and smiling at the camera, she sees me off to Denver. At the airport in Phoenix, Arizona, Najla will always be seeing me off to Denver in my mind's eye. 'Safety journey', she says.

Safety journey, Najla, wherever you are.

18. WATER CARRIER

Probably you are wondering (and when I stop to think I confess I am also astounded) how you can read so far through a story about Palestinians, about travel (c/o Sahhar Bros., PO Box as I've told you) and yet, for all the airports and cars and trains, the criss-crossing from Newport to Jerusalem to Arizona to Amman, the dashes to Baalbek and Baghdad (even Venezia, even Siena), and although we are far from where we started and quite a way through, what you have not heard about yet is a donkey.

Let me remedy that.

Here is a Donkey.

This Donkey is on a postcard I receive in the mail from an island near Athens where three friends convene for a holiday (a holiday I am supposed to join them on). They have dispersed again when the Donkey arrives, although earlier they send me a photograph of a mountain donkey on stone steps sunk into the side of a hill. It's conveying an old man up – they run to the window at the sound of the hooves – and then down again. The Donkey in my postcard looks gentle and foolish, dressed in a suit, captioned *We found the Groom*, and when I write my thanks, Sary recounts, *I might have squealed when I found it.*

Sary tells them my story, which is a story my father tells me about donkeys, and it might be his story (but it also might not be).

This is the story of the Donkey (a Palestinian donkey, I presume) who is invited to a wedding, and as any donkey would be, our protagonist is excited. *An invitation to the wedding!* this Donkey is overheard to think to himself (and my father adds to this story that the Donkey is bragging to all his donkey mates about the invitation and they say, 'Are you sure? Probably they've asked you to carry the water'). As the Donkey arrives it becomes apparent (increasingly so) that his invitation is not as good as the invitation others are given. 'Donkey!' they say, 'Can you carry this water that way?'. And then when our Donkey gets *that* way with his water they say, again, 'Donkey! Since you'll want to go back to where you came from, would you be so good as to take that firewood with you back again?'.

Water, wood,
water, wood,
backwards and forwards,
backwards and forwards.

And Dad says this adds to the pathos, all the donkeys predict the invitation will be as a water carrier, but wood too!

Dad laments, when the donkeys ask, 'How was the wedding?', our protagonist is just too disheartened to say, a doubly sad but true story of how they treat the Donkey who was a guest at the wedding (a story Dad tells me again and again because I love this one, which he relates with much resignation, as he ferries me thanklessly all around Melbourne).

I am staying in Newark, which is and is not in New York, an Amtrak away from the dense city blocks of Manhattan I will stay among later. I am staying with the son of a Tony (this Tony is the Tony who places the call to Rose in a Japanese restaurant, who once writes to my aunt the most staggering letter lamenting the things that are missing which he struggles to pinpoint until he visits the family severed from him in Australia, and when I share this with his eldest son, who I do not meet until eight years later, he writes, *oh my, that's the most eloquent I have ever seen my father to be in writing*).

That morning my cousin wakes me very early (and two dogs, one of whom later goes missing) around six or maybe earlier, and he feels that he has just cause although I am also disorientated when I come to my senses. He wakes me because he needs a witness, a family member, he says, as he kneels at my bed in the last dark of the night before dawn light, to attend his baptism. And although we have only just met for the very first time on the previous evening, he requests I attend this ceremony in the facility of a Mormon chapter some two hours drive away (and I am, as I imagine you are, stunned, although I have heard that it is not long after my visit that he is indeed baptised into that faith, and that the Mormons do, after long searching, hold all the things he had hoped they might hold for him). So it is true I disappoint him, and after he leaves it is true I cannot sleep, so anxious am I about what family means, and I spend the morning in deep conference with his wife, who laughs when I tell her what's happened and says, 'Well, you know, religion is just his thing' (and she tells me more stories I won't repeat for you here because although I am telling a story, not all stories are mine to tell).

When my cousin returns from the service we get in the car with his wife and we drive to another neighbourhood, also New York and not Manhattan, to visit his uncle George, my father's cousin. I have never heard of this George before, but what I learn at that lunch is that the extent of the family is far more significant than I had ever imagined (but a thing I still do not understand on this occasion, a lesson still nearly a decade away from my comprehension). George is an upholsterer, something I recognise, he carries on in the family industry I have not yet spoken much of, called Sahhar Bros. only.

It is winter, and the light is dappled through the bay window at the front of their house and we eat lunch together and George takes out (I still have it) a copy of the letterhead of the furniture business at 94 Mamillah Road. George sees, although I am struggling to place him specifically, that I am a person who collects stories; or maybe what George sees is the daughter of a man (his cousin) of whom he has heard very little in fifty years and of whom, circling round in his head, there are a number of memories and no-one to tell them to.

After lunch, George unfolds a plan and it's this, he says, 'Would you like me to place a call to your parents?'. And of course it is clear at this distance that George asks this because George would like to speak to my father, and so we sit at the rotary phone and dial a string of some twenty numbers from a part of New York that isn't Manhattan, to Canterbury, Melbourne. When Dad answers the phone I tell him there's a George wanting to speak to him and he says, 'Right, who's that?', and I explain (as best as one can explain in a room full of listeners), just where I am and who I think George might be and Dad says, 'Right! I don't think I know him', but he's a good sport and I pass him over to George, and I can hear his confusion through the earpiece until his voice changes and he says, 'Oh! Is that Mahfouz?'. And apparently it is.

It might be Mahfouz or it might be my father who tells me this story; it might be a story I overhear on the phone by the bay window or one I hear once we've rung off (or from my father later, but I think he is too young to recall this story in all its detail, although he has a memory, but I think that it is a memory of a story with him in it, and that it is a story that someone has given him). When Dad says 'Mahfouz' there is a light that enters his voice, and I can hear it through the crackly international dial of the landline we are sitting around like a fireside. The story is this: that as a young child, my father is put on somebody's shoulders, it might be Mahfouz or his brother Tony (because they have walked a long time and Dad's legs are too tired to carry him, so someone carries them for him). There they are, children together, lost on a road between Bethlehem and Jerusalem. The older children confer, not sure where they're going (and I know that nowhere is far; Amro says in Amman that from where his house is, it is only a six-hour walk to Jerusalem) and one of them says, since they are walking with a donkey who chaperones them between places, 'Well the Donkey knows Jerusalem, let's follow him!', and sure enough the Donkey does know the way and takes this collection of tired and lost children home with him.

I've always found it difficult when someone asks you to name your favourite animal to choose just one (and though I cannot imagine it is ever a serious question, to children it is a matter of great moment). But when my father is small this is not a hard question, because *Donkey* is definitively the answer, and this is what he tells the water carrier in Amman when he is old enough to tell him. No running water in the camps of Amman where the Palestinians settle for a time (and some settle still, although not in the place I am thinking of, on Hashemi Street near the stream, prime real estate now. I don't have a picture of this house but of the neighbouring one. It's the picture with Dad, again, in a sister's dress and Pa's black shevro-lett). The water carrier, who delivers water to all these struggling people each day on a donkey, stops to talk to my father, small boy, who stops to talk to the Donkey. 'What will you be when you grow up, my boy?' he asks him and Joey says, 'A water carrier, so I can have a donkey!'. It is reported that the water carrier's answer must take into account the planned emigration of Pa and Ellen, and the five children they are steering through Amman in the years when my dad is the youngest child. What does the water carrier say? Something like, *if you want to be a water carrier you may as well stay where you are*, or maybe, *better to stay with your parents and get an education*. His answer is fairly specific in dissuading Joey from this water-carrying aspiration, whatever it is, and the delightfulness of donkeys is certainly removed from contemplation in that question.

There is one more Donkey to speak of (or two, but I will let Disney do both, as it did for me as a little girl when I did not know that donkeys ran in our veins) – the Donkey that is purchased by Joseph (my father's name also) and Mary to convey them to the stable in Bethlehem where Jesus is born (and also Ellen). A little cartoon that was played at Christmas, which I loved and still love, and which I am still heartbroken by when I see it, *Small One*, which tells the story of a boy (like my father) who must sell his tired donkey. And he takes him to market and the people laugh at him – thin, old and haggard, they crow, insulting our noble Donkey protagonist. And towards the end of this film, in despair the boy is approached by a kind-faced man we are meant to understand is Joseph, who looks encouragingly at the Donkey and says he is perfect. It is not comforting to me that the Donkey passes out of the *Small One* narrative to become important (nativity scene, birth of Jesus). I am always left with the immense sadness and a lump that does not dissipate from my throat for some time afterwards as I watch this sweet donkey called Small One, and the boy who he loves, embrace one last time, and I tear up now, as I write this.

19. MA'AMOUL

I start writing a poem when Ellen is still alive, and it is the first thing I write that I am proud of. It starts with a title (it is part of a sequence) or maybe a number, and then: *I was afraid of Easter / stuffed with walnuts and dates / moulded then sugared / (why mould if you're sugaring?).* I forget the next part of the verse, which concludes: *moulding and sugaring and Eastering Arabic cakes.* Even approaching ninety and losing her sight, Ellen would make hundreds of the cakes I am writing about, called ma'amoul (and I have subsequently learnt that we really did Easter these cakes, cakes also made for Muslim festivals like Eid).

These cakes are shared across religions, although I wonder (but do not know) how Muslims account for their iconography, which I understand as follows. One cake is moulded with many ribbed lines which converge at the centre in the shape of a dome – a cake filled with walnuts and rosewater or sometimes orange blossom water according to preference. This is said to represent the sponge of vinegar offered to Jesus (a man who is terribly thirsty, a thirst he expresses in Aramaic and I do not know what that utterance sounds like, although I can say that whatever the language, in the mouth of our saviour, it must have sounded painful) when he is nailed to the cross. There is also a cake filled with dates, and one year I burn out the engine in two different blenders until they are smoking toxic grey-plastic plumes into our faces, and Nader says, 'Stop!' and I say, 'I'm nearly there', and all we can do is laugh as I try to pulverise the brown sticky mass of a kilo of dates and just as much butter. And later Dad reminds me that Ellen would grind dates in a hand-operated meat mincer (which makes sense in the context of the blenders).

This cake can be made in two different ways. You can use a mould – a flatter shape than the walnut cake – which is a nest of concentric circles that radiate out to the circular edge. But Ellen does not use a mould for the date cakes (Dad's favourites). Instead she rolls the ground dates into a log, and then she rolls pastry around it and slices the log into pieces and joins each piece into rings with a hole in the middle. This cake represents the crown of thorns, which tore through the skin of Jesus's forehead (and which as a child, bored by interminable Masses and sitting beside my mother, I would stare at for those long hours until I believed that what they had wrapped around Jesus's brow was barbed wire). Pa makes a tiny set of tongs from scrap metal (you can see the imprint of a serial number in them) used to press little patterns around the edges. These are delicate pinpricks far from the teeth of the thorns they are representing, which Dad says are made so the dusting of icing sugar catches and does not slide off.

The production of these cakes is quite epic, more so when you consider that Ellen would make trays for all her children (minus Vera in Adelaide) and all the grandchildren old enough to have separate families. We arrive in shifts; she has made the dough, which must sit for twenty-four hours, but the crushing of walnuts, the hand-mincing of dates, the moulding and cooking and cooling and sugaring, is a task for many hands and the kitchen is set up in temporary work stations. Ellen shows me how to knock the mould on the table so the walnut cake comes away with the pattern printed and the cake intact, and after several hours she says I'm the best at it and I wear this endorsement as a badge of great honour always.

When Ellen dies, the daughters (my aunts) sort carefully through all the articles of property that belonged to her and to Pa at Mirls Street. There is no argument in this process and each of us, all of the grandchildren, is asked if there is some specific item we would like to keep before the rest is packed up and sent to the Vinnies on Mason Street. Vera is here (from Adelaide) and so is Sylvie, and it falls to these aunts, this task of fulfilling requests, of searching through the pieces in a gone mother's house for each of us. And at first I can't think what I would like or what I am even allowed to ask for, but I ask for this, the ma'amoul mould from Syria, the finest mould I have ever seen, heavy and deep, for making my favourite cakes, the walnut ones, in the shape of the vinegar sponge.

It is carefully put aside by the time we arrive at Mirls Street for the very last time at Ellen's wake, and Vera and Sylvie both tell me what happens after I ask for it. Vera says, 'We couldn't find the mould and I said to Sylvie, never mind, we'll buy her a new one', and Sylvie says, 'She doesn't want any one, Vera, what she wants is that one!'. And Sylvie is very prescient in this and quite right, and I am pleased they do find it, and it is placed into my hands on the day of Ellen's funeral and it has always been exactly where I know it to be ever since.

At Ellen's funeral I find that I cannot cry. In the days between the day that she dies and the day that we bury her, my father takes on the task of writing her eulogy because he was disappointed by the minister's eulogy done for my Pa. He sits up on his bed with his magnifying spectacles halfway down his nose, and bare summer feet crossed at the ankles, and he spends these several nights writing – very little – onto a paper napkin, which he leans on a book, until the night before the funeral when he hands me the napkin at last and says, 'I've got the bones of it down, you finish it'.

On the day of the funeral we print out my work, to which Mum adds, *Vale Grandma* (and I say to my father, 'What's that doing there?', so incongruous do I think these two words, and so unlike Ellen, to which Dad says, 'Well, all I know is your grandmother's dead and your mother's still living'). Dad says he will drive me via the university first, to submit the slew of November assessments that are due that same day, because even on this day of all days to be bothering about undergraduate essays, we're a team, Dad and I. And after I submit each paper through the slots in the doors on different levels of the John Medley Building according to subject, Dad turns and he says as we sit in the traffic, 'I'm an orphan', a thing his own dear dead father, Pa, would say too. And I wonder then if *orphan* is a word that means something to a man of fifty-six on losing his mother and last parent (but can confirm at the age that I write this that, should I outlive my parents, it will be for me as it has been for my father).

I find I cannot cry on the day of the funeral or for many nights after the news of Ellen's death arrives, and it is as if I am stunned by this loss, as if I am too close to this absence for it to mean anything yet, until two weeks later when I take the handle of the mould in my hands, and lay the flat back of it against my cheek and I cry and I cry. I do this same thing for many nights, late at night, listening to Lucky Oceans compering *The Daily Planet* on ABC Radio National, and it is the first time that I actually understand what people mean when they talk about *catharsis*.

There is something quite marvellous about this mould and it is marvellous to this day still: when you hold the negative space of the impression it will make on a cake up to your nose, you will not smell the butter and semolina that has been pressed into the hollow (I do not exaggerate) thousands of times; what you smell is the most delightful emanation of the scent of Mirls Street, of Ellen and Pa, of the kitchen where cakes were made, each Easter, twice over (first for the Roman Catholic and then the Greek Orthodox calendar). One Easter when Shukry is visiting, a cousin nearest my father's age and more like a brother to him than his own, he tells me, and Dad tells me later, that they used to share all their cakes to make Easter last for as long as it possibly could (which is why I mention the asynchronous calendars of Christianities). Shukry also remarks that Dad and Irene were small nuisances, eating the hand-minced date paste before Ellen could give it a second life in the crown-of-thorns cake. Dad recounts no such story of Shukry and perhaps these were not Shukry's favourite, or perhaps my father, the younger of the two, can find no fault in his memory of the older boy. On the back of the mould is stamped 'Made in Syria', and I believe that this mould is part of the legacy of a trip that Ellen and Abdullah make in the late 1960s (after Nakba hurls them to the edge of the world, to visit their family) and when I ask about this stamp, it is the first time I learn of that trip.

20. ITALIAN HOSPITAL

On my first trip to Palestine (in the autumn that will be remembered for *Pillar of Smoke*, as are the euphemistic names of these 'operations'), I do not intend to stay in Amman but something happens which means that I do. Amro is waiting for me at the airport, and I don't worry about whether I will recognise Amro, so like Ahmad is he, this brother, and he waits a long time because I am inside and he is outside and once all of the baggage has been collected from the carousel of my Gulf Air flight, it turns out that my bag is missing. Some weeks later Amro will sit with me again in this scene of chaos when I am leaving, and he will order us coffee, only to announce, 'What a mess, the waitress is missing and the coffee's on fire!', a direct Arabic-to-English translation so much more vibrantly capturing how Arabic coffee bubbles up high and floods out of the pot if no-one is watching. At the lost luggage counter I am given a number. 'Call tomorrow', they say, 'we should have it in forty-eight hours', and Amro will say, 'They won't have it a moment before then either, they won't lift a finger until they have to'.

I have slept at the Istanbul airport, almost missing my flight. I have run through the transit at Bahrain and the ground staff have driven me out on the tarmac to meet the plane. Now Amro drives me back to his house, which is set on a hill and is solar-powered. His wife Nour wheels out a rack of clothes she picks out for me after a shower – the rack because Nour is a fashion designer and she tells me one of those airport stories about the weight of her luggage, when she shamelessly wears three heavy coats and five ball gowns onto the plane for a Dubai exhibit. And their son is there too, small angel; I will send him *Possum Magic* later, and I am pleased when Ahmad sends me a picture of a page in that book which is heavy with finger marks where the page has been turned. And my own copy is just like this one because it is my favourite book as a child, which is read every night, first *to* me and then *by* me (for three years and six months, this drought of variety my parents endure).

No-one expects my visit, least of all me, and Amro and Nour are not free the next day to show me Amman, but they give me their driver, a Palestinian man named Ali. I have not thought much about what to do in Amman and when Ali arrives and asks me what I would like to see, I can think of only one thing, odd request for a tourist, but Ali fulfils it and places it first on our itinerary (a list which he adds to himself as we wind through that day) and we set out from the house on the hill to the Italian Hospital in downtown Amman, located on a street that is eponymously titled Italian Hospital Street.

It is perhaps from my mother I hear that my father has no copy of his birth certificate, though Dad later uncovers a fragile and heavily folded piece of paper, stored in a small velvet pouch for jewellery, and written in Arabic, which Dad cannot read (which he claims may or may not be that document). And I tell Ali, and he says, 'Khalas! We'll get him one', since my father is born in the year of the Nakba, here in Amman, at the hospital we are now visiting. Ali and I walk through the entrance and into an older wing, which looks like a wing that might have been there from the hospital's founding, or at least from the time when my father arrives, twenty-two years later. We are looking for the Hospital Registry Office, and we walk along corridors and up a flight of wide stairs and there are pictures of earlier buildings and the Italian nuns and Ali says to me, 'They are very nice people here, you know, when my wife had our children they helped us, although we are Muslim, and we had no money, but at the Italian Hospital they will help *anyone*!'. And he looks at me kindly and I suppose he remembers the arrival of his own precious babies, and he steers me into the office which is marked in Arabic as the office we need to be in.

Inside, there are quite a few people waiting stretched out on plastic chairs, and I can see that Ali feels important, guiding me to the registrar behind a built-in island in front of a door, beyond which must lie all the records, including the one I am looking for. Ali says, 'This woman is from Australia and she is here to collect a proof of birth certificate for her father', and the registrar is quite sympathetic and asks me the date and I write it down in English and also Arabic (scant things I can write in Arabic but numbers are some of them). She looks at the date and then her eyes open wide. 'Forty-eight!' she says. 'You should see the files from that year, it's a mess, it will take us some time to find this.' Ali is undaunted; he gives them his number to call when they do. But I never have heard if they find this precious file of my father's arrival, or if Ali is called, or if someone, maybe Ali or Amro, was sent the paper on which it notates the birth of a baby who is now an old man, my dear dad, born in the year of our Nakba.

Leaving the hospital we look down to where Ali says you could once see the Seil running through Amman, and at the bottom is Hashemi Street, though even this resolute geography of steep peaks and troughs is all redeveloped now. On Hashemi

Street, Ellen and Pa and their children live in a house, or a hut, of one or two rooms, and it has a dirt floor which is swept with such vigour that it is a firm and smooth surface where little eddies of dust are not permitted. At Hashemi Street there is a toilet in an out-house and Vera says it is around this structure she acquires a scar on her face, because they are playing a war game called *Jews and Palestinians* and the older children lock her in, like is done to the Palestinians in Jerusalem, and she is distraught and comes to whatever grief is the grief that befalls her, at six and three quarters, to leave her with this scar and lasting memory of Amman. In the dwelling at Hashemi Street, Vera would often say to Ellen, 'Mum, you should have let us jump on our furniture because now the Jews have it and they are probably jumping on it!' (and if that is not literally true you will see that metaphorically Vera sees accurately into the substance of the politics she lives through, and which is now history).

When my father is born, Abdullah and Ellen have four children already, and already a son, and it is upon this eldest son that their duty is discharged (*as usual they name the first son the name of his grandfather*) so there is no great weight or moment attached to the naming of my father. Ellen and Abdullah invite a couple without children, who live in a hut quite near them in Amman, Jerusalemite Armenians who are also displaced in this year of our Nakba, to name the second son they give birth to. And this couple name my father for the name of the husband (no skipping of generations between names, it would seem, for these Armenians) and my dad is named Yousef, and no-one now remembers the name of the wife, because her name is not given to any of these children. I hear that they loved him and after he is weaned would often take him for feeding, an honour they arranged with a system of broken mirror pieces flashed up and down the hill, catching sun, to attract one another's attention.

On my phone, forgotten at Amro's, I will later find two messages waiting, one from Juju and one from my uncle Tony, who is particularly enlivened by this trip and who I do not recall contacting me until this day in October when I am visiting his childhood. Juju and Tony both want me to know about the night which followed the birth of my father, these oldest children, who remember his birth, and now it is only Juju who carries this with her. This is the story they tell me, and one I have told on the radio and which I will tell you now too (and his siblings have teased my father all his life, calling him the Urdouni, and when I finish my PhD, Irene gives me a keffiyeh in red, the Jordanian colours, and they laugh again, and Dad says, 'Micaela knows who I am' – which is Palestinian).

When Ellen gives birth to my father she is running a fever and suffering the hallucinations of delirium, poor woman who has left her loved home in Jerusalem not a week earlier, a departure from Palestine which is not the last one but is in many ways final, precipitated quite specifically by this baby's arrival. So Ellen gives birth to the boy that my Pa refers to (oh so lovingly on the tape) as Joey, and once he arrives the Italian nuns say to her, 'Shall we put your baby in the nursery to give you some rest?'. And Ellen, who I tell you is sick, fights vehemently to keep the new baby beside her before going to sleep. On January 16, Ellen wakes to the news that the nursery at the Italian Hospital in Amman has burnt down. And she becomes quite hysterical until the baby is produced and placed in her arms and they say, 'Look! Here he is! He has spent his first night beside you'. And in hindsight we see that the life of my father surely hinges on the capacity of Ellen to fight (not once, but twice) for his life, which ensures my newborn father survives his first night on this earth, and the many more nights that will follow after that first one is over.

Later, I begin to wonder if the woman who writes to my Pa is not in love with him. There are two similar accounts. A Swiss woman and later an American couple attempt to adopt Abdullah. He is already a full-grown man.

21. REVENGE

Revenge is a very satisfying word, I have found, in moments of anger, which comforts me although I have few causes in which to use it. Revenge is a word that lingers on the palate (you try it, *revenge*, that springy sound with some grip to it, *revenge*, which does not do the work of its meaning half so often as the production of the word does a work of satisfaction, stamping its way around my mouth). I do not often think of the word before 2018, and since 2018, when I think of Revenge I think of a poem with this name by Taha Muhammad Ali (which when I first hear it, conveys to me an apotheosis of the Palestinian condition). Revenge is one fantasy among the many fantasies we Palestinians harbour, wielding our title deeds and brandishing our keys, and I long for the house that my Pa built and in which, like his business, he gave a share to each of his brothers. 'I write it in the four names', as Pa says on the tape. All these proofs of our lives in a place we are told has never existed, and that we are told is a place in which we have never existed either.

So I go to a play about Taha, and I go with my father (and the love of my life, who I wait a long time to meet and who waits even longer to meet me) and Dad is enlivened by the sight of the Palestinian community who have turned out to see this work at the Arts Centre Melbourne's *Big World, Up Close* season. And I have to ask Dad not to point when he recognises faces – the handsome Palestinian! And the curly-haired one! Friends whose names I am not sure he knows or remembers.

The poem begins, *At times ... I wish / I could meet in a duel / the man who killed my father / and razed our home / expelling me / into / a narrow country*. This is a poem by a man and maybe revenge is a masculine fantasy. *And if he killed me, / I'd rest at last, / and if I were ready – / I would take my revenge!* This first verse nurtures something in my heart and in all the hearts of the audience at *Taha* who are Palestinian. *Yes!* we think, *yes! We are here and you will not deny it when we take our revenge.* In the first verse of this poem, all our bloody fantasies are recognised, because you cannot negate the existence of hands that seek to annihilate.

Until I hear this verse I do not think I have harboured such violence inside me but it feels good to hear it (springy word, stamping about), and it feels also like another great apprehension of that elusive catharsis. I wonder how this play is received around the world as it is toured and performed, and I remember a footnote I read once about Elia Suleiman's *Divine Intervention*. A motif in that film is a red balloon printed with a caricature image of Yasser Arafat, and at its first screening in Ramallah the Palestinians cheer, and throw up their arms, as the balloon swoops over Qalandia Checkpoint and soars high to the gold glittering Dome of the Rock in Jerusalem, marking a flight path unthinkable to a Palestinian audience in Ramallah, with inferior West Bank permits issued them.

But the poem does not finish there, and our poet has cause next to reflect on the victim of his fantasy (the victim who has victimised him) and he says, *But if it came to light, / when my rival appeared / that he had a mother / waiting for him*, and here Taha wends his way through all the caveats that depict the value of a life, even a violent one, to the people who love him. Here I return to the measured teaching of what it means to be a Palestinian, and to a day around a month before I submit my doctoral thesis, my supervisor and I, sitting outside at a café on a windy day (and he is hearing impaired and cannot hear me over the wind, and I am clutching hundreds of pages of an unbound manuscript, trying to take notes and restrain these loose papers) and he says, 'You know the hatred of the colonised is neither equal nor opposite to the hate of the coloniser', and although I do not know of a study on this, I know he is right. And I think also to the other great lesson he imparts to me, some years earlier when we are sitting outside (again) and we are combing through the draft of a chapter and he says, 'Don't be an angry Palestinian, be a clever one', and Taha finishes his verse, *then I would not kill him, / even if I could.*

Revenge is a fantasy with mercurial properties, and as Taha describes it (a word which is satisfying to repeat again, and I entreat you to do it) he also cuts into it, like the geological dating that is done on all the layers of silt on the side of a cliff. And as I listen, I return to fantasies enshrined by Anne-Marie Jacir in *Salt of This Sea*, a film that encapsulates all the fantasies of the diaspora, of people like me. In that film we watch the protagonist, Soraya, do all the things that we dream of doing, here she comes from America with her papers and memories and first she says she is from there, and she argues with the Palestinian Authority, 'You don't get to say with a piece of paper whether I am or am not Palestinian', and then she goes to the bank with a ledger of savings and she says she would like to withdraw this balance and they take her into a room and they tell her she can't and she says, 'Well, the bank is still here!'. In Jaffa she visits the house that her grandfather built, laying the stones and afterwards the tiles inside it, and the woman who lives there invites her in, but Soraya won't leave and the Jewess says, 'What do you want?', and Soraya is full of rage and she shouts, 'What I want is my house!' (yes, this is the woman I wish I was, when I stand at the border between Jordan and Palestine and I tell the Israelis that I am Australian and I tell them that my father is after all born in Amman, and I wish I could say, *you know and I know that I am from here* but I never do say this).

In the final verse, Taha reflects on what he would do if the subject of his revenge was in no way connected to the life of another, and it begins, *But if he turned / out to be on his own – / cut off like a branch from a tree* – and the play has been building to this great recitation and then the final phrase: *Instead I'd be content / to ignore him when I passed him by / on the street – as I / convinced myself / that paying him no attention / in itself was a kind of revenge.* And what Taha does best is to explain us to ourselves, and in this luminous line to convey also, for the international audiences, our staggering gentleness in the face of a moment in which we might take our revenge – and do not – and the staggering humility of the gentle Palestinian who defers this satisfaction, whose dream they have tended for a lifetime, and walks away.

At the end of *Taha*, the audience sits stunned for a moment before this too breaks, and they collect their coats and personal items and one audience member is heard to say, 'Quite something to hear the story of a Nakba survivor'. And my dad is still seated, but then he stands and turns to me and he says, 'That's me! I'm a Nakba survivor', but the crowds have drifted away, and my father grows smaller and smaller in the emptying theatre, and now there is no-one to hear him, but me.

22. FIL MISH MISH

This expression I have heard translated in just one way but interpreted in two and I will explain both of these idioms to you now. One version is my father's, who thinks about this phrase quite literally; the other has lived inside me for many years. Fil mish mish means *in the time of the apricot*, something I learn in 2005, when I see *Divine Intervention* and when I hear a Turkish Cypriot poet discuss this film. My encounter with the poet is a glorious chance, I see flyers announcing her talk in the lifts of the John Medley Building, and the date has not passed, and I am astonished to find that a film nearly no-one has heard of in Australia could be a whole field of study for people elsewhere.

There is a scene in *Divine Intervention* when the auteur and filmmaker, Elia Suleiman (who appears in many of his films, maybe all of them) is driving his car in the West Bank on a road demarked for Palestinian cars, which are forced to drive long perilous routes in a vivisected homeland. Where he is driving is near a checkpoint (never far between checkpoints for Palestinians) and along the length of the monstrosity which Israelis have called *the separation fence* and which we call *Pathetic* (see: Amro). On his drive, Suleiman is eating an apricot, and when the flesh is all gone and the stone is the only artifact remaining, our auteur throws the pip right hand to left window, since cars arrive to Palestine in Ottoman times, and despite intervention the Mandate is too late to change this (though one wishes that the small matter of drive-sides could have been the

Mandate's most lasting legacy rather than what it is). In the next scene we see a colossal explosion, like a planned detonation, rip through the length of the wall that Suleiman is passing.

The visiting poet directs her participants to examine this scene, which she says is an articulation of the concept, fil mish mish, an idea that performs our fantasies of restoration (an idiom in English you might be familiar with is *when pigs fly*, which I admit as a child I viewed not as an expression of hopelessness, but an enticing invitation). Maybe I misunderstand her meaning but I carry fil mish mish with me as a more elegant expression of the general use concept *inshallah*, which is also deployed (politely) when Palestinians have no real intention of carrying through on a suggestion.

Divine Intervention is a cinematic work punctuated by what is described at the time as magical realism (though I have since learnt that this genre is too often imposed on real magic and also multivalent reality). But even with these misgivings, the form works well for the narrative of Palestinians, and it sets me to thinking about reality and why it is that colonial structures beat imaginative multiplicities out of us (if they can). Which is to say that for Palestinians, the most unlikely part of a story is in a superlative sense the most accurate, such as when our diaspora hero, Edward Said, describes the true but unbelievable instance of the society of sheep raisers in Israel who are sent half the funds requested for immunising their fold, since the Ministry of Agriculture has *no certain knowledge about mixed marriages among the sheep, and that lately some difficulties about the conversion to Judaism were encountered*. In this example, Said teaches us, we must reject comparisons to Kafka, because life for Palestinians, or anyone, is a life (not a parable), and because this is *the possessive exclusivism which has been imposed upon reality* and by which only an occupation is served when we do not chase dreams.

My father and Vera remember this expression quite differently (and I have already said, quite literally) as a very brief period when apricots arrive to Ellen's tree and have to be harvested quickly – too many to eat, so Ellen makes jam to preserve them. When I say fil mish mish to my father he says, 'That's a very brief period of time', a halcyon moment, perhaps metaphorical, which can exist in real life but disappears if you are not looking before you have noticed it. Apricot season is summertime, and Mirls Street is hot, notwithstanding the Kelvinator which fills a good portion of the wall in the lounge room, above the couch with the tear where Pa sits with his key and remembers his own fil mish mish in Palestine. Dad remembers that during this season, late at night, Ellen would stir large pots of the cut-up flesh of the apricots, and she had bare arms and the puree would spit and leave angry red welts where it hit her.

One year when Ellen is making jam in apricot season, and fortunately in several batches, the children discover that one packet of sugar, a packet she is already using, has become a destination for a whole colony of ants. Ellen is distraught but my father comes up with a solution, which he laughs about now on the phone as he tells me, 'It was quite brilliant, really'. Joey says to his mother, 'Let's put two crosses on the labels of all the jam jars that have apricot jam without ants', and Ellen gasps, 'Imfadaheen! (you embarrass me) What will we say when people ask what do these crosses mean?'. And Dad is still laughing when he reflects, 'I suppose it would have meant we re-lived this embarrassment as many times as we gave people jam and they asked *what do these crosses mean?* And we would have said that these are the jars without ants in them!'. I ask what becomes of the second-class conserves and Dad says, 'Well, in the end we put the crosses on those ones, and we ate them, but we knew how to pick out the ants'.

There is also a story of Ellen and eggs that her eldest son brings her, and when he arrives he discovers either there are too many eggs in the fridge (*why don't you eat them?*) or none (*why do you give them away?*) and one time my father arrives before Tony, and Ellen says, 'Well, your brother is coming for lunch, better put those eggs in the car', and when Tony arrives Dad says he spends the whole lunch amusing himself by subtly referring to them. After Tony leaves and Dad is still there, Ellen heaves a sigh of relief and says to him, 'Fadah-nah, I was holding my breath all the time, I thought you were going to embarrass us!'.

After the talk I attend by the Turkish Cypriot poet, Alev Adil, I fruitlessly search for her book, until finally the scholar who hosts her finds me a copy, *Venus Infers*, and the poet writes a beautiful note on the endpapers. I cannot remember that our meeting was one in which we exchanged personal words, but she writes (and I am surprised to see the warmth of this inscription some fifteen years later) *with much love for the shared dream of new worlds*. In approximately the middle of this work is a poem called 'Refugee Memories: Baggage', and it shocks me, the opening line posed as a question, one which I recognise and which is a question I have lived with all of my life: *Do you still wake up in the night / and start listing what you'd take ...*

As a child I grow up in a house with an outdoor toilet that someone, before we live there, has renovated to make it inside, and the floor is concrete and quite wide, and there is always a pyramid of toilet paper there, some hundreds of rolls neatly stacked in this shape. And when you walk into the laundry to wash your hands, should you open a cupboard, then you chance the possibility of tens of stacked-up boxes of Omo Matic falling on top of you, a cupboard Dad fills with products bought at the best prices on pink-slipped rain-checks, and which he drives all over the city collecting on Saturday afternoons after closing the pharmacy. I live at this time with the knowledge that this is unusual (no pyramids or heaving cupboards at other friends' houses) and also with the knowledge that this is how we live (mundane but also special). And later I am telling Sary and he says, 'Oh yeah, us too, we stored hundreds of cleaning products', and when Nasser moves recently he says, 'My god! Mum had thousands of tins and I said, do we have to move these? And she said, *they're not hurting anyone*'.

These products are not (since you're asking and I'm telling) the things we would take, but the things we surround ourselves with, we Palestinians, to be prepared (we are trapped, don't forget, for a time in Jerusalem and I have mentioned this before and I will say more later). When my family takes flight they take with them some scant array of possessions, they take armfuls of photographs (I've told you) and the beads of a broken necklace – and it is said that some Palestinians leave meals on the table, and that the Israeli government moves in Jewish families so quickly that the meals are still warm and they eat them. There's also a rug (in my parents' house) and a Bible (or several) that Pa writes in, and there are many things they don't take and things they regret not keeping. When I am born I am born with this in me, this word which precedes me, this knowledge that that which seems permanent is also an illusory state of being. And what I can say is this: that there isn't a Palestinian living who hasn't considered this question, of what they would take in the night if a Nakba should ever befall us twice, and we could grab only this one small suitcase before we took flight.

23. MR SETTLER-COLONIALISM

This is what they call him, my friend, and also now called the late, great Patrick Wolfe (and I don't know when late is left behind and we just recall someone as great), who dies just a month after my thesis is examined. How pleased I am to tell him that, how generously he hears it, Patrick who calls me very early one Saturday when my poem is published in *The Age*, and asks, 'How did you get that in there?'. Patrick, who calls one afternoon, and at his emphatic opening line, like a poem – *The State / of Israel / Must / Be / Abolished* – I settle into the couch because I know this will take some time.

My very first meeting with Patrick is not so remarkable when it happens, at a café on Rathdowne Street around lunch-time, but I learn it is remarkable afterwards. Patrick is introduced to me by a friend who is Patrick's colleague when I am scouting for supervisors for a project not yet fully fleshed out in my mind (a project that later is born as *Occupied Narrative*) and we write back and forth and it transpires that Patrick thinks I'm a man and also that he has formed the impression that he will not like me even a little bit, not even at all. And I wish I could trawl through those mails of our first correspondence to see what gives it away, these misgivings he has, but they are lost in long-ago email accounts, and what is special about this is not clues but that Patrick tells me himself, years later, after our friendship has been cemented.

So I am sitting inside, and Patrick outside, or maybe the

other way round, and Patrick is waiting for a man and I am not sure who I'm waiting for, and just as each of us is ready to abandon the possibility of our meeting we collide in the doorway, and we talk like we've known each other a very long time for all the rest of that day. Maybe it is 2006 or 2007 when this happens, this meeting, and Patrick is immediately an ally from that very first day (and I his), and he tells me then that he likes meeting students who read his work. And I am honoured he tells me this, this discussion of students when I am a student, because immediately he makes us conspiratorial equals together. And I realise now that Patrick did not work to make me an equal that day, dear Patrick just saw the world in a way in which he was always surrounded by them.

What happens between the time that we meet is no great story, just a story of friendship. The wine at Jimmy Watson's when I get my doctoral scholarship, Patrick buying; the car rides together, most memorably a twenty-four-hour return drive to Sydney when we reverse part-way up the Hume in Patrick's Hi-Lux and he says, 'If you're going to make a mistake it's important that everyone can see you', and he honks to a pollie who turns off to Canberra – *good driving companion*! – and we eat warak einab straight out of the tin on my lap; and all the exchanges that are miscellaneous between two people until one of them dies and then you reify these things and collect them together as something partial and precious. And you regret all the fragments which are intangible and which, like people, are things you can't keep anywhere but in the unreliable eye of your mind.

Not long after I meet Patrick it is the dark northern winter, when Gaza is relentlessly bombed from the air, and which is now known by the name of the military operation *Cast Lead*. An Israeli friend says that in Hebrew, 'It's even more visceral, because the Cast should be Molten. It comes from a song that Jews sing to each other, this song a recent invention of Zionist culture, on one of the many miserable holidays they celebrate, that reify destruction and terror'. But on this characterisation I have since reflected, and will share with you the contents of Tamar's rejoinder, who writes that one ought to take pause over a leftist Israeli position that Jewish holidays are miserable ceremonialisations of horror; rather she describes very eloquently that *this passionate secularism sort of sneaks a disavowal of (their own) secular colonialism through the back door by implicitly blaming the Occupation on religious barbarism*. This, Tamar notes, is done by and in the spirit of an ideology that is even more purely colonial (so beautifully put, dear friend).

Patrick sends me a photograph of his Brunswick rental, and here it is summer, an absolute scorcher, the year of the Black Saturday bushfires (and devastating to Patrick, who loses his own house but who with his characteristic humour will tell me that following this destruction a man showed up with some paint to give his old van a face lift, and over the smoking skeleton of it between them remarks, 'It'll need more than a lick of paint, mate'). I am dividing my time between cold showers and protests in front of the State Library. And at Clarence Street, where from the porch you can hear Bessie Smith or the Philharmonic Orchestra, Patrick has hung a huge Palestinian flag. He reports: *This flag's proved universally popular in our street. Everyone but everyone passing by comments favourably. I was waiting outside afraid that the house might be attacked. Nothing of the sort. People just about cheer* (and this thrilling report is precisely what Patrick says in his email).

But the story I want to tell you is this one, it's about Ramallah and Palestine and Patrick and me, and how we are there together and how we don't know it, but this is the end of his life or very nearly, and retrospectively this infuses something already special with the knowledge that it was a very brief period (fil mish mish). It begins when I meet a Jewish woman at a conference (who becomes a good friend, and who looks a bit like me) and Tamar reports similar stories of meeting Patrick, charging through protests in a city in America wielding a Palestinian flag together and forging a friendship. Patrick sends me an email entitled *Tamar!* and both she and I and also Patrick are pleased we have found one another, although Patrick confesses that he had often considered, but always deferred, our introduction on account of global distances and time differences (and when he hears, he remarks, *some things simply don't admit impediment!*). And as it turns out, Tamar is the one who works it out, that we, that is Patrick and I, will be in Ramallah at what she thinks is precisely the same time (and we, Tamar and I, are drinking Malbec together in a hotel bar in downtown Denver at the time she discovers it).

I had forgotten the anticipation Patrick and I share (and frankly apprehension) until I read through the long emails we send over several days that December, and most of all these are about crossing the border from Jordan to Occupied Palestine. Patrick writes, *and I'd like your advice (if you have any) re getting through immigration*, and I write a long missive which begins *my advice is the advice of a paranoid Palestinian*, and when I read it now I remember (something I had forgotten) that my little cousin had just recently been strip-searched at the border on less provocation than the provocations I write to Patrick should be extracted from both your thoughts and your luggage. And I marvel now at how Palestinians forget these extraordinary events that would be seared into the minds of any White citizen for the outrageous indignity of the situation; and although we too think this is a situation of outrage and also indignity, we find we cannot hold onto all these sad details or we would be crushed by the weight of so much trivial information before we arrived anywhere – not least the beginning.

When Patrick finally arrives in Ramallah he has been waiting to arrive in Palestine for over a decade (or perhaps, as with firsts, a lifetime) and he has said to Tamar that he never would visit until the time when the Palestinians invited him (and at last the Palestinians do and just in time too). And when Patrick arrives there's a buzz at the conference that I am attending, because Wolfe is well known to the thinkers and arts workers and NGO representatives, and they all plan to see his paper at Bir Zeit on Monday, and when I ask what Patrick is presenting, he says, 'Oh, nothing new, just the stuff you've heard me banging on about for years and I'm glad the book's out and I can start on some new ideas'. He says this when we are sitting in a café in Ramallah's old city, and we remark on the incredible capacity of Palestinians to do ordinary things like have lunch in a café amidst Occupation, and in one vivid scene, Patrick returns from the bathroom with a long skein of toilet paper fluttering behind him, attached to his shoe. And he says when I tell him, 'Well, I'm glad that's what it was, I saw all these people smiling at me and I started to wonder if we'd been introduced!'.

Patrick has a good sense of geography and we walk to the Palestinian Martyrs mosaic and Patrick says, 'Let me take a picture', and he does, walking backwards, further and further until he is standing on a zebra crossing, holding up traffic, and the drivers can see what Patrick is doing and they honk in the way that Palestinians press their horns when they're cheering (and the picture has all of the mosaic, and all of me, and Patrick lines up the frame so it looks like one of the figures depicted, a woman, is steering my shoulders as support from the dead to the living). And Patrick is excited as we walk past a house, old-Arab-style architecture (or just Arab) and also abandoned, and he says, 'Hey! Want to live here with me?', and we plan out which floors will be our common spaces and we don't worry about how we will buy it with all of the no money we have between us, and he swings me around on the pavement like he does in the hotel lobby when we catch our first glimpse of each other, and he says, and he writes, *yeeeehah!* with a glee I can almost touch when I think of him.

I am reminded of a time (the time we drive to Sydney) when Patrick is worried the other guests will be abstemious, and we stop at a pub in Glebe to ask the way and we have a red wine (him a second) before we get back on the road towards dinner. In Ramallah, Patrick himself is abstemious, he's tired from the crossing, and I take him to a bar with a broken docket system. And despite the huge angry queue the bartender knows me (he has rescued me one evening on the second occasion I am lost in Ramallah), and he serves me two beers free of charge for Patrick and me. As Patrick walks onto the terrace the men from my conference all cry, 'There he is! Mr Settler-Colonialism!'. And now they look at me in a new way because I hand Patrick a beer and he beams to these colleagues, 'I'm just here with my friend from Australia' (and Tamar and I will never not feel a deep sense of gratitude for that friendship, and for the one that he forges between us and which we still cherish).

Patrick writes, *'til soon, dear friend* and maybe I'm still in Jerusalem then, but already we have parted, and he asks for some feedback, and I send him some poetry, and by then I am back on the balcony at Ahmad's in the third circle of Amman. We plan to drink wine in the summer (*beside the churning waters of the mighty Chum!*) and he says how sorry he is and how painful it must be to leave a homeland. The poem Patrick likes best is one whose imagery is derived from the fact I have just seen him and because when I first meet Patrick he tells me his beautiful daughter is practising the art of tattooing on pig skins. (And when I ask Maeve she agrees that pig skin is a good gauge to practise tattoo depth as it is much more like human skin, but that in the end she used oranges owing to the unbearable stench of it). Patrick writes of this sequence, *I have a little foothold in your stunning poem which makes me very happy and proud at 6am*, and then later, *dear friend, but your writing cuts into my skin – it's dark and beautiful. I'm aglow that we've caught up.*

Patrick and I are in Ramallah together in December and he dies the next February. I think of him always in these months, and also at Nakba, omnipresent with loss of all kinds. I think of the mails he signed off in his signature ways, *in haste*, or *love always*. And between the living and the dead, love always remains transcendent.

24. ROAD TRIP

My oldest school friend gets us tickets one year to the Melbourne Comedy Festival show *Extreme Rambling*, and I am apprehensive about this excursion. *What*, I think to myself, *does a middle-aged Brit have to tell me about Palestine*? But my fears are not realised, this rare show that has something to offer the pair of us, to someone who knows just a bit about Palestine, and to a Palestinian who often feels she knows a great deal more than she cares to.

Extreme Rambling is one of those few orchestrated experiences where I have ached with laughter and had to keep going, tears streaming, that excruciating hilarity in which you can scarcely draw breath. And I recall Mark Thomas describing a visit to Qalqilya Zoo in the West Bank, more than an hour from Ramallah and as the crow flies closer to Jaffa. The zoo has almost no animals but what it has is a giraffe that was killed in the Second Intifada and then taxidermied (quite badly) so it stands on a tilt (which Thomas speculates is how the giraffe appeared in its final moments, gasping for breath), with garish green golf balls in place of glass eyes that make it goggle and leer at the patrons. And this is a thing we both laugh at, painfully, this description of the zoo with a taxidermy giraffe in it. But when I tell my father later he says, 'It's quite sad, really, these people are just trying to live and enjoy their lives'. And while it seems quite a stretch that a stuffed giraffe is a thing of joy to anyone, I am sobered, and now in my memory, by the difficulty of living a Palestinian life in our vanishing landscape, that only some of us whether through accident or tenacity managed to stay in.

The father of my little cousin Rasha says to me at lunch on my last day in Ramallah, 'Why doesn't the family visit? They need to see this!'. And I'm not sure what I say in response but I recall at the time that Sary is preparing an exhibit, *Unpicking Jerusalem*, which centres on the Palestinian commercial district of Mamillah and the colonial accretions of a redevelopment that comprises the Mamillah erasure (although it retains the original name, which causes a distressing disorientation for anyone wishing to walk the old New Jerusalem). He sends me the fliers and I ask Juju to come and she says, 'Why would I do that? Why replace my beautiful memories with all the ugly things that have happened?'. But Ramzi has lived through it all and he says, 'Some people don't get the luxury of looking away', and I say, 'Well, I guess I am looking for everyone'. And Ramzi takes out a bottle of crisp white wine made with Palestinian grapes, and laments that our vintners are blocked from large-scale international exports by the Israeli strangulation of ports.

Rasha comes to collect me and we drive to Bir Zeit to see Patrick, and then we drive past a store which smells like hashish and I learn that mloukhiyeh is in the same family (and the only green leaf they are selling there) before we arrive to her house, where her mother makes a mahshi I have never tasted (nor tasted again), which is artichokes stuffed with the usual fillings, and it is the best food I have on that visit. Since then Rasha has won a competition for script-writing and made a short film, nothing like the earlier manuscript I have read, but better, luminous depictions of Bethlehem where her family hails from (unlike mine, *chasing dreams*). And Rasha is also luminous and kind, and after lunch she and her father will not hear of the bus station and undertake, instead, to return me in person to the doors of the Kenyon Institute in East Jerusalem.

For many nights of my stay in Ramallah, each night, there has been the sound of minor explosions and strife which I hear from the room that I rent, and which I see, illuminating the sky from my window. It is 2015, and the Western media speculates about whether a third intifada is imminent or whether it is already here. And the Palestinian news is quite different; Ramzi has turned on the television, no sound, which is looping and magnifying the moment in which an Israeli soldier saws off the door of a civilian car (and don't ask me what happens to the driver standing between the tank and the vehicle). For the nights of my stay, late at night, in the street there are men loping about nursing injuries just acquired and warning us all to take cover. 'Have you heard of the Israelis?' one says (most thrilling question I have ever been asked, as if anyone could entertain the possibility of a reality without them suffocating us).

So the three of us get in the car, Ramzi driving, and Rasha behind us, and we steer out to a road that is closed, littered with canisters of tear gas, grim metal objects that are disturbed by the wheels of our car. Then we drive to a second, closed also, and Ramzi says, 'We'll have to drive north towards Nablus and swing down from there to the Jerusalem Road', and we are still in Ramallah but we stop to get petrol and Rasha goes into the station and buys a shopping bag full of water and snacks for this road trip, though the distance between Ramallah and Jerusalem is not many kilometres and Ramzi says, 'About fifteen minutes as the crow flies' (as only the crow does now in these times of Occupation).

We drive through the fading light, going north for what must be an hour, and on our way we pass refugee camps where Palestinians have been displaced twice, first Nakba then Naksa, and Ramzi winds down the windows to let in an appalling stench that we all gag on and he says (eyes watering), '*That* is Zionist excrement that runs down the hill from that settlement, and literally onto the heads of Palestinians beneath them', and Ramzi knows a lot about sewage and town planning and he says, 'Make no mistake, they are trying to smoke us out'. And he reclaims this colonial imagery as he is saying it, describing the latest neo-liberal strategy of voluntary departure, one arm of Sari Hanafi's spacio-cide, when life becomes too unbearable. Later at a meeting in Jerusalem an anthropologist says, 'It's just so difficult to find an *authentic* Palestinian, they've been spoiled by the years of NGO interactions and they've adopted their language' (and I am astonished that Orientalist tropes about Arabs continue in academia to go unexamined).

At some turning point on the road we begin driving south again, and as we approach the lights of Jerusalem, Ramzi tells me a story about his family's property in that city and one of these stories involves a building which houses a foreign embassy (before 1948 and after it too) which his grandfather built. The story is this, that for some years after the end of the Mandate, that government continues to pay the Palestinian owners a rent until they realise they really don't have to, and there is no Palestinian, owner or otherwise, to enforce it. So these diplomats stay on in the style of an occupation and maybe they are still there in this grand old building in Jerusalem where they too are complicit in stealing the wealth of all us benighted Palestinians.

We drive from the West to the East (rarely enough according

to the compass and also colonial language), circling down past the Ambassador Hotel and a madrassa to the Mount of Olives Road. And the door in the wall of the institute is hard to see in the dark, which I instruct Ramzi is beside one of the Nashashibi's houses, now a museum. Ramzi is a true Palestinian gentleman, and he hoists out my case once we park on the pavement and I wrestle with the lock and then we fall into the garden, and Ramzi cries, 'My god! Look at what the British have done to us!', as he trips on a series of half-broken steps cut into the soil that ascend to the mansion. And all he can see as a man who remains in a homeland when others (my family) depart, is the neglect of these premises in a contemporary sense, and not the romantic resonance of a long-gone life that I, returning grand-daughter of the Sahhar Bros. Tours and Motor Service, attribute to it.

25. MAMILLAH

Mamillah Road in Jerusalem is still called Mamillah, and that is not to be taken for granted in the geography of Palestine where much is renamed, and *Hebrai-ized*, as Ilan Pappé has called it, to make Jewish-Israeli citizens feel at home as they go about life in the stolen landscape of their unnatural state. So Mamillah is still Mamillah and you can visit it, but as I have said the accretions of a colonial redevelopment have left precious few buildings to indicate what it looked like in the years before Nakba.

Mamillah is also the name of a district, then and now also, an ancient pool and a cemetery that was in part transformed into an *Independence Park* (some decade after the so-called occasion) and in part planted out by an *Independence Garden*, which was funded by a gift of the South African Zionist Federation. And you may have heard of the exhumations from the cemetery, and then injunctions, and the flood and then the drought of funding that was raised for a *Museum of Tolerance*, designed by a great but hapless architect, to be un-ironically erected over the bodies of dead Palestinians. Mamillah runs west of the Jaffa Gate from the Old City and is positioned between there and the property Abdullah builds at Asa Street (more later). There in the New Jerusalem (as we called it) Mamillah spills out from the Roman city that was once in its middle, before commerce boomed and Jerusalem with it, in the late Ottoman period.

I have told you already of the correspondence Pa saves from one of his earliest clients, Miss Sena Bowman of the ABC crowd (as they call themselves and I call them). Miss B renders me a service now as I write this, in faithfully noting the dates on her postcards, which helps me to narrow down the moment when Abdullah opens an office on Mamillah (which Pa affirms on the tape – 'We open an office on Mamillah Road' – but otherwise fails to dwell on, less vivid one imagines than the actual business of travel). By 1935 the offices are established and there is an advertisement the Sahhar Bros. take out in a guide book, *The Traveller's Companion to the Holy Land* co-produced by a George M Sahhar, a man who Jerusalem still remembers and who writes at least two guidebooks during this decade. Pa must place an advertisement with George, his cousin, though his grandson and I cannot quite make out the relation (though we know that there is one), and you can find it on the bottom half of page fourteen in the later and larger volume from 1935. And later again, when I trawl through *The Palestine Post* (a Zionist paper that is cunningly renamed and continues to this day under a new title), I find an advertisement dated April 12, 1944 that on page two announces: **5 Day Tour to Petra** and beneath, ***Exclusively for H.M. and Allied Forces*** in bold, and the tour is starting in May and you are advised to apply to George and John, c/o. Sahhar Bros. for more information.

I'm not sure what my Pa thought of the soldiers whose forces filled Jerusalem like a scourge in the 1940s, but he was a man of business and here you can see that he sees an opportunity. There are two photographs I have of Abdullah from this period, after he is married and all of the children who pre-date my father are born, in a tarboosh that the photocopy I have has made black, and in one he is sitting in front of five soldiers and in one he is standing behind about double that number, and both of these photographs are taken in front of Qubbat As-Sakhrah (which maybe you know as the Dome of the Rock). And I hear that one of these officers he meets, and who might be in one of these pictures, is a royal from somewhere white-skinned and English-speaking. When I ask Juju, she asks in return who the foreign minister was in Churchill's government, before proposing that the identity of this dignitary is one of the Queen's uncles, who appears a much thinner man in the picture I have than in portraits available on the internet.

The Sahhar Bros. have a working relationship, or so I surmise, with this George M Sahhar, and George's first job is with the Fast Hotel at the junction where the Jaffa and Mamillah Roads once split around the triangular corner and edifice of it. The Fast is such a landmark that it is noted on all the tourist maps I have seen of Jerusalem in the first half of the twentieth century, and there is even a picture of Australian Prime Minister Robert G Menzies there with Australian troops on his visit to Palestine in February 1941. In the late Mandate era, during the Second World War, the Fast is renamed Australian Soldiers Club as is affirmed in a 1941 *Steimatzky's Palestine Guide* map which lists *Hotel Fast (Soldiers Club)* to capture this; though whatever its final name, the iconic Fast is now demolished.

By 1935, the Sahhar Bros. advertisement states that their offices are to be found on Mamillah Road at number 94. I am told by an elderly Jerusalemite that the enterprise is two shopfronts, leased from an order of Catholic nuns, the Sisters of Charity or perhaps the St Vincent de Paul Hospice. Part of the store is a showroom for the carpentry business, and the same man recalls, *I can never forget, and I still see in my mind's eye, the display behind one of the two shop windows with a beautiful double bed dressed in a lovely satiny, light-honey-coloured-cover with a couple of similarly covered pillows, though of a lighter shade.*

And an even more elderly Jerusalemite, the neighbour of George's grandson, tells me she worked for my Pa as a teenager. But I'm sad to say I learn no more from her than this fact. On the letterhead for the business that I am given somewhere outside of Manhattan, there is no number denoting the shop. And on the tape Pa recounts, 'I became sort of very well known', so maybe a number was superfluous.

The furniture business, a business simply known as Sahhar Bros., makes fashionable modern furniture and this can be seen in a bedroom setting they picture between their address on the letterhead, in English on the left (read left to right) and their address in Arabic on the right (read right to left). I have two copies of this, one a photocopy with a *2* written underneath the picture and the other, what I think is an original (the one Mahfouz gives me) with a date written out in beautiful script which reads *March 28th, 1949.* This is not a significant date except it illustrates that they are still there on Mamillah, Issa and maybe Emile, ten months after Nakba has turned the Mamillah Road district into a no-man's land (Israelis report in their official histories that the region went into a decline). On the wall of the office at 94, I imagine Abdullah had framed a certificate from the Arab Chamber of Commerce, Jerusalem, which attests to the fact that the above named *has been duly registered as an active member* of the aforementioned, all in flowery script, right side Arabic, left side English.

In the catalogue notes for *Unpicking Jerusalem*, Sary explains how the Mamillah Road, due to its pivotal location, was *quickly established as the new commercial centre of the city.* It is proximate to the new Jerusalem-to-Jaffa railway line's main terminus, not fifteen minutes on foot from the district. Mamillah later became the home of the Palestine Broadcasting Service, and this hints, Sary writes, *at how Mamilla* [*sic*] *had taken on a cultural significance within the city by the time of the British Mandate.*

In Jerusalem today there are desirable upmarket suburbs, now in the West, which were built (and not sold) by Palestinian families; although there is a transition period when Mamillah, made derelict by Nakba, is *a grimy industrial suburb* of workshops and garages. As far as I am aware there are just two buildings today which remain in their original places. But there are also several buildings that Sary notes in his exhibition, which the Israelis number and take apart, stone by stone, and then re-insert back into the re-developed landscape; and they adopt in the process Palestinian architectural aesthetics and the celebrated Jerusalem stone, and Sary says that in doing this, they make a claim *to have always been there.*

The ghost of Mamillah Road is still a short walk to the train station but there are no trains to Jaffa today (or on any of the days since the line was closed down, or even since it was reopened in its postmodern way, that distresses the old Palestinians who have remained). I would need the old registry of land parcels, or the help of my Pa, to discover precisely where his showroom was located. I have walked the Mamillah complex as it currently stands, all the long length of it, behind an off-duty soldier with a rifle slapping his fatigues while he licks at an ice-cream and laughs with his girlfriend. Like the Fast Hotel which marked the bifurcation of roads, the Mamillah I write of is also effaced.

26. THE MAPS HERE ARE USELESS

The art of cartography is surely a colonial art, which hails from the earlier Age of Discovery, when the Americas are mapped, quite inaccurately, and the unknown lands of Australia are marked twice, on the left-hand side of South America and again on the right-hand side of the Dutch East Indies. Maps tell a story, as many have observed before me, like what do you put in the centre, and what the periphery? And sometimes powerful figures are depicted on top of a map, like in the Ditchley portrait of the first Elizabeth, or the Cape to Cairo image of Cecil Rhodes, to communicate in more than a metaphoric sense their assertion of ownership. And sometimes also a place that has been depicted for centuries and known for millennia disappears from the maps overnight, as if inexplicably, and this marks how maps serve colonial narrative. So what I can say is that maps are a poor measure of knowledge in place, and all the old Palestinians knew place better than any map – that conceals their home – can relate.

We all of us now, in the twenty-first century, form impressions that precede our visits to some several great cities, like London and Paris, like Rome or New York, and perhaps when you visit you feel like you know them, the buildings, the rivers and monuments and how they connect together. But for me this is how I find Jerusalem to be, or Al-Uds as the Jerusalemites say it, dropping the sound of the Q, a hometown I have never seen, until my thirtieth year when I arrive at long last in a city I know like the back of my hand, and although I consult not one map I have a geography of stories, and I am never lost in it. And I look at the city, and the city at me, and we both say in our way Ahlaan, which is the sound of a welcome that lights up your eyes and tells the recipient that you couldn't imagine anyone better to see: *Ahlaan, Al-Uds, ahlaan!*

My dear Pa, who attended services at the Williamstown Gospel Mission on Electra Street after Nakba (where his funeral was held and fifteen years later, Ellen's) enjoyed church in the Jerusalemite spirit of mixed denominations. For instance, when visiting my parents he would go to the Mass with my mother, who said, 'Mr Sahhar, communion is for Catholics', and to which Pa would say, 'Don't worry, Maxine! God recognises me!'. And what I think he liked most is the way that the Bible so very immediately evoked the landscape of his youth, in whose descriptions he revelled until the end of his life. I particularly like a story of Pa attending a service with the Baptists on Sydney Road, where he turned to heckling the minister who was describing an oration presented by Jesus, and to which Pa intervened, 'No, brother, no! If you're standing facing down from that mount then the olive groves are surely not on your left but to the right!'.

In Jerusalem, I walk a city demarked by Old and New, not East and West, when I am walking our history, and I walk to the re-built King David Hotel and the YMCA building opposite. And I am reminded of a story from when the infamous bombing occurs, and I have seen an image of the explosion that resembles a mushroom cloud, which is held in the Imperial War Museum collection, in that now-faded metropole, London. What I hear is that on the day of the explosion, Juju and Tony are sent home from school (early) and they are neither adults but also not children, and they make their way together over and through the crime scene which is as Jerusalem appears on July 22 of that year.

Tony tells the story that on the corner beside the King David was a boy who the schools did not require, and during the day, all day every day, he would go to this corner and set up a game of marbles. And as Tony tells the story, the boy is here again on this July day of 1946, playing marbles before the explosion, and he is one of the casualties after it, and as Tony and Juju pass by what they see is a corpse blown to pieces, his skull (literally) open on the pavement. Tony says he recalls that some of the marbles had rolled into the boy's exposed brains, and the force of the bomb was so great that when they walk past, the marbles are still moving inside the skull of a boy who is remembered by Jerusalemites everywhere. When Tony tells this story Juju says, 'I must have seen it too but now I don't remember', and later again when I ask Juju what happened she says she was at home on the balcony at Asa Street eating grapes, and what she saw was the plumes of smoke that hung on the skyline for hours.

This story places my uncle and aunt in the landscape of a particular day that is an important catalyst to the unfolding national trauma to follow, and when I return from Jerusalem, I recount it to Ahmad on his Flinders Lane balcony and he stops me halfway and says, 'I know that story too! My aunt was there and she saw it'. And I store these anatomical details of the boy and the marbles into myself and recount them on the hotel pavement to my Hebrew translator; and later in the Liberty Bell Park I will say, 'This city is alive with stories that only we know', appalled by the hubris of colonial ignorance, that can swallow a city without even seeing it.

I have walked many times on Salah Ad-Din Street, and if you are facing towards the Old City you will arrive at the turn for my cousin's bookshop, who when I ask for the address simply says, 'You don't need it! If you are lost, ask anyone, everyone knows where I am'. This is the confidence of geography which people who have been in a place a long time are born with, like all the great families of Jerusalem in the cemetery registries. I am always delighted when the Palestinians recognise my name, inside and outside Jerusalem, like a Palestinian ambassador visiting from London to whom Sahhar means something, who engages me in pleasantries at a conference, that suspend one reality we live in for the one that we wish to be in. Jerusalem is a city I know in my heart, that makes the map useless, whose geography I inherit as a memory and that I remember (like the Donkey) and which, like my surname, is something fused into my being that nothing, not even a bomb, can succeed in wresting away or parting me from.

Not Beirut, nor Rome, Ramallah lacks the repository of images that inhere in some cities. Nor Jerusalem, for which there can be no substitute.

27. VISIT PALESTINE

This iconic slogan which most people know (and maybe you too) begins its life on a modernist poster produced by the Zionists who are trying to encourage Jews, the world over, not just to visit this place, but to live in it. The poster is designed by Franz Krausz, an Austrian, drawn to Zionism, and he moves to Berlin and does art and design and as Hitler rises to power he moves next to Spain and then Mandatory Palestine. By the time of the poster, Krausz and his wife, a photographer, have arrived in Jaffa and move to Tel Aviv, which is protected now by UNESCO, the White City they call it, constructed in just a few decades on modernist principles and designed by architects hailing from Europe. Here they all coalesce in the largest Jewish settlement in Mandatory Palestine and give birth to this city and Krausz to this poster, *Visit Palestine*, in 1936, for a body then called *Tourist Development Association of Palestine*. Though the Zionists have since claimed that 'Palestine', note the inverted commas with which it is written, did not have a political connotation, this is merely a fiction maintained by people it suits to maintain. It ignores the agency of Palestinian political newspapers fomenting demonstrations, strikes and revolts across these Mandate years, which Palestinians deployed to communicate their rejection of British decisions and the Zionist seizure (though it ends as one might expect and as we all know, for the plucky Palestinians, who lack the resources of a colonial infrastructure they sought to oppose).

The most long-lived of these poster images is known as the 'Jerusalem' version, which is reproduced in limited edition in the mid-1990s owing to the community sentiment Oslo generates. Later it is reproduced in unauthorised versions by Palestinians, and sometimes it is warholed with a wall dividing the foregrounded tree from the stylised dome behind it, and later again the Nasser brothers will Gaza it. Since the earliest production of these posters many objects have become endlessly reproducible and they derive their value, in those cases, not as objects (the original) but through narrative (the infinite).

I grow up quite unthinkingly with two souvenirs from Jerusalem attached to my desk lamp, a keyring depicting an espaliered olive tree above an enamel rendering of that city's English name, and a wooden Jerusalem cross of medium size, threaded through a ribbon and dangling from the neck of the light. Added to these was a Palestinian coin, five mils, with a hole in the middle which came to me after an Arabic-speaking customer of African origin brought it into my father's pharmacy and attempted to use it in payment for a PBS prescription. And this coin is silver and slightly greened from all the handling it had between the year of production – 1935 – and the year it went out of circulation in a shop on High Street in Preston.

I am contacted by a curator at the Immigration Museum about an exhibition they are producing to represent the Palestinian community, and I arrive to a meeting in a room near the Seafarers Mission on Flinders Street, and they are already planning. The men say, 'We have many documents to show, passports and coins'. And the curator says she does not anticipate cabinets of coins to comprise a particularly gripping exhibit. How do you render a diaspora in a museum, I wonder, when all the saved things we have are not things we would easily part with, even in alarm-sensored cabinets and beneath lock and key? None of the objects we save, even broken beads from a necklace, are things we *can* spare, not even to prosecute our story in a museum. And as we discuss the vanishing avenues of possible objects to showcase, the men are not diverted by curatorial wisdom, and they press again, 'But what of the coins? They are a proof beyond reasonable doubt that we were there before we were here, and that there was a somewhere, and that somewhere was ours!'. The coins are an argument, *Palestine* incontrovertibly emblazoned on currency.

Souvenir culture by contrast leaves many more traces, and not long ago when you visited Jerusalem there were shops full of found artifacts and old tat, retrieved from houses, like old cigarette packets and trinkets abandoned on coffee tables. Souvenirs travel as is their conception, to spread far and wide and even as far as Australia, and in an antique shop near my parents' house I find two brooches in mother-of-pearl, a large Star of Bethlehem, like Najla's Bible, and a smaller less weathered design, and I ask at the cash register where the vendor of stall 29 acquired these objects and the cashier is vague, 'Her husband's a doctor and they travel a lot to odd places'.

Souvenirs continue to proselytise the fact of our nation, and I am always pleased to see them with Palestine inscribed for all to see on their backs or their bases, and later I am given a brooch which is a very fine example of Jerusalemite filigree with that nation's name stamped into the silver back of it, and which I carefully polish to brighten the origin. The mother-of-pearl is from Bethlehem (see: wedding hats) and most of the nativity carvings you see (sometimes including the apartheid wall that cuts through that city) are also from Bethlehem and usually shaped out of olive wood (and the Israelis are pulling up our ancient groves with such speed that there is more wood than can be carved into nativities, and more roots than there is space left to plant them in).

Issam Nasser has documented nineteenth century portrayals of Jerusalem as follows: holy, biblical, devastated (*'Tis horrible! Is there no hope?*) and orientalised. This third attitude, devastated, captures what Nasser (who incidentally is part of the tree of my family, recalled by Ellen in her dying days under the name of his father's village, and not by their surname), says came to characterise the gap between a tourist's long-awaited encounter and the real Jerusalem which *often aroused in the visitor a grand sense of disappointment*. The infamous Baedeker writes that while to most *a place of overwhelming interest, but at first sight many will be sadly disappointed* ... He continues, *[i]t would seem at first as though little were left of the ancient city of Zion ... and little of it indeed is to be discovered in the narrow, crooked, ill-paved, and dirty streets of the modern town*. An English traveller, Robert Byron, will describe in what I deduce is the early years of Mandatory Palestine, the Church of the Holy Sepulchre, our local parish, as *the meanest of churches. Its darkness seems darker than it is, its architecture worse, its cult more degraded*. It is in this connection I have always enjoyed the legend of unsavoury souvenir items that the credulous modern tourist pilgrim might have sought in the streets of the Old City (in a biblified time but quite recently), holy relics, for instance. And I like to imagine the Palestinian merchants of a morning, clipping their toenails and then their children's and saying later of these abject offerings: *this big toenail costs twice of that little one*, claiming to each relic a provenance from this or that patron, and perhaps in Jerusalem even that of our Lord and Saviour.

Somewhere in the Old City, past the Muslim grocers and the pomegranate-juicers, who crush the flesh of these fruits on their citrus presses, I am approached by a vendor who remarks on the amber beads I am wearing and draws me into his shop, a place I feel trapped (this delicacy of being a Palestinian in a Jewish shop in Jerusalem) and there is nothing I want to buy there but feel awkwardly obliged. I pick through the replica posters and select the ubiquitous *Visit Palestine*, now framed in my house, and when I visit a friend in San Francisco he has the same one, but in a more blueish tone on account of the variability of reproduction.

Later that day I am sitting in the shop of a jewellery seller and he sends his son out for a coffee to serve me. He takes from a cabinet something he particularly wants to show me but which isn't for sale, his grandfather's passport, that notes, unmistakably, the existence of Palestine. This man has seven children, laughing that they are a demographic timebomb, and we sip our hot drinks and I remark on the slender wrists of the brides who wore the silver bracelets he's selling. I purchase three wooden boxes from the jeweller, who imports them, he says, from the Palestinian camp in Damascus (which is by then a suburb, but now I fear may be indistinguishable from other neighbourhoods of that once-beautiful city, after a relentless and deadly decade for the Syrian people) and it is made with some several woods, including from lemon trees, and intricately painted on every conceivable surface in the pattern of an inlaid mosaic – for which we are famous – and which you can see at Jericho or in the Shellal Mosaic at the Australian War Memorial in Canberra. Into these I will later place bougainvillea clipped from the fence of my Pa's house, which, though dried, has held its shade with resilience (and this is no less than I would expect from a plant that has remained in continuous habitation at Asa Street). The jeweller and I chat for some hours, looking over his photo albums together like old friends, and he tells me stories about his family's continuous presence in this city our ancestors shared. And he recognises my arrival as a returning, and as I am leaving he welcomes me home to Jerusalem.

28. FRUITS OF THE LOOM

I am sitting in Juju's dining room which is divided from the kitchen by mid-1960s cabinetry, with glass sliding doors above the bench. I like watching Juju through the glass while she is at the sink washing just a few dishes, a chopping board and a blunt knife, and you can see all the way through to the laundry and over the sunroom through the eclectic selection of glasses that could have been transported from Ellen's kitchen at Mirls Street, and maybe they were. There are stories that this house was architect-designed but also a kit home that a plumber once built for his family. It doesn't much matter, since the wall of glass windows that overlook the gums and the variegated ivy has for fifty years been Juju's own sanctuary.

She brings to the dining room table a series of photographs that we pore over together after lunch is cleared and as we sip our small elegant coffees in finjans and pick at the fruit platter. There are photos people have sent, maybe to Ellen before she died, and Juju looks at their faces and says, 'Do you want some of these? You seem to know these people'. She folds a selection of weddings and birthdays and nothing particular into a card and the card into a small plastic bag which I take home at the end of my visit. There are some Christmas portraits, whole families with children (now adults older than I am) and even of Hanna, Juju's grandfather and my great one with sweet George, Ellen's brother, wearing ladies' boots on the wrong feet in my mind, and after whom there are several cousins, also named George. One of those namesakes, the youngest George I know of, is pictured with his wife in a studio portrait from the 1980s, which you can tell from their garish disco clothes and shoulder pads, and they are grinning wildly with fabulous long hair (George) and a terrific and characteristic perm of that time (his wife). But the pictures I am particularly taken by on this visit are just a few small black and white images about the size of my palm, and these are in Amman and they are of people I know very well, my aunts and my father; and people they know very well, their aunts, Ellen's sisters.

Juju appears in two of these pictures and each image contains one of Ellen's younger sisters, sometimes Rose, sometimes Lily, and what is clear to see is that Juju is of their generation and not of her siblings, and they too are like sisters. I think they must help her with herding the three small children in front of them and I'll call this *Amman #1* although there is an earlier photo with Dad that I've told you of, scudding around the car that my Pa transforms, such is the magic inherent to our good name, into the price of the berths required to reach Australia. *Amman #1* depicts five people, my little father in a dress again, at the front, between Salma and Vera, and you can see how little Vera is and how she has tucked her cheek into the baby's small arm (and to this day those two speak most mornings, one in Adelaide the other Melbourne, chatting about ordinary things families talk of like what is for lunch and the best way to stuff kousa). Salma and Dad are dressed in garments patterned in just the same fabric, and Salma's that awkward age when no-one knows how to dress young girls who are neither little nor women, though for refugees this is of less concern than it might otherwise have been.

Juju and Rose are bent slightly behind the children who are smiling (maybe bouza is promised) and this picture is unlike the others, because there are trees and dry-stone terraces and a handsome stone house at the top of the photo behind them. Juju and Rose, there are just a few years between them, speak often I hear, until Rose dies (the Rose who says, 'When are you coming darling?', sounding like Ellen, the edge of a laugh at the corners of her direct question). Juju is in an elegant frock, and I have read of the Palestinians in Amman that they were *'well-dressed', an indicator that many of those leaving Palestine … left well-off homes and assets behind* them – or so says Jack Flowers, staff correspondent for the *Sydney Morning Herald* during Nakba. Rose looks less elegant, dolled-up with a frilled collar and curls pinned out to the sides, and now that I study it, I notice that around the same age I would prepare my hair just as Rose does here without knowing it.

The two other photos are different to *Amman #1.* There is a small one of Juju and Lily, looking much like Ellen, who stand at the left-hand side of a rooftop terrace, and maybe what they are trying to gesture towards, in the vanishing point at the centre that they are not standing in, is the proximity between Amman and Jerusalem. If you know the right route then this is a walk of not more than six hours. The back of this picture says 1952 and maybe that's true (*Amman #1* is less certain, maybe 1949 or 1950, Juju's note wonders) but it is hard to follow the movements this family makes over the four-year period between the birth of my father and the voyage they make on *The Roma.* The last photo is Rose, on her own, and she stands on the same terrace as Juju and Lily but the camera is positioned differently to show the tiers of small houses that crop up in the years of the birth of the refugee crisis (and maybe this is above Hashemi Street and this terrace and those houses are long past demolished now). Rose looks like a young movie star in this one (Elizabeth Taylor) in shapely slacks and a close knitted sweater, her hair shining black and her skin completely untanned as she squints at the photographer, who may be her niece, Juju or sister, Lily.

When many years later Juju reads a collection of stories, *Seeking Palestine*, she jots down some notes which she gifts me as the precious document they are and she says, it *jolts my memory to places I've been to*, and what she does not note down is that it jolts her memory to the place that she's from and the cities she's lived in. One of these notes pertains to Lily – Lily on the terrace with Juju in Amman, Lily who fights for the necklace with Najla in 1932 when these sisters are still small children and they are still in Bethlehem. Although I don't know where Najla and Lily and Rose go to school, nor Alice who will later be employed as a school principal in Beit Jala, they are surely educated, and by the late 1940s, Lily is a teacher in Jaffa (great port town and jewel of the Mediterranean, now subsumed as an outskirt of the Tel Aviv settlement, liminal and luminous city the Israelis want to live in and are also wary of).

Something happens in Jaffa which perhaps Lily never recounted to her niece Juju, and the Palestinians are forced to flee, and Lily among them, and they flee on the back of a utility, Lily and many others. Juju states: *we had no idea where she was.* Eventually it transpires that Lily is found (suggesting she is lost, although one might imagine Lily was always acutely aware of her whereabouts) in the Jordanian city of As-Salt, of which Juju remarks that Lily reports just one thing. Such was the state of the town and the extent of the crisis that people had to drink their own urine. With Juju again on the rooftop in Amman,

Lily grips the wall at the back of the terrace and maybe this is a trace of the time in which Lily was absent, a clue that just four years since the start of our Nakba, she had lived through a lot. Even on a day of photographs, family and bouza, you can see in her body already that she carries sumud.

In the late 1960s Ellen has already been parted from her sisters for near twenty years, and they plan a ticket first to Syria then America. Not long before they depart, Pa suffers a heart attack and Ellen insists that he shouldn't fly and my father recalls a scene in the lounge room at Mirls Street with Ellen crying and gripping his arm and Pa standing resolute and saying, 'Well, it's up to you but I'm going!'. My cousin Di says my Pa gives her a present at the airport (coming or going, she doesn't remember) when she is a small girl and Fouad must be there, horrified as I have said by the state of Ellen's dresses. She sees Badia, great seamstress (more later), she sees Najla who so desperately wanted to follow her to Australia. She sees Lily and George, who fills up her suitcases with safety razors and American clothing (and I think of Najla when Dad and I visit, who is quite certain that we need to make room for a kilogram packet of freekeh, which she advises will keep you as young as good clothes do).

In Syria, Ellen stays with Alice, whose daughter obtains a degree at the great old Damascus University, and Ellen buys four thobes with gorgeous tatreez (which, it should be stated, is not something that urban Jerusalemites are in the business of embroidering), one each for the daughters. Juju shows me hers now, which has a note attached to it, explaining that in the event of her death this garment is not to be taken to the op shop but given to someone who'll wear it, and after she reads me the note she asks if I want to be on the list to receive it. Ellen is given, perhaps by her sister, the mould for ma'amoul that I will one day inherit. I am not sure that Ellen procures a gift of any significance for my father, but he says that out of the safety razors and boxes of Chiclets chewing gum and clothes heaped up in his parents' suitcases, there were dozens of packets of underwear, Fruit of the Loom, and this is something he's given when they return.

In the past when I have thought of the hoard of oddments that fill Ellen and Pa's cases I wonder why they bring all these everyday items home with them, but as I get older I understand that this is what families do at an easy distance unthinkingly (like 'Do you need soap or tissues?' my father often says at the end of my visits). This splintered family who will never be all together again are trying to recreate this ordinariness in an extraordinary instance, taking their one slender chance to revel in the mundane.

Rattling around in the green enamel box, Juju finds a ring and she says, 'I forgot I had that'; and later when I visit her, wearing it, she says, 'I forgot I had given that to you, it looks nice!'. At the Los Angeles airport, Rose is there with the others, farewelling Ellen, when she suddenly takes this ring off her finger. 'This is for my little friend Juju, I miss her', she says as she folds it into Ellen's palm.

And so a little gold and blue ring comes flying back over the seas, and this is the last thing that passes between Rose and her niece, my Juju, both younger than me when they were last in arms' reach of each other. And now there is only Juju who remembers the day that these portraits were taken, or the imminence of that separation, or how an aunt may appear as a Hollywood star a lifetime ago and many continents away.

29. PA AND THE TURKS (IN PALESTINE)

My Pa was a man who told stories and who (as I've told you) became, by misfortune, the eldest, and Abdullah often felt the weight of his mother, Taata Barbara, and four other children while Pa's father, who dies quite young, is seemingly free of this burden. Yet it is beside his own father, Andoni (also the name of his son), that he wished to be buried, in a cemetery on Mount Zion, and when he tells Juju she says, 'We will try, Dad'. And later, perhaps after an epiphany about the meaning of bodies or one about the rigidity of borders, he tells her the body is merely a shell and his spirit will be with the Lord.

Pa speaks of the Ottoman period on one of his tapes. He tells us Andoni is requisitioned like property by the Turks but forbidden to fight, since they do not trust the Christians, nor do they pay them. Pa recalls that his mother would sell her clothes and jewellery in Beit Jala, where nobody knew her to know the disgrace of this thrift. And on her journey to market, Taata walked past the Church of St George and the Dragon (patron saint of Palestine and other Mediterranean places, where he was reportedly born and lived out his days), on the road between Beit Jala and Bethlehem.

Juju says later that her grandfather's job in the army was to carry food, on poles, for the Turkish soldiers and to dig their trenches. Her recollections are of a man with dry wit who says the Turks fed them soup and bread, and says also *you had to be a good diver to find a lentil in your soup.* Andoni would run away to visit his family and hope that he wouldn't be caught. But this period is a terrible period, my Pa recollects, in some sympathy I suppose, with the Turks, 'It was sort of unbearable, even the Turkish soldiers were hungry and they used to come to the Christian quarter, and pretend to be Christians'. Perhaps because Andoni dies in Palestine, and is a man of whom my father has no recollection, in my imagining he is often on the brink of being a scoundrel. This impression is aided by a story of his dying days, when Pa drives Andoni around to the doctors for second and third opinions, and all of them say, 'This man's surely done for, let him smoke and drink as he pleases'.

'The alternative', Pa remarks on the tape, with a wit that fortifies the now-distant sadness, 'would have been to cut off his head'.

Juju has few recollections of him either, but as the eldest it would seem that she thought to ask her father (my Pa, his son) and Abdullah recalls *that grandpa Andoni was a gentle and generous man.* Pa remembers his father's humility before the altar of poverty, he recalls him *sitting at the table having a drink and waiting until all the children finished eating before he ate.* And then I get one glimpse of Abdullah as truly small, eldest son who is made to be old before his childhood is done. Pa says he *remembers his father lying on a bed with his children climbing on his chest and listening to stories he loved to tell – while the children asked him for favours which he always tried to fulfil.* There is maybe one photograph of Andoni, a slim man in a tarboosh at the back of a frame that features people I know with their feet in the fountain at Asa Street, but there is no-one left to identify him.

And I see also now that what Andoni does, in running away to visit his wife and his family, is surely an act of bravery. Pa describes in some colour the punishment for those who were captured, 'They used to hang them on the gates of the city, and supposing they wanted to hang three of them, then they would want to hang one of them Christian, one Mohammadan and in the morning people would come to see them'. Pa remembers that once a Turk was found to be innocent, but already he swung on the gates.

According to the articles published by Alexander Aaronsohn which formed the text of a volume, *With the Turks in Palestine*, the Turks had initially conscripted all fighting-age male inhabitants of Palestine, and only later revised this position in which men were placed, like Andoni, in the working corps *to conciliate and flatter the Mohammedan population, and at the same time to put the Jews and Christians, who for the most part favoured the cause of the Allies, in a position where they would be least dangerous.* Yet when I am asked to launch a re-issuing of this text I conclude that *while British intervention may have been conceived of as liberationist, supporters of the Ottomans, to the contrary, styled the continuation of Ottoman rule as a rejection of Western imperialism. Instructively, one sees that in neither of these positions is a religious motivation paramount.* Accounts of colonial and imperial interests, be they Ottoman or British, too often conceive of Palestinian life as incidental to grand narratives.

I see Abdullah walking from Bethlehem (a family strapped to his shoulders) back to Jerusalem, where his uncle Dawood, a carpenter and also a miller, hires him. He is taught about engines and millstones and works there for a year before Dawood's business partner sacks him, to create a role for his own orphaned nephew. Pa tells an honest story, he says, 'When they sacked me I didn't know what to do, so I walked over to a place near the Damascus Gate, a flour mill, which had three big stones to grind for the public and then four smaller stones to grind wheat for the Turkish government'. The picture is desperate, he says, 'In those days there's no work, there's no food, and the people were begging'.

Several sources record that Abdullah works all day every day and all night every second, he sleeps once in each forty-eight-hour period, but he doesn't complain. He says, 'I used to run the engine for them and sharp the stones, the stones I used to sharp them with a chisel, and one of the chisels fell down on my foot and cut it from top to bottom near my toes'. A foot swathed in bandages yet he carried on working all the same.

Late in the war, the Australian forces arrive under Allenby's command with (light) horses, and the Turks need more soldiers. Pa recounts that there was an officer for the Ottomans who hung a brass sign under his neck, and who started to round up malingering boys. When he came to the mill, Abdullah hid himself between the roof and the ceiling at the back of the biggest mill wheel. When the brass-signed officer discovered the scheme he made it his practice to return to the mill quite often, where he sought not Abdullah, but payment to keep what he knew to himself.

The mill owner was, one supposes, a canny businessman though not especially kind, and though he could not spare Abdullah, it was from Abdullah's own wages that he paid off the Ottoman, shedding not one cent that he missed, dividing that meagre pay between the authorities and Abdullah's mother, who would come to Jerusalem collecting his wages. Pa recounts that finally, one day or one night, he announced himself to the officer saying, 'I'd rather go because probably I would have a night's sleep'. But even then he is spared, indispensable to his boss and his mother, so the mill is where he continues, long hard years he remembers (not metaphorically) as years of slavery.

Pa recounts his travails from what is once called the Great War on the couch at Mirls Street, turning the key to Asa Street over in his hands. And though he does not say it for this tape, my father tells me Abdullah is one day conscripted yet somehow hides under a bridge and escapes. Pa does not say, but I know, it's a very poor life for the eldest child, who shouldered a family at the age of thirteen, and from whose care he was never relieved until the day he was laid in the grounds, quite near the sea, of the Williamstown Lawn Cemetery.

30. CYPRUS

The grandparent my father best remembers is Taata Barbara, who lives quite a long time, and she is old enough to have children by the turn of the twentieth century, and she lives for more than half of it. Taata Barbara spends the last decade she lives in Australia, where up at the shops she is never not disgusted by the monolingual reality of the shopkeepers, exclaiming without fear of recognition, 'Hmara!', as she rolls her eyes and turns to her littlest granddaughter, not yet at school, in appeal. You have seen her already, walking from Bethlehem to Beit Jala, and she washes Andoni's uniform, which is filled with lice from the soldiers and trenches (and I think how incredibly itchy these men must have been, every day, all the time, something people don't mention when they are telling you about heroic exploits).

Taata Barbara lives at Asa Street in one of the five apartments her good son, Abdullah, will build for his mother, and she lives there with Yousra until Yousra is married and repairs with her husband to a Greek Orthodox complex in the Old City. Taata Barbara is widowed for quite a long time but she is married a good while too, and when she is still very young, she exchanges a name she has had since birth for a married one. When she is twelve her father-in-law spies her on one of the streets of Jerusalem's Old City and makes enquiries – it is said she has long blonde hair – and this father-in-law (I surmise an Abdullah as is tradition) calls his wife (a Salha, recalled by my Pa as the name of his sister who does not survive, who was named for her grandmother) to identify this child who will make a good match for one of his sons.

When I think of the colour of Taata's hair I am reminded of the half-known story of where she is from. Was it Izmir, on the Aegean, with Athens just over the way, and beneath the Mediterranean, in the eastern corner of the sea of the Roman Empire? You can see how close are these places and how a family might travel unthinkingly between them, presuming as people have done throughout history that they will return as they please and whenever they choose to. Or maybe this is the story of Taata's family, since at age twelve, there she is, small girl with fair hair, wandering the narrow streets of Jerusalem where my Pa's grandfather first sees her, sipping his morning coffee and surveying the great Roman architecture.

So Taata is married, not Taata then, just Barbara, and for five long years there is a marriage but no children. And you can see how my Pa loved his mother, he says later, 'How could she? She was only a little girl at the time'. And in these years the father-in-law often embarrasses her (more farmyard imagery), he calls her a mule, until she has eleven babies, of whom we know two names of the ones that didn't survive (and four more who are lost to history). And then there are five remaining who live through their childhood and make it out of the Nakba alive.

When she is older my father recalls (a fact he is interested in, professionally speaking) that she has immense respect for medicine and she likes to take pills, and sometimes other people's when she hears they are doing them good. Dad says in contrast Ellen's mother, Ajia, is not so interested in this institution, and in consequence, there is little I have to tell you of Ajia because she dies quite early, before this family despairs of their homeland. When I think of Taata's obsession with health, I think it makes sense; the oldest texts of medical science hail from the region she lives in and where her family live for generation upon generation, around the seas that connect the three great continents you see on the T and O maps that centre the world on our hometown, Jerusalem. (Those maps, incidentally, were devised by an Isidorus, who was central to converting Visigoths to Catholicism, and I imagine that highlighting Jerusalem may have helped to convince them.) Taata was a lady who cobbled together medical facts with a mixture of fables, a woman who believed for a time that more was most certainly more, and my father recounts a day when she had learnt that kerosene was a very good rub-down for arthritic joints, so to get the most out of it she splashed on a bit and then splashed on some more, on her skin and her clothes, until she was covered in burns all over her poor arthritic bones and the skin that held them in (and I do not know, but suspect, that Taata thought twice before doing that again).

Pa takes his mother to Amman, to Jerusalem, to Amman and as I have said, at last to Australia. But before this happens there is one famous trip that they make, to an island between Izmir and Jerusalem tucked up in the Mediterranean Sea and diagonally adjacent to Lebanon. It is 1950, and Ellen and Pa take Taata Barbara and their newest son Joey to Cyprus to meet Nicola (who by now has been all around the Empire and is running a café with the wife we all know about, though I cannot say if they are on the Turkish or Greek side of the island, though they are in Nicosia, but this too is divided). I am asking my father about this trip, a trip he has little memory of, and I call Taata, *Taata Barbara* and Dad says, 'I never knew Vera was on that trip', Vera who is named for this grandmother and is teased mercilessly for it, until she changes schools and also her name with it (and I am sorry to say this is Dad's mishearing, as Vera could have been a good lead).

So they take my young dad with Taata and they jump on a boat or a plane off to Cyprus to visit Nicola because he is emigrating and Taata is certain she will never see him again; and perhaps she reminds Juju, who is reading the Brontës and Austen, of one of the more comical dowagers among their pages. I have an image in Cyprus, in my mind, of the backs of my Pa and Ellen with suitcases. It is probably hot and they are weighed down with baggage and I guess they're not sure where they're going. They have been walking for hours and Joey is throwing his arms in the air, each step of the way, saying, 'Can't walk, carry!'. And added to this, Taata Barbara is trailing behind, somewhere on the day she has lost a much-loved shawl (and you can understand how after Nakba that no loss is an opportunity but simply a loss) and she is adding her voice to the din, lamenting the shawl, until my Pa (gentle Pa, who loves his mother) stops in his tracks and declaims, 'If I hear another word about that shawl I'll hit the baby!'. Dad laughs, 'Two birds with one hiding'.

There is nothing more of Cyprus that we remember (my father or me) but Dad has fond memories of Taata. When they arrive in Australia there are quite a few pictures of her with the original weatherboard house at Mirls Street, pictures they take to reassure Yousra and Issa, both gone to America, that Taata is fit and alive and being looked after. Taata has sore swollen legs at this time and is suffering from a miscellany of ailments for which I presume she receives treatment gratefully, and she lives in the house with Pa and Emile and their wives and their children and this is no uncommon thing for Arab families, whether you are still in your home (Jerusalem) or forcibly removed, as this family is, to Newport in Melbourne.

One object that Juju presents me with is a small faux-leather-covered diary from 1957, produced by a *Youngs Transport Agency* (pictured on the cover inside of a gold-embossed star that looks like the Star of David). Youngs are customs agents for imports and exports, offering *a complete transport service to all Australian ports* (and even some places I am not sure are ports, but I suppose there are ports without seas and the desert has ships, and for terrains so different, what you find is that the imagery is quite often shared). All of the entries are written in Arabic, but in a few places Juju makes a summary in the blank spaces of what Pa is saying. Here on the 8th of April (a Monday) Juju has written: *he stayed home, Joe sick. He took him to hospital. Did not go to work. Worried. Only 2 sick days left.* Pa writes nothing more in that week or the next.

My father is taken to hospital at the age of nine years with an inflamed appendix, a condition the family has earlier diagnosed as *malingering* to get out of the dishes. Dad's classmates send him a box full of comics, 'beautiful ones hardly read', he says now, but when he gets home his parents say that the comics, now stored in a fruit box, are a fire hazard and will have to be put out the back. 'They didn't last long there', Dad tells me. When my father returns, he finds Taata gone, a woman who would sit in the kitchen and with whom Joey would shell broad beans and peas, his small fingers slipping them out of the pod and Taata collecting them into a bowl. And when Joey complained that Taata hadn't helped very much she would say, 'Il-asher mish-ham, il-lam il-ham', a rhyme in Arabic, 'It's the one who collects them that matters'.

Pa's diary fixes the date of the hospital but not of Taata dying (it is just my surmise), and this absence is the kind of *caesura* that Pa must feel at the loss of his mother, orphaned, around the same age as my father will be in the future. And these blank pages, the unusual absence of notes, must be as my father experienced his taata's absence, most of all in the Mirls Street kitchen when he remarks, to whoever is listening, 'And now who will help shell the peas with me?'.

Of jam: when my father sees ants in the sugar these days he says *quick, we better make some jam.*

31. SNOW FIGHT

It is recorded that as the new *Sabras* took root in the land of my forefathers their poetry got better, more specific, the knowledge of how sun fell on their backs and how far salt travels. And it is said also that our poems grew narrower and narrower, our cities receding like forsaken treasures.

Fouzi El-Asmar recalls at the 1958 inauguration of the Arab Writers Union in Haifa, a program for the state-controlled radio, *Voice of Israel*, broadcast proceedings but declined to record the poems expressing political sentiments. This, he observes, would have given a listener the impression that Palestinians only cared for love and descriptions of nature. Perhaps this is where that idea comes from, along with a myth that doubles erasure, that you must be in a place to write well of it. But Palestinians know a myth when they hear one, since stored in our memories and passed carefully down are the minutest of details like the length of a walk or the colour of tiles in a grandmother's kitchen. Palestinians, as I have told you, know place, and they know about origin, and while I tell you that Ellen was born in Bethlehem, the Bethlehemites say, 'Well that may be, but the name's from Jerusalem'.

In 2002, during the Second Intifada, Benny Morris interviews the former prime minister, Ehud Barak, about what had gone wrong since Rabin's assassination and to help explain to *Guardian* readers the collapse of the Oslo Agreement. The article's title is quite prejudicial, *Arafat Didn't Negotiate –*

He Just Kept Saying No, and it is something in hindsight that even the centrist Zionist Peter Beinart has questioned (and in no small part as a result of this questioning, Beinart has now transcended that ideology to champion our Right of Return. And to champion too the practical plans of repatriation that Dr Salman Abu Sittah has proposed, which might allow every one of us who wishes to return to do so, even to our occupied homes). But what Barak reveals is really quite special, a thing which makes sense for the inorganic interpolation of a modernist movement over a whole ancient people, and Morris says:

> [Barak] seems to think in terms of generations and hesitantly predicts that only '80 years' after 1948 will the Palestinians be historically ready for a compromise. By then, most of the generation that experienced the catastrophe of 1948 at first hand will have died; there will be 'very few "salmons" around who still want to return to their birthplaces to die'. (*Guardian*, May 23, 2002).

And when Barak says this Palestinians say *we are salmons* (more flattering anthropomorphisation than the *human animals*, *vipers*, or *pigs* Israelis have also called us). How little, how little indeed, does he, or anyone who says this, know about Palestinians.

The winter of 2012 brings snow to Jerusalem, and that December an Israeli friend shows me a series of photographs that his sister has sent, making snow angels and smiling crazily, and while he has lived an hour away from Jerusalem for most of his life he tells me he can't remember a snow quite like this one, snow in the Israeli state arrives as a novelty that winter. The next morning after this conversation takes place I wake to a note from Juju which says: *weather forecast for Jerusalem minus one. Will be snow on our windowsill on Christmas Day from memory.* And what this says to me then is that Palestinians know our place better than anyone, and you can ask any Palestinian who has never returned in their lifetime, and yet they will describe to you the entrance of their house or a fruit-laden mulberry tree their great-aunt ate fruit from each year. One semester I teach a boy who tells the class he's Jordanian, but as the course presses on, me in my olive tree necklace, me in keffiyehs, he asks where I'm from and he changes his answer, and now he's a student from Al-Khalil. And although he's never seen it, he describes with great care the landscape of the neighbourhood he wasn't born in but knows, with the forensic intimacy that Palestinians pass down with our names and our Nakba.

I know snow in Jerusalem from Yousra's great trove of photographs, where there is something new to find each time I examine it, and on this occasion I find three pictures that pertain most directly to snow. Two are taken quite close together (*snap*, then the insurance shot, *snap* again). The other is grainy and worn, like a picture someone must have folded up in their breast pocket and removed on occasion (at night in bed I imagine), to trace their finger over the barely distinguishable faces which are hard to identify now that this love has done its damage. A handbook on Palestine, produced in the British Mandate, notes that snow was not an uncommon sight during winter in Jerusalem, and perhaps the compiler has asked the Palestinians, since this book is published in the 1920s (and how would an administrator for the Mandate know at that time what is or is not common for Palestine?). And perhaps this knowledge is premised on what Palestinians call the Big Snow, which became a kind of turning point and helpful marker of both snow and of time for people whose births were unregistered, as was common enough in an era when such pedantry was not a condition of travel, and age was understood relationally (such as eldest) rather than precisely (date of birth).

This other photo is quite a theatrical image, a scene set like a stage, three men at the back and one crouching at the front in the middle. Their faces are hard to make out (unrecognisable even) but the man in the middle could be one of Yousra's brothers or maybe her husband. To the centre and the right of the composition, these three men wear bone-pale winter coats and on the left is a man who is dashingly handsome, which is less that you can see his face but that he stands like he knows he is handsome, and he is wearing a dark black overcoat which might have medallions on his left arm (our right), or maybe just snowflakes glittering against the black of it. The man in black is holding, centre front of his body, a huge white snowball, and the man on the far left has a snowball too, this one poised in his hand as if the photographer was the target and after the shot he would throw it at whoever that was. There is an urgency to their pose, and I am convinced that after the picture they will shout, *snow fight*! Or whatever that sounds like in Arabic. The men stand in the garden of one of the Jerusalemite mansions, the premises of one of these men, or a relative or friend, and there is an expanse of snow between them and the photographer, and behind the men you can see low stone walls depicted in bright white snow edgings, and the high dusky walls of the house (and snow on the windowsill, for Christmas).

The other photographs show (unmistakably) a portrait of my family, and you can see they know snow, they have built the most intricate snow queen and she has her hair in great tresses and a beautiful carved waist depicting the belt of a fashionable dress. There are two pictures like this, and I now know that the location of this scene is in the Old City, where Yousra lives as a married woman in a Greek Orthodox compound, which Evan visits quite recently and photographs himself with the same iron railing you see here. There is Yousra and Taata and the faces of eight children, two I can name, and the others perhaps names that those children still know. When I find these I show my father, the first then the second, and when I show him the second his eyes glitter with pleasure and he says, 'There's Taata smiling!'. Although there are pictures enough of Taata, this is, so far as he knows, the only photo in which she smiled at the camera. This must be a day when Taata walks from the Greek Colony to visit her daughter in the Old City, and the children build an elaborate snow queen and then someone whips out a camera and they capture this ordinary moment after the children have done as children will do, making a monument to this day, built out of the snow.

Photography arrives in Palestine early; there are archives of pictures full of Jerusalem, although often without many people (a fact which is later deployed in campaigns to disappear Palestine before our eyes, even while we are still there inside it). Photography arrives, and the Palestinians take great pleasure in photos. There are photos of big things, and small things, and ordinary days. There are studio portraits and there are photos like this on location. And there is some great photographer, some documenter, who is a member of my family, who takes photographs of Yousra and Taata, of people in summer with their feet in the fountain at Asa Street. This amateur photographer is a person about whom I know very little, nor can I say much more than this: that the photographer who pictures my family was surely a quick and good shot, a person who knew Jerusalem and probably lived in it. And above all I can see that as all the Jerusalemites knew, so too the photographer knew about snow.

32. (NOT RUNNING), IN RAMALLAH

I have no particular interest, as a child, in Ramallah, and in fact I resent it – I resent the way it is foisted on me in a class about conflict in the brutalist building of my school which architecture recalls as significant (my history teacher less so, who is there at a picket the day they demolish the Victorian mansion this building replaces). In a literature class we are reading Brian Friel's *The Freedom of the City*, and the teacher is building a context and she asks us all about contested terrains and I say, 'Like Palestine', and she writes in thick chalk, *West Bank* and I say, 'You've left a lot of it out', and so she writes two more words (I can still hear her deliberate scratching) and when she turns I can see she has added to this, *Gaza Strip*. Of course I protest, telling her I am quite sure that Friel is on my side in this question, and she says 'Yes, well, of course the Palestinians want their strip too', and I am really incensed, sixteen-year-old anger I suddenly find I am carrying and I say, 'It's all ours, not just Gaza'. We are caught on the horns, each of the other, until I sweep with adolescent finality out of a room to which I will never return, after the vice-principal makes a call to my mother, herself a fierce advocate, who says, 'Everything my daughter has said sounds quite reasonable'.

It is not just on account of this incident but also many others that I never ask Ellen about Ramallah, though you already know Ellen thought it was *bee-yout-tiful*. I put Ramallah almost entirely out of my mind ('No', I say at a bookshop, 'not the capital'). I work hard to ignore it, until the time when I finally visit Palestine and there I am at the border, preparing my story, no trip wires to catch myself out in. I am a Christian (I am) and here I present for a tour to visit the Holy Land (and Ramallah is no site for pilgrimage and I do not mention it, and later I learn they are suspicious of single young women, common profile of activists). I am standing in a queue which is short but moving slowly, and the metal detectors are whizzing in overdrive and I remove all the obvious things and then the unobvious ones, which include my bra, glasses and hairpins (and an Israeli, who is holding my bra aloft in one hand as I walk through the security arch with no shoes on, says 'beautiful eyes', and I think this scene captures for you the intimacy of structurally ingrained oppression).

For forty-five minutes as I stand in this queue I am trying to remember my Catholic upbringing, and in particular I start to fear they will request a recitation of the Hail Mary as a condition of entry. I am thinking desperately *what is the second verse of this prayer?* stuck on the first, which loops endlessly until a moment when my subconscious finds the next lines, and I realise I have been saying the Hail Mary, quite audibly, for nearly an hour already. As the second verse wells up in me I am almost shouting, triumphantly; *see how Catholic I am?* it declares as I roar 'Holy Mary, Mother of God!'.

Only then do I notice that more than a few heads are turned. No bra, no hairpins, no spectacles, I am emboldened by blindness, chanting my way to the front of the line and the interview is a quick one, a silver-haired man who makes a call to my friend in Tel Aviv to confirm I am staying there. Then he waves me through after a small scuffle about stamping my passport, which is about to expire. I say, 'Go ahead, stamp it'; he says, 'I'll stamp a piece of paper'. I say, 'No, stamp the book', but with a flourish he hands me the separate paper and says, 'Maybe you want to go back to Syria?', tapping a visa from several years earlier emblazoned there for him and anyone to see. (And I am reminded of applying for that visa, filling in the form to send to Canberra which asks, *have you ever visited Occupied Palestine?* I say to my Syrian friend and at that time office-mate, 'Why do they care?'. And he says, 'Because that is the name they still use to describe the whole area and the state that replaced it'.)

From my room at the Rocky I walk to the centre of the new city in search of stationery, which is a reconfiguration of two towns, Ramallah and Al-Bireh, a Mandate innovation for the purpose of surveillance. This shift has enabled the city to be shut down rapidly, a possibility deployed by the Israeli Defence Force during their 2002 West Bank invasion and later, in the almost forgotten *Operation Brother's Keeper*, an event largely eclipsed by the 2014 bombardment of Gaza. I purchase an A5 size notebook and unfold the map I am given to retrace my path back to bed for the evening. The map has a circle around where I am going and I am standing in Al-Manara Square, which has five stone lions at its centre. I am trying to re-orientate my walk, but each way I progress I find myself back at the lions again. Then a red sports car drives past and someone calls out my name and it's a woman I met at the border with her Hamas boyfriend and they wave me into the back and I join them on a visit to the tomb of our ambivalent patron, Yasser Arafat (whose popularity is revived in that 2002 operation when he is trapped in his compound, and I read somewhere that he requests, in exchange for an interview with a foreign journalist, a chocolate bar). After a juice, at one of the ubiquitous but no less glorious Palestinian juice bars, they put me back out on the street somewhere closer to where I am going, and I find some street names and sit on a wall and try again to make sense of my uncertain geography.

I am near the Friends Girls' School again and I pick my way over the white dusty road and I pass Darwish's garden (again, its moving dedication, *From Palestine – to Mahmoud Darwish*) and although I am faithful to the turns I make on the map, the map is not faithful to the city I'm walking in (*the maps here are useless*, such a resounding lesson I am still learning). As the sun slips into the dusky horizon it is clear I am on the wrong road (and later when I am researching maps someone says, *well, I don't know about maps but I know if you ask a Palestinian they'll soon have you on the right road*, which is anecdotal but also true to all the stories on this subject I have ever uncovered). So I think to myself, *Jerusalem is a fifteen-minute drive as the crow flies.*

I walk down the road, past the stone terraces and through olive groves, and two riders are mounted behind me, and then they pass me, and later they pass me again in the opposite direction. *Why don't I turn?* you ask, and me too with this retrospect, but I don't, I continue, walking and breathing deeply to the rhythm of the clip of the hooves behind me and then before me (and breathing deeply in Ramallah is quite a delight, one I notice acutely on my second visit, when I come from Jerusalem and from strife, and I exhale with relief as the juice-seller mistakes me for the relative of a favoured old customer of his, maybe something about my eyes). Is it an hour or two that I walk between Ramallah and Jerusalem, poised in a space in which no-one could find me, an insignificant woman lost on a road?

On this walk, first night in my homeland, but still far from home, I am propelled through the roads I don't know in a place

I have not often thought of, and I steel up my nerves and I flag down some headlights that belong to two men in a utility. When I say where I'm going, and ask if I'm close they say, 'Well, you're not too close but you're not too far, hop in, we'll drive you'. This is a thing I never would do in Australia but I don't think for a second about doing this, and it is the second car I have been in that day with strangers, and they drive me first to their shop for a coffee and we share some sparse words (not much English, not much Arabic). When they drive me home they ask, 'How long are you staying?', and they laugh at me kindly and give me a card with their numbers on it, saying, 'Give us a ring next time you're lost and we'll find you'. And I never do see them again, but maybe one of their names is *Bassam*.

33. OWL

I remember my father drives me to school before he drives himself to the pharmacy. On cold mornings he takes out an ice-cream bucket of hot water to throw on the windscreen, and I am anxious because we are late again and this is both of our faults and we keep Arab time, but Dad is somehow never late to the shop. Driving to school with my father is an excellent education, and as we get in the car I always request a story, and I like the repeats, and to hurry me up he says, 'Today I'll tell you the story of the owl' (and sometimes the frog, and sometimes the donkey). Sometimes the morning story is a parable, Dad knows all of the Bible although he does not practise religion. And when I am little I love looking at the books in his bedroom at Mirls Street, especially *Silver Chief*, which he wins for attending the most Sunday school lessons, and it has a bookplate glued into the front with the year, maybe 1959. Dad says, 'We never had money for holidays'.

Dad's interpretation of the Bible is one I have come to value immensely; it is secular and also evangelical, because the stories when he tells them speak directly to me, even when the story is complicated and hard to make sense of. I am thinking, for instance of the troubling incident in Genesis, when God tears Isaac at the very last moment from the altar of Abraham's sacrifice, and you might ask what a merciful god means by demanding a man show his devotion in the death of a son, or what a father is doing when he consents to fulfil this command.

On mornings when I have fought with my brother, Dad tells the story of his namesake and the Amazing Technicolor Dreamcoat (a story which occurs to me as Lloyd Webber wrote it, and I have a tape until I don't have a player with a young Jason Donovan singing the part of Joseph). This is a complex story too; no son wants the burden of being the favourite, or the cruelty of brothers who abandon him on a wreckage that flows down a river (brothers who resent this young son whose arrogance puffs up his chest). And maybe Dad likes this story because it's a story of youngest sons, and he and my brother are both the youngest (and it's a terrible burden to be the oldest, I tell you, a thing that neither my parents know of first-hand).

At Mirls Street things are quite tough; Dad says baths consist of two buckets of water tipped over you, and the soap is kept in a cage so you don't waste the last little slivers. Dad remembers a day he stays home because he can't find his school shoes and there's no other pair of shoes to go to school in. Ellen is an excellent knitter, and she makes for my father a vest, see him there on a swing with Irene, wearing it. The photo is in black and white, and to the unknowing eye this vest is two-toned – but when Dad sees it he says, 'Oh that vest! I was teased mercilessly for it', and the vest is his own technicolour dream vest which Ellen has knitted together out of all the odd ends of wool that are left.

Dad and the amazing technicolour dream vest. I imagine him sitting in the Mirls Street fig tree, where he sits with Irene, overlooking the suburban football ground behind them, no penny to pay for the entry, and where they become great fans of Australian Rules Football. To the fig tree Ellen hands up home-made chips fried in olive oil for them to eat, and the kids are not all that thankful, they want chips from the shop up the street where the proprietor fries them in old grease, and either chicken or fish. Out in the west there is only one team, which is Footscray, a team that reflects best the spirit of the game. Dad is too young or too newly arrived to recall their 1954 win, first premiership in his lifetime, but he makes up for this with delirious joy in their unlikely 2016 premiership from seventh place on the ladder. Dad once told my brother (Dad, like Ellen, gives stories to people who need them) that he never did know if they'd won, unsure how to tune the radio into the game on weekends, and he'd ask other kids at school on the Monday (and I suppose they laughed at him, eternally hopeful Joseph, *as if they won! As if! Fil mish mish*).

Ellen says to my mother one time how sad she is that the youngest children never got to be princes in Jerusalem, and Dad says, 'Well, we didn't mind, we never knew what it was we missed out on'. Ellen smiles her teleological smile directed at no-one when she hears this (as I imagine it in my mind). Dad is a quintessential fan but not great at sport, unlike my brother who is an excellent sportsman, and who Dad drives all over the city, to tennis and cricket and Auskick where he doubles as umpire. One year Dad wins a trophy for umpiring the under-nines, and although my brother has many trophies it is Dad's trophy he's proudest of. There's a story about Dad as a kid, volunteering to swim at the Willie High carnival, and it's unclear if he gets in the pool or not before he recalls that he can't. And swimming is something Dad learns as an adult, when he and a lady called Helen are the stalwarts of the slow lane, and Dad's still quite young and she's already a grandmother, and he never does get any faster. And there's another I like about a gymnastics performance, a presentation they do at a local hall, and his parents are there and it's Dad's job to somersault through the middle of the squad's formation. He dives into the roll and comes out of it flat, he's collapsed, and the audience gasp, especially his parents, and I'm not sure if the show does go on after this shocking development.

When I'm still little, Dad watches *The Wonder Years* with similar commitment to his watching of the Bulldogs, and there's a beautiful episode in which Kevin is asked by the sports coach to pick out a team. First he picks Paul, his best friend who is always picked last, and then he picks all the worst of the players and it makes them feel good, all these hopeless young sportsmen, who get up their spirits and manage to win – or if they don't win, then in my memory at least they are winners. Because here they have experienced the great kindness of a peer, and also a reprieve from the cruelty of competitive children's sport, and the excruciating length of the physical education period that fills bookish types, the world over, with dread. Dad has a similar story. He is put in the tunnel ball team, and they work out a system and get quite far through the Victorian State heats as a well-oiled bunch of non-sportsmen, who apply great organisational skill to the competition. These boys don't run fast, but they don't drop the ball, or push it too hard, 'Typical tortoises beating the rabbit', Dad recalls.

In the car, Dad is quite experimental, he likes π. O. and other word artists, and sometimes he makes up poems (he's ahead of his time) with just one word repeated over and over, sometimes my name, in different registers and then I do it, these yawps. And it makes us feel good in the morning together, driving to school and exhaling out words, although I'm fearing detention and the tiny theatrical man presiding over the gates, writing out slips and terrifying the girls with his officiousness.

Not all culture travels successfully and this is true of the owl story Dad tells me (and which Ellen tells him, apparently). The Owl is asked by some greater being to choose the most beautiful animal in the forest, and of all the gorgeous menagerie on offer the Owl chooses her owlet and this story says, *see, every child is beautiful to their parents* (and in football they roar at the stadium, *face only a mother could love*, and they do). In Arabic, there is an insult, *you owl*! Dad and I are in the cinema together, and someone says this in the film and Dad whispers, very audibly, so that everyone in the surrounding rows can hear him, 'In Arabic this is an economy, what they are saying is *she's as ugly as an owl*'. Gentle soul that he is, undeterred by people shushing him, Dad finishes, 'but I don't know why they think it's an insult, the Owl is a beautiful creature'.

34. SKELETONS

Every family has skeletons, and ours is Nicola, and I know who he is, but not much about him, and this is a well-buried skeleton, and the stories are buried with him, and Abdullah and Ellen, who lie side by side, in the flat neat plots of Williamstown's Lawn Cemetery.

Out of the blue, my cousin sends me *The Palestine Gazette*, dated October 28, 1937, a document full of statistical information about the movements of businesses and people under the British Mandate. One function of the *Gazette*, for instance, is to document the vast number of people changing their names from something European to a name legible in Hebrew. The date of this issue falls in the second year of the Great Palestinian Revolt, and on the front page is a notice:

> The Officer Administering the Government deeply regrets to announce the death of
>
> **Mr. Avinoam Yellin M.B.E.,**
> Senior Inspector, (Jewish Schools) Department of Education,
>
> who succumbed to his wounds on the 23rd of October, 1937, as the result of a dastardly attack on his life while proceeding to his office on the 21st October.

The Revolt begins in 1936 as a popular uprising against the British Administration and in particular the policy of open-ended Jewish immigration, pursuant to Balfour. This has turned, by the date of the *Gazette*, to something more violent after the British systematically repress Palestinian expression of identity, and deny the specificity of a homeland (ours). What is left for Palestinians to do but to prosecute their outrage, publicly, about the expropriation of this loved land, before their own eyes and while they're still in it?

I do not know if this is why Uncle Nic leaves a homeland behind, by choice and not by disaster, but the reason my cousin has sent me this edition is because there's a listing for the Sahhar Bros. business, under the section *Registration of Partnerships*:

> Statement of Nature of Changes in the Particulars of the General Partnership: Sahhar Bros.
>
> A. Change in the partners or in the name or surname of any partner:
> Nicola Andoni Sahhar has left the partnership.
>
> B. Change in person or persons authorised to sign on behalf of the partnership:
> Abdallah Andoni Sahhar, 'Isa Andoni Sahhar and Emil Andoni Sahhar jointly or severally.

And you'll note the fluidity of Arabic vowels and doubled consonants in English transliteration.

So Nicola leaves Jerusalem, before the Second World War even, and before he appears again in Cyprus or again as the sponsor on Pa's immigration papers, he goes, I believe, to

Great Britain, though specifically where I'm uncertain. Here he acquires a wife and they give birth to two daughters, one named Barbara in honour of his mother, but no-one knows much of these nieces, granddaughters or cousins (and since they were – I presume – abandoned long before they were grown, they have had, if they are still living, understandably little interest in who it was that abandoned them).

I picture Nicola, in his wilderness decade where little is known of his movements, rambling at weekends in the British countryside, much like the walks one takes in Palestine. In his undocumented thirties, I wonder if Nic is earnest but confused or just roughish and relieved to be away from the network of obligations he has left in Jerusalem. He is dashingly handsome, according to a photograph of Nic in his twenties, leaning on the runner board of one of Abdullah's taxis, scarf tucked into his suit and a tarboosh in his right hand, and wearing the smug smile of a man who knows he is beautiful. Perhaps he charms the English girls with his Mandate gentleman act, more British than the British, in a well-cut and brushed suit. It seems he leaves little trace of himself in Jerusalem. The remaining brothers buy out his shares in their business and also his share at Asa Street, although I have never heard that he lived there.

Someone must know what happens to Nic's English wife and his firstborn daughters, but if I know anyone who knows this they have kept their secret. Since nothing is known of this first wife, to say Nicola *runs off* may be ungenerous; there are numerous and intimate particulars that might make one person leave another. Sometime between Jerusalem and Cyprus, Nicola must meet Joan, a woman I don't recall ever meeting (though I attend her funeral) and as we drive from the church to her wake Dad speculates that they are living together in Williamstown when they get word of a lost wife's passing. Dad remembers his uncle vanishing that day with Joan, and he supposes they quietly get married in Melbourne, and maybe they've already had children themselves and nothing much changes. And though there is an authority hunting for Nic, who gets as close as the Mirls Street door, the children who answer the door are pressed away, as I've said, by the adults. The family never divulge what information they have, and given what institutional bodies and authorities had done to this family in both general and particular ways, they had really no reason at all to co-operate, and plenty of evidence to the contrary that co-operation is not mutually beneficial, and quite often lethal.

Nic is a businessman, unsentimental, and I'm not sure he misses Palestine as much as the others (and this is maybe how emigration works best when a person leaves of their choosing and not with a gun to their neck). In Melbourne he runs several businesses; I've already mentioned the milk bar, where he sips wine from small tumblers and eats garden-era. Later Nic has the licence to run a kiosk at a public pool on the outskirts of Melbourne in the other direction from Newport. One year Joey works there, Pa driving him out and back again. Dad remembers it was hot and tiring work and that he never had a swim in the pool. As an adult, Dad learns that his cousin Shukry swims when he's working and Dad says, 'I guess he just asked, but I was too shy to'.

Uncle Nic is one of the reasons that Ellen and Pa and all of their children arrive in Australia (hostile and suburban, Juju writes, *stay where you are!*). On the tapes my Pa says, 'And thank God, we are happy to be here', but I have always wondered if he wondered if ASIO was listening in when he said that. Pa's story does not include the departure of Nicola from Palestine but just that Pa was a fair man, who gave everyone an equal share in the wealth he acquired which flowed like a river, he would say, when he remembered it. Whatever the skeletons of romance or finance might be, in recounting these fragments I am reminded only that my Pa loved all his brothers, his sister, his mum. And if Pa could live with Nicola charging him rent in Australia, one of the scandalous things about Nic that I knew in my childhood and which was periodically stirred up at family gatherings (and Pa gives him, remember, a business and also a house in Jerusalem) then who am I to hold this against Nic's memory?

When we lower Joan into the ground, her daughters, my aunts, my dad and their cousins, someone says, 'I went to Rome and I was surprised by how much I loved it, and then I thought, well, but I grew up in a Roman city'. And they discuss again the price paid for some cutting-edge formula of scientific destruction in the First World War, which was Palestine, they say. I look at the dates on the headstones, beginnings and endings of lives, and I can see that Uncle Nicola and I share some time on this earth, but in truth I have no recollection of him.

35. THIS WAY TO THE BOMB SHELTER

My first arrival to Jerusalem is via the old Bethlehem Road, a name now concealed in the bland 'Route 60'. It is unlike my other arrivals to Jerusalem, wending through the East in local Palestinian buses, when the young boys' faces flash past me as if they could be my young father's – weaving on bicycles through the undulating streets or shouting 'mai barideh' while they stack ice-filled eskies with bottled water by the Damascus Gate. On this arrival, I am in the front passenger seat of a car with an Israeli friend. We have visited Al-Khalil to meet a Palestinian journalist, who lives with tens of family members in a house on the edge of an Area A section. They point from their house to some land out the back which they are trying to build on, demarcated as Area B. Though building commenced long ago, it is also stalled by withdrawn approval for plans and an injunction, and the preliminary structure is falling apart, a ruin already. Her elder brothers were meant to live there with wives who quite soon will be too old for children.

When we are planning this day we talk about places my friend can visit; she says Bethlehem's out. This is significant, I discover later, when my activist friend casually mentions he has been in Bethlehem. I know this is not possible unless he is there as a soldier, and that is how he is there, at the age of twenty-one, stationed in a tank that is part of the Siege of the Church of the Nativity. He tells me he cries in the cabin and then he cries harder as he understands all at once the brutality of service for himself and most of all for the people he is literally threatening to kill in his tank (and I do not ask if before that he's smiling). We drive through the West Bank on settler roads and we drive through some settlements and I keep my head low when we do that. In the car is a filmmaker she knows, who is from Russia or Poland maybe, who is describing the places we drive as *Judea* and *Samaria*, and my friend apologises to me privately before we get going. 'It's just what they call it here', she says, while I shell half a dozen eggs for the drive that she cooks in the narrow mouth of an Arabic coffee pot.

The filmmaker is sitting behind us, and anxious not to stumble onto politics with a woman who is travelling through *Judea* and *Samaria*, I ask her about Joseph Trumpeldor and Tel Hai, and not for one moment does she pause or think it's remarkable that I know something of the inner workings of Israeli national psychology. She talks as if everyone knows, and I am riveted as we pass the main town of Al-Khalil when I first learn of Baruch Goldstein, and that the Israelis have created a memorial to this man who perpetrated the Cave of the Patriarchs massacre (because even if *Plan Dalet* is not a plan, the state is never not pleased, whether by accident or by design, to see the back of a Palestinian, however they exit this land or this life – and in this massacre, both happen together). My friend who is driving becomes quite hysterical about the Goldstein memorial, it's like we're digging up skeletons, she says it's an awful place and we do not stop there. She is trying to shield me, too late, from a horror that has already happened, and one that continues to happen, if not specifically at this site then elsewhere.

This drive from Al-Khalil to Jerusalem is a great favour my friend does me, she is uncomfortable in Jerusalem then (years later, she will meet me in Sheik Jarrah, less anxious and with her wife, although I send careful directions because the maps don't work in East Jerusalem. 'It's to discourage Israelis from straying there', she tells me). As we drive the road on this short trip, there are a collection of people at a turnpike hanging their thumbs and waiting for lifts and she says as she pulls up the car, 'That's what we do here, although you don't in Australia since the hitchhiker murders'. Two people get in, a young boy and a man with a gun. As we drive I am gripping the edge of the door and my knuckles are white and she says, 'You ok?' and I say, 'Yeah, strange thing for an Australian' (and I do not say 'Palestinian', because there is a man with a gun behind me) and we let the man out first and then the boy and we drive to the centre of the city together.

Once we park at *Safra Square*, she is wary, and she takes my backpack and I'm wheeling my luggage up Salah Ad-Din Street and she says, 'What if we get attacked?' and I say, 'Drop my backpack and run!', laughing. And later the activist I will stay with affirms, 'It's a street full of families buying sweets for their children'. We meet up with the activist at the Institut Français Chateaubriand and watch a film there, which is the first time my Israeli friend and I do this. I mention this because there is another time when we do not watch *Salt of This Sea* together at a festival; she is harrowed already by an Israeli documentary, *To See If I'm Smiling*. The film's title is derived from the reflections of one IDF subject who cannot bear to revisit a photograph, a relic of her service when she is pictured with the bodies of dead Palestinians. And she can no longer access the memory of what she must have felt to pose for such a picture. The film we now watch in Jerusalem is a film about kites that children are flying on the beaches of Gaza, which is also where Palestinian children are murdered. I often think of some young cousins on a fishing beach playing soccer in the summer of 2014, when they were killed instantaneously by naval missiles fired by the most moral army in the world.

Afterwards, we all walk to the Jerusalem Hotel and drink with the people who used to drink there, journalists mostly. There are two women fresh from London for the *Guardian*, and it's the Arab Spring elsewhere, and the one who is most naïve is looking for stories, a search she interrupts to say to me, 'What are *you* doing here? Just look what you've done to the Aboriginals!' and I say to her, 'The problems of Australia and Palestine are both of your making', and I offend her so badly that I hope that she learns something while she ignores me for the rest of the evening. Later we get a lift home, my Israeli friend back on the road to Tel Aviv, and my activist host says, 'What now?' and I say, 'You live very close to Asa Street, I want to see it'.

The activist lives in an old Arab neighbourhood, in a new block of flats, and above him lives a Black Panther who is surprisingly racist, and who has a brother in Melbourne that he requests (even more surprisingly) I visit with a bottle of spirits to help mend some old estrangement that has grown up between them. Where am I staying? A ten-minute walk or thereabouts from the house that my Pa built, and it is midnight or maybe after and we walk through the hollowed-out neighbourhood and then we are there at 8 Asa Street, home of my Pa, and my certain origin in Palestine. On the fence there is a swarm of bougainvillea and jasmine, like at Mirls Street, and later Juju asks if the passionfruit vines are still there. They are not, as I learn, those are vines that do not last many years without care. On the fence also are some large Hebrew letters, and I think it's graffiti, and the activist says that it isn't, and then he translates: *this way to the bomb shelter*.

This is a skinny street without pavement, Asa Street; there are just some white lines drawn on the bitumen, and we sit behind one of them, opposite the house, and I breathe in the intoxicating smell of the flowers which is stronger at night. And after some time, a single figure turns into the street, and then into the gate at the place we are sitting and I call out to him, 'Hey! You live here?'. And he does, and my translator says, 'This is Micaela's house that her grandfather built', and the man says, 'But how can that be? This house is only eighty or a hundred years old!'. He tells me (does he say it in Hebrew, I cannot recall) that he grew up here, in the flat that I think my Pa rented out, fifth flat in the complex, with a roof-garden-terrace. He offers to show us some pictures of him growing up in the house if we want to come back at a more usual time. But I do not accept this offer, I cannot bear the thought of his memories crowding out mine, so carefully comprised by my aunts and Abdullah.

I pick from the fence swathes of bougainvillea, and back at the flat we position a branch in an unused coffee pot and I dry out the rest and place it in boxes, one for Juju and one for my father, but Juju does not accept this gift when I give it to her. I am thinking about how it can be that a man who lives in a house his whole life has literally no idea of the length of an occupation or the existence of Palestinians. I recall the advertisements that boast *Arab style* when I am the truth of how they are just Palestinian. I learn later, one Nakba, that Nakba is simply not known of among young Israelis, sometimes they have heard of the word and sometimes they haven't, and curriculum is surely the way to raze a whole people out of a history (their own), by the state that replaced them.

This activist says that *this way to the bomb shelter* is not graffiti but a practical marker. Sometimes people are told to get into them when the IDF is shelling the West Bank or Gaza (I am reminded of a story in which the only injury to an Israeli citizen during one such shelling is to a Holocaust survivor who, forced to wear a gas mask, becomes deeply distressed before he trips over in it). This is a state that keeps people frightened of people like me, who might knock on your door and say, 'All this is mine and I'm here to reclaim it!'. When I think of that night, I hope I became that young man's ghost and that I haunt him when he turns up the street after midnight.

When I tell Juju and Tony about the sign they both nod their heads and they say, 'Makes sense', and they tell me of a well down the back of the premises, which from a structural perspective would be a good place for a bomb shelter. So I have taken you as far as I have ever been at 8 Asa Street, but there is more to say about the house my Pa built and where we lived, in the city we come from. When I tell Evan he replies, *we own that house in a way that no-one can ever take away. It was made for us.*

Sidewalk letterers in Jerusalem must be used to writing such things.

36. *TRAVELLER, WELCOME!*

A book, in truth not much more than a pamphlet, arrives, wrapped in lilac tissue and thick brown paper: *Traveller's Note-Book for Palestine*, price, fifty mils. The foreword is dated December 5th, 1931, and I suppose this is the month it might be published in Jerusalem, by the Commercial Press. I purchase this text when I discover it online, written by P Afif and one G M Sahhar, initials which I am sure relate to our family names, and the more obvious surname itself. Here, I find my family in Jerusalem and in Palestine under the Mandate.

G M Sahhar remains a mystery to me for close to a decade after I recover this text (though I discover the G is for George in the foreword, whose author praises his friends for their 'literary venture'). Slim volume, the first half devoted to Jerusalem and the remainder to Palestine (making good on the promise of its title, one imagines). There are seven black and white photographs reproduced in the volume and one advertisement. The first and the best of the images is a classic panorama of Jerusalem including the site (or the sight?) of the Haram Al-Sharif complex, but you have to fill in the glittering iridescence of the Dome in your mind (black and white, nor yet the glittering gold which King Hussein will lavish upon the mosque in a later restoration).

There are two epigraphs set out at the start, and one of these is a rare clue to the sensibility of the authors. It appears three times: in Arabic script, transliterated and also translated –

shuf el rafiq, qabel el tariq – take a companion before you decide on the route. Later I learn this is a popular Palestinian expression and this part is only a half of it, which continues el jar abel el dar – know your neighbour before you choose a house (which does, in the context of national calamity, seem particularly pertinent).

Beneath is the verse of Psalm 137, headed ***Jerusalem***. It offers the 1930s tourist an indication of the tenor of this guidebook but also, when I read it now, it offers the Palestinian (me) a guiding hand in my quest of returning:

> If I forget Thee, O Jerusalem,
> Let my right hand forget her cunning.
>
> If I do not remember Thee, let my
> tongue cleave to the roof of my mouth;
> If I prefer not Jerusalem above
> my chief joy.

The Christian Palestinian families of Jerusalem displayed, it would seem, fine skills in entrepreneurship. I have told you of Pa, Abdullah, and cars, and the people who wrote to him, like the ABC women. Later, a woman in Australia sees Tony in a University of Melbourne job-scheme publication, and she too is a former client who writes to my Pa, and he takes her out for the day with Ellen and the two youngest children. My father recalls that they take this lady, a Miss Brown or perhaps a Miss Green, on a picnic, and when they arrive my little dad dashes out of the car and pulls the rope of a bell in a bell tower. And as it reverberates, Miss Colour says, 'I knew you'd do that', and Joey is astonished, 'How did you know?' he asks. My gentle father tells me that many years after that day, when he is a student at pharmacy school, he visits this Miss on her death bed, second and last time that he sees her, and that she begs him for sweets which he returns to her with.

For the mercantile Christian Palestinians of Jerusalem, it is perhaps a thing that they sensed, the pilgrim's need of the dragoman-Palestinian intermediary to teach them to see their imaginary past in our present, and one finds in this text the evangelist coming of Christ in our lifetime. These authors have little to say of ***Nazareth***, remarking on the unremarkable-ness of that town, and the entry concludes: *there are no buildings of antiquity except the greek-catholic church* [*sic*], *which is claimed to stand on the site of the Synagogue where Jesus preached.* But this lays a foundation for the next section of notes on ***Tiberias.*** The entry commences: *Leaving Nazareth for Tiberias we pass a public fountain called fountain of Mary. It is the only one in Nazareth and there is no doubt that the Holy Virgin and her divine Son drew water from it.* These businessmen have a good eye for a myth they can sell, don't you think? And I admire George and Afif as they describe the progress of Jesus and offer an idiosyncratic history in which *the year 21 of our era* makes a town (Tiberias) comparatively young.

The advertisement on the endpaper of this slight text is for the Hotel Fast, Jerusalem, a hotel I've mentioned before and where George holds his first job. I learn this when I am connected at last by an excellent if proximate chance with a man who can identify what the middle initial stands for, and his name is George also because (and perhaps you have guessed it) the man I have found is G M's grandson. And George tells me what he knows of the enterprises of his sedo, G M Sahhar, who may have owned a cinema in Al-Baqa Al-Tahta (but I find no evidence of this when I look for it). One of his first business relationships is with the owners of the Fast, an Irish-held business at that time, his grandson believes (and I have heard very little of the Irish in Palestine but there is a long-held and natural affinity between ours and the Irish experience). In 1946 (and in retrospect what terrible timing), George opens a hotel in Jaffa, Qasr Al-Bahr, which is repurposed as a sea-view hospital after Nakba (it 'becomes', his grandson says; too much 'becoming', I think, these unbearable *becomings* that overwrite – to the best of their ability and without trace – the myriad things they negate). It was a magnificent building, his grandson says, but I have found no pictures of it. In the one photograph I have seen of George M, a tall man in a double-breasted suit, perhaps taken in the year of the Sea Palace's opening, he is posing on a stately flight of steps that run up to a house, and I surmise it is his house, which is not far from ours, in Jerusalem.

In 1931, George M Sahhar has a connection with the Hotel Fast, and Abdullah has opened his touring business, Sahhar Bros. Perhaps to develop a reputation independently in this market George prints his text with Afif, the foreword composed by a man of the Mandate, one Robert Haydon Jones; given to the flair of Calvino he writes: *Traveller, welcome, and behold the Promised Land! Pilgrim, here is the object of thy yearning!*

> Look about you and you will see back through the centuries – back for two thousand years. Listen and you will hear a murmur of ancient tongues. The presence of the Saviour is felt at every turning; history breathes from every stone ...
>
> You, reader, do not know me; and I do not know you. But we have met through these pages, and we have one common

> bond: we are both travellers. Then listen, as one traveller to another: Keep this book, as it will make Palestine a place worth living in ...

There is a sense in Jerusalem, and in Palestine too, that the objects are living. If you listen quietly perhaps they will speak to you. Later, Edward Said will formulate a concept known to music but less so to thinking, the notion of the contrapuntal, and one wonders if such an idea was informed not only by the pianoforte but by the multi-planar existence of being a Palestinian in Jerusalem (or missing it).

To my knowledge, George M Sahhar makes one other contribution to the field of travel writing. This text has a different tilt to the first, although at first glance, they seem similar: *The Traveller's Companion to the Holy Land: Being a concise and accurate guide and easy reference when travelling through Palestine, Syria and Transjordania* (ironic title with not much concision about it). This volume, from 1935 (first edition) is reviewed in the *Palestine Post* on February 3 of that year: *More Aids to Tourists. We have received two pamphlets of slight or doubtful value to the tourist*. The first is described as an index, most carefully cross-referenced, of biblical place-names in three languages (which the review concludes *is certainly a useful compilation but not for the everyday tourist*). Of George M's second foray into the publishing world, co-written again, this time with no images but a quarter devoted to advertisements including the Fast and also the Sahhar Bros. Tours and Motor Car Service (a half-page entry positioned, my Pa would have liked the coincidence, after three and a half pages devoted to the Church of the Holy Sepulchre) the *Post* writes:

> its merit lies in its brevity. It is wholly 'Palestinian-made' – Palestinian printing, spelling, syntax and misprints all complete in generous measure. It is composed in the genuine language of the dragoman. We like the book's opening sentence: 'Numerous books have been written claiming to be a Guide to the Tourist'.

Surprisingly in this volume one finds a good deal less Jesus and a good deal more Jew, both Torah-derived and contemporary to the time of its writing. I do not know what sources are drawn on for a review of *Jewish National Fund* projects in the *Yishuv*. There is a long entry on a place called *Emek Zebulun* – a reclaimed swamp land attributed to Jewish ingenuity (a particularly strange claim for Palestinians to make as this project is one iteration of the destruction of complex biosystems wiped out by colonial monocultures and a misunderstanding of terrain) and as they tell us, a hub of investment and transport:

> The J.N.F possess 33,000 Dunoms [*sic*], and the Palestine Economic Corporation of America and the Haifa Bay Development Company have another 15,000 Dunoms [*sic* again]. The Government has appropriated land here for the railway workshops and an aerodrome, and in turn leased large areas of sand-dunes to the Jews (p. 60 of the above-named work of which I very much doubt you will be successful in finding a copy).

Emek recurs in the name of a street near our house, and means valley I believe and the one near our home, *Emek Refaim*, is translated two ways, the valley of giants or the valley of ghosts. From an aesthetic perspective, I think it very likely that the second is accurate and intended by the early Zionists, who are left in no doubt about what they have done to the Palestinians. But *emek* aside, I find this entry quite inexplicable, this description by a Palestinian tour guide of *Jewish National Fund* plans (the same *JNF* who will plant our villages out, and us with them, deploying sometimes eucalypts and sometimes pines as a ready and inexpensive method for 'holding land').

What are you doing here, George, when you say this? We are transported into the images now of the last supper of Jesus and I am not sure if you are a disciple, who saddens the heart of our Saviour, or Judas Iscariot, when you write this passage (if you write this passage) that seems to conform with the mythologies we have spent more than seventy years unpicking (and which works its mischief here in Australia too, the great colonial caveat *improvement*, by which the method of acquisition is purportedly cured). And at least briefly it is worth revisiting the seesawing myths of wilderness and civilisation or other frankly horrific word games that purport to negate whole societies despite their manifest cultural wealth or sophisticated geographic embeddedness.

The grandson of George tells me the story when I am last in Jerusalem that as a small boy with his father they enter a shop, and on the wall is a map that his grandfather made, along with Afif, and his father is transfixed to see it again and my cousin tells me that now this map is in his home and he sends me a picture of it. It's a beautiful map with inset images of the glorious city our family has lived in for centuries. And I can see that whatever a guidebook might say, this man is a fine one with no knowledge of how a national catastrophe might cast such a book as a difficult legacy.

I progress in non-linear fashion through these volumes, the second particularly, always on watch for some vital clue that this work is designed for the tourists who bought it. And later his grandson says that many of the tourists drawn to Palestine were people who believed in the Bible as a tool for exclusion and colonialism. He concludes: *this does not mean that our ancestors were like-minded with these groups, but in their time no-one knew what we know today.* Or, to adapt from the Bible again, if tomorrow is not promised, then neither is it foregone, and it appears that even in the middle of the Mandate the great conflagration of Palestine was not yet the only road for the taking.

If I had to stake anything, my pride or a wager, on what George M Sahhar intended, decoding our home to the welcomed traveller, then I would return to the first little pamphlet and the one line of Arabic that offers a glimpse of his character. A line, it is true, without the power of prophecy, but one filled with the hope of a journey and the wisdom of choosing your travel mate wisely. This is an aphorism that survives the rift that divides a home from a catastrophe and which strains commerce and politics with irreconcilable contradictions. It is a rare thing, those things that are true on both sides of a Nakba, yet I am certain that *shuf el rafiq, qabel el tariq*, is one of them.

37. JERUSALEM SYNDROME

How do you walk off the script of a family? I confess I don't know how it's done. A family has things in common, including a family far-flung. We grow up in our parallel lives and if we do not contemplate one another, then we contemplate at least the forefathers who carried us to the edges of Empire. Each of us is aware that something is lost, a place and the people in it; and somehow the generation of immediate leaving maintain their whole lives a sense of each missing other. For me one of these absences is felt in the loss of our language. One day I fight with my father, 'Why didn't you teach us?', and Dad says, 'Nobody wants a thick accent in the school playground'. He tells me about the embarrassment of lunch swaps as a boy, when no-one would swap their lunch for his excellent one, which lacked, to the primary-school palate, the appeal of a Vegemite sandwich. All Dad can see is this burden of not belonging.

When I am just graduated I fly to Canada and I spend some nights in a hostel in Toronto. This is a city that reminds me of Melbourne and also Milan, a cold city with Victorian architecture and tram lines. The hostel has an uneasy atmosphere, and though there are three of us in a dorm, there is an American woman to whom we all accede the room because she has broken her leg and despite immobility she is also having a lot of sex on the bottom bunk in that room. The other inhabitant and I take turns using the pay phone; she is enmeshed in a torrid breakup with a woman in Sydney who won't answer her calls. Later, we sit downstairs and drink whisky together. She plays the guitar and I sing a little bit and we live together on the margins of a hostel room and of our lives, and although I have never seen her again the world is a small place for similar sorts of people. Perhaps I will meet her at a poetry launch one of these years, something we spend long hours discussing as we leaf through the Carson and Purdy I buy, and *Wide Slumber for Lepidopterists* which is grappling as we are grappling with the stages of sleep (though it does not contemplate an American woman with a broken leg).

I walk between Union Station and Koreatown marking time, nursing jetlag and fighting through snow, and I am tolerated by two affianced friends as their third companion. We scour the bookshops and apart from the poetry I am searching for Elizabeth Smart – whose book is easy enough to find in Canada – along with its neglected companion. I will find *The Dead Seagull* at The Strand in New York, and as a young woman I am fascinated by the candour of a man, Smart's lover, the now overlooked George Barker, who is negotiating the architecture of fraught emotion and who will later say, 'I've stirred the facts around too much ... It simply can't be done'. These two texts remain on my shelves (though not side by side) yet I cannot bear to revisit them after I learn of the great Angela Carter's quip, that she wishes to establish a press to foster such titles as *By Grand Central Station I Tore off His Balls.*

At Union Station I will board a train to Montreal's Gare Centrale to stay with a man that I think I have met some years earlier. I am young and shy and when I write *I look forward to seeing you again* he tells me he doesn't believe that we've met. Although many years later again, I find pictures from Mirls Street when I am three with my handsome young dad, wearing slippers and a stripy bomber jacket, and Evan is a tall gorgeous teenager in a university sweatshirt.

Evan is the eldest, I can tell from his name (first named for the grandfather) and he lives in an apartment with his wife, who in retrospect I see is not much older than I am, and their fairly new daughter who is in her first winter standing. The snow is dense and deep and they are delighted that I know less about snow than these two newly migrated Californians know, and they lend me a hat with fur flaps and some thick snow boots. The soft black leather of my boots is already wet through in the distance between their back door and the car they turn on, to warm up the engine, while we're still sitting inside in the kitchen with cats on our laps or the windowsill, watching. Evan's taata is Yousra, the sister of Abdullah, a wonderful cook and great keeper of photographs. After she marries her husband, who is so handsome that my dear Juju as a girl wished to marry him also, they move to the Christian Quarter of the Old City.

Yousra I think must be around the age of my Ellen, and there are some beautiful portraits of them in a studio, taken together with Ajia, Ellen's mum (and copies of these live on Najla's dresser, and I wonder where they are now that Najla is not there to tend them). When I look at the pictures, I think Yousra and Ellen must have been good friends, flung together by family and prised apart by Nakba. Her name is often spoken of in my childhood and though I apparently never meet her I have a memory of a meeting Dad says never happened. It is around the time when I am wearing slippers and a stripy bomber jacket that I also store twenty American dollars in my money box that I believe she sent me, whether I met her or not. Yousra's father-in-law is a Greek–Palestinian man who paints Christian icons of saints, and there is a story that this painter named his daughters after the saints who are pictured around Queen Eleni and King Constantine. This is what it says in Juju's handwriting on the back of a copy we have of the icon, but Evan tells me he cannot remember his great-aunts having names from an icon.

Where I am sleeping, the room is lined with books, and I study them with growing amazement. Evan has first editions of Bukowski's *Women* and other dream books on my wish list. I ask his wife about this and she says, 'Well, don't mention it to Evan, it's really too sad, but he'd written a whole creative writing PhD at Berkeley and then the disk got corrupted and he lost it and he left all that writing behind him'. I am staggered then and again when I think of this. I have just finished an honours thesis in creative writing and no-one I know of among our family is particularly inclined to writing until I learn this story of Evan – like a glorious apparition of Adorno's theory, that what is alone must be somewhere else occurring, as I find is true in this family too.

The second-hand bookshops in Montreal are remarkable. I wish I bought more from a place that had a treacherous flight of external steps, covered in black ice, where I find a beautiful copy of *Men in the Off Hours*, with jagged papers that mimic, but were never cut, by the reader (the cutting of pages one of life's lost pleasures I think; for two pounds at a National Trust thrift store in Nottingham I buy a Charles Lamb, tickled by the wisp of history embedded in the object – awarded, which a bookplate records, as a grammar school prize around 1925, but much of it never read by the recipient, as revealed in the uncut pages). I present my hosts with this find at the end of my visit. We eat Quaker oats and clementines shipped in crates from the citrus state, and drink rye and red beer, which are cheap in Quebec as I remember. And we talk about Burning Man, and I am in awe that they've been to this festival I've only just learnt of, watching a late-night documentary of some American artists engaging with the structural problems of producing an enormous replica of Marcel Duchamp's urinal. And though I am appalled by the vast efforts that are reduced to one spectacular conflagration, people taking off their clothes in the Nevada desert to celebrate, Evan and his wife are wise about both the permanence of things and of human nature. These two people I've only just heard of who feel as I feel about the world, who read the same books, who attend festivals I dream of. These people, I think, are people I would want to meet with no family connection to hold us together. And it is not long later I discover that one of the last great cycloramas of Jerusalem, at Sainte-Anne-de-Beaupré, was only a three-hour drive away from where they are when I visit them, a vista now closed to the public after one hundred and twenty-three years of continuous operation.

More than a decade after this meeting, Evan decides to make a visit to Jerusalem. We plan out a time for a phone conversation because if talking about Jerusalem isn't as good as being in it, it is still always thrilling to speak of it. We talk of the crossing, of what he should say, and where he should go, and who he should meet: who is there in the city we hail from and in the surrounds where our family is pressed to, successively, in the sacking of the New City and then the so-called reunification of the Old (so many euphemisms used to describe our erasure and to make it *contested* or just *disappear*, depending on which good liberal interlocutor you are talking to, who supports human rights and in the same breath may wonder aloud if the Palestinians could be said to have any left). I send Evan a pamphlet I have, a suggested itinerary from the Sahhar Bros. Tours and Motor Service, and he checks over the list and he ticks off the sites in Jerusalem, guided by the spirit of these great uncles of his and also by photos from Yousra. I delight in his picture by the railing where, some seventy years earlier, the snow queen is so resplendently pictured.

When Evan goes to Jerusalem he takes a picture of himself in his hotel room dressed up in a sheet like a biblical costume which he captions *Jerusalem syndrome.* It is a strange curiosity of medical science, this illness, and sometimes tourists attributed with the syndrome go missing. For instance, recently in the *Negev*, a British tourist, who is never found – what he leaves behind him are just ripped-out pages of a Bible concerning the part in which Jesus goes into the desert for forty days and forty nights, and also his wallet and passport – by which the search team work out he has not crossed a border despite having vanished. Jerusalem syndrome is a perplexing problem, averaging one hundred cases annually, around forty requiring admission to a psychiatric unit in Jerusalem which houses a dedicated treatment centre for the condition. A district psychiatrist says, 'It is not a mental disease by itself but is usually superimposed on top of a background of mental distress', but an article in the *British Journal of Psychiatry* calls it 'severe, Jerusalem-generated mental problems'.

Apparently, it is difficult to find a true case of the syndrome, considered to be a disturbance among people with no particular regard for religion or underlying triggers. These are the more interesting cases I think, cases which highlight the way in which people have regarded ownership of our hometown for centuries, that when they arrive they are fulfilling some messianic prophecy. I am reminded of the British Israelites, a faded chapter of evangelism, who regard themselves as the true inheritors of that part of the earth, much like the British regard themselves as true inheritors of much of the rest of it, I suppose. When I first hear of Jerusalem syndrome it strikes me as having a relationship to the way people dress up at the turn of the last century to amuse themselves. Like Virginia Woolf in blackface, a picture largely obscured now in the preservation of her literary memory and as the darling of other marginal identities she championed, so I have rarely heard it mentioned.

Evan's picture, I know, is a joke, a big poke at all the orientalising people who arrive in our city and make themselves sick with power, who find that unlike our countryman, Jesus, they are not made of the stuff of messiahs. I have never heard that a Palestinian returning was so possessed, since we know what it is to carry our pasts and our futures between our shoulders and in our bones, as we have done for all the years of our ghorba, a count we continue.

38. OUR LOCAL PARISH

There is a story Juju tells, and one she remembers directly, concerning the moment at which Abdullah and Ellen convert from the Orthodoxy to some roving form of Christianity which is not, I don't think, specific, but certainly evangelist in nature. Perhaps they have converted some time before, but the story concerns the day when they confess to Ellen's mother, Ajia, this embarrassment to Orthodox propriety. Ajia reportedly comes out in a quick-cold sweat, visiting as she is at 8 Asa Street, and collapses in a dramatic faint onto the chaise-longue, upholstered in sky-blue velvet. There, she thrashes from side to side when she comes round, calling for smelling salts to revive her more fully (and to better address this shocking news, which has remained unchanged in the time between her loss of consciousness and regaining it again).

I had imagined that Abdullah and Ellen converted in a similar mode to Alice, face-down on the floor through the night and astonished to wake to a morning again. This would, I think, be a good explanation for why you exchange one staunch institution that has failed to protect you, for an old crow medicine show with vials of snake oil lined in neat rows. Perhaps it offered at least a sense of decisive action if not a solution to the predicament people find themselves in, in Palestine in the late 1940s, watching a country disappear before them.

But the reasons why my Pa converts are more opaque than that; perhaps Abdullah is just a good fortune-teller who sees what is coming, who relinquishes his local parish for the promise of miracles and to hasten the second arrival of Jesus. Or perhaps, as is true with some evangelist chapters, Pa prefers the idea of a portable Jerusalem, which though his is a city he will soon be parted from, and one he will never lay his own eyes on again in his lifetime. Jerusalem is a city quite central to faith, as Blake highlights in his hymn which is sung like a second anthem in many institutions and also some countries (Britain for one), and a researcher on Israelite genealogies asks one of his subjects, a Coptic monk in Egypt, whether he *cherished the idea of visiting Jerusalem*. And the monk responds, 'Jerusalem the Holy is right here, in and around these caves ... Jerusalem is here, right here, and all spiritual riches of the Holy City as found in this Wadi'. This is, I suppose, what Abdullah must feel like, and certainly my Pa, who records on one of those tapes in the 1980s a Holy Land Tour, and he begins, not dissimilarly from the monk, with the Holy Sepulchre, 'Where the empty tomb of our Lord, Jesus Christ is to be seen'.

Pa will take us inside. 'There's Helena, she's the mother of Constantine, two hundred and thirty years, or something like that, after Christ.' Now he says, 'The floor of the church is all mosaic which shows you the whole of the plan of the country, and the midst of it there' (he trails off) 'of course, it's too far to go but I'm just mentioning it'. And now he shifts to the centre of this great plan, the design of our country, made of mosaic, 'And we go through the old streets', he says with a reverent care as his voice takes the virtual traveller by the hand and says, *Traveller, welcome, and behold the Promised Land!*

Abdullah is sent to three schools in quick succession. He begins at a Greek Orthodox one, where he spends not a day before running back home because the boys were nasty and bad to him. So his father sends him next to the Frères in Bethlehem which is where he learnt, Pa says, to speak good French, and the Frères as you know are Catholic but not very pushy about it. Pa says, 'They were not sort of insisting on you to come to Church', and Pa doesn't report what effect this has on a young Abdullah and whether he was devout in the care of the Brothers or not. But the Frères did insist on money, and Andoni had none of it, so after a year he changed schools again, to the Salesian Don Bosco school, Italian-run and more charitable one supposes but also more devout. They force little Abdullah to church and to prayers 'concerning the Santa Maria or whatever it is', Pa says. He reports that the lessons were taught in Italian and when they spoke Arabic among themselves, the boys were punished. But it must be here that Abdullah learns a good Arabic hand, and although he leaves school after very few years, perhaps the fourth or fifth grade, he is proud of his written Arabic all of his life, and writes in Arabic when he can to his dearest firstborn so that she can admire it. I remember an evening when Juju is sitting at our dining room table reading a missive aloud, and my dad feels important because although he can't read the Arabic, he can understand to translate it.

There are not many clues in this history of Pa's checkered, and later abortive, encounters with the education system, other than that Palestine is a home to many different Christian denominations and also to many schools. Ellen is at the Quaker Friends School I have told you about earlier, although she is there later, some thirteen years younger than Pa. Perhaps it is the plurality of religion that encourages him, that a child can be at a Greek Orthodox school one morning and a Catholic the next, to think of it as no great thing to choose yet another denomination a decade or so into marriage. Or perhaps it is something more immediate, like the story of what happens to his second-born daughter, third child, Salma, who at six years old is beaten so brutally on the back of her legs by the nuns for being left-handed that she is obliged to lie face-down on her stomach for three whole months before she can stand to walk again. It is Vera who tells this story, and Vera and Salma who follow their parents in faith until the present time, and maybe there is a kernel in there, this beating, before the youngest are born, and the older two children are too old to care. Maybe this is what happens, when two concerned parents are confronted with the barbarism of a school administered by a great pillar of organised religion.

So they change religions and the new one is not into make-up, perhaps it's even forbidden, and Juju again says she kept lipstick hidden in her purse and she would put it on after she left the house and wipe it off again before she returned. Pa would say to Ellen, 'She thinks I'm stupid', but as there were no consequences attached to the lipstick this was just a loving remark from a man who appreciated his eldest always, and appreciated her even more once they came to Australia. At Mirls Street there were a few placards hung around in the kitchen and lounge room with quotes from the Bible, and these punctuate Pa's stories, who liked to open or close different parts of the tour with precise pinpoint references. Here he says, 'In front of this empty tomb there is a previous part of the church which belongs to the Greek Orthodox Church, and inside the tomb there are three depictions of the resurrection – the Greek, the Catholic and the Armenian'. He explains, 'They have their own part, not within the Greek Orthodox Church, and then the Coptics have got their part, back of the tomb from the outside, and the Abyssinians from the Catholics'. I do not think this apportioning out of the Church was decreed in the Bible, but no doubt it speaks of the tomb and Pa concludes, 'The gospel according to St Matthew, Chapter Twenty-Seven'.

Pa is inviting us into the sections now, he says, 'It's wide enough to go in, just bending your head' and then he explains the etiquette, 'We go in forward and we come out backward'. The church has Greek priests there on shifts and also guardians, who are not Christians, he says, but Mohammadans. Around the same time as Pa is thinking back to this tour he is guiding us through, from the couch at Mirls Street, the traveller, Byron (not to confuse him with the more notorious poet), writes an account of the Church of the Holy Sepulchre. He reports similar things: low doors, inner sanctuaries, the divisions between Greek, Catholic and Armenian. He is talking to a man from Mount Athos and Byron is unimpressed by a wax Virgin who is draped, he recounts, *in a pawnbroker's stock of chains, watches and pendants* – a description which our Lord and Saviour would, I imagine, find more than offensive (and no doubt would have screamed at this Byron to leave his temple, or at least the Jesus that Tim Rice ventriloquises would say it).

Byron's interlocutor, Gabriel, is also well versed in the Christ narrative and he shows him some holes where Jesus was bound by the legs and tortured. Byron says, *But is that in the Bible?* and Gabriel says, *Of course*, and like my Pa he offers another story. Byron is suspicious, *But did Alexander ever visit Jerusalem?* And Gabriel says, *Certainly. I only tell you the truth*, and Byron (author of his own story) gives himself the last word. He says, *I'm sorry. I thought it might be a legend.*

I think this puts a fine point on what it is Palestinians are up against, these wise old men filled with stories they are willing to share, and which, when the visitors hear them they disbelieve and the storyteller's honesty with it. I am reminded of this in a secular context when the gardener in Jerusalem, Sami, is telling me about a spate of what he calls knife-killings. In these, Israeli soldiers throw down knives at the feet of young Palestinian teenagers and compel them at gunpoint to retrieve the weapon which they claim is the child's. This sets in train a sequence of violence resulting sometimes in murder, which is hinged on the manufactured dispute about the origin of weapons. And search as I might, I find nothing of this in English and when I tell other Arabs they say, *well, yes, they are deviously inventive*, and when I tell non-Arabs they say, *it doesn't help your people to make things up or exaggerate.* And there we are confronted with the same problem you see here between the suspicious international traveller Byron and my Pa.

Pa is taking us into the city via the Damascus Gate, so called as he says, because it's facing Damascus. In Arabic the gate 'is Bab El-Amoud, or the Gate of the Columns, because in the olden days', as he says, 'there was a big column dividing the streets', one of which leads to the temple and the other to our local parish, the Church of the Holy Sepulchre. One curiosity of the church is an eighteenth century arrangement, which is known as the Status Quo, and which refers to an agreement that is made (to a backdrop of much disagreement one supposes) about the status of Holy Property and the roles of different denominations and other custodians. On the date when this is decided and affirmed in an Ottoman decree, which is reaffirmed a century later, a tradesman is out to lunch (I suppose he had slipped in through the window and out into the square beneath it to buy some). When he returns, he finds that his ladder is now permanently part of the façade, and whoever he is (and who knows) his ladder is surely well known and it is called, legendary thing it becomes, the immoveable ladder. There is much consternation some years later, after several lifetimes of weather have degraded the ladder and it has to be moved – albeit temporarily – to receive some much-needed repairs.

There is a proud story Pa tells, of the time when his carpentry business on Mamillah is by then well known, like he is, and there's a door at the Garden Tomb which sits outside but near the Old City through a small entrance on the Nablus Road, in need of repair. This is where many Protestant Christians go in the belief that though the tomb in the Church of the Holy Sepulchre is empty, it might be here where our Lord is resurrected. When I visit the Garden Tomb I attempt to inspect all the old wooden doors looking for the stamp of the Sahhar Bros. furniture company. There are too many groups from America, Malta, France and Sri Lanka breaking out into spontaneous song and sermons and losing (if they haven't already) their minds, to examine these doors as I would like to. I wonder if Pa accepted payment for this proud repair, or drew up a bill? Perhaps Pa thought it was God's work, or perhaps he thought these are wealthy institutions who can pay. A receipt would answer my question, but the absence of it makes no difference to this speculation, since what I have is vast tracts of absences which reveal loss with great clarity; since it is hard to distinguish between an absence that was always absent, and an absence that marks the fragmentation of a documentary record.

How convinced was my Pa by evangelism in the end? Did he sit on his couch and think, *Jerusalem is here, right here* when I ran in to kiss him? Did he welcome members of his evangelical chapter into his lounge room and think to himself, *here we are in the Church of the Holy Sepulchre*, as he poured them all drams of non-alcoholic grape juice to imbibe the blood of Jesus? Surely my Pa walked for much of his life in the footsteps and also in the shadow of Christ. But I suspect that he would have been as surprised as any of us to learn that Jesus was literally among the neighbours, who came for the finjans of coffee and squares of Hilbe, conducting his weekly Bible discussions at Mirls Street.

39. HANDS

My Pa has large hands and his wedding ring spins around all of my fingers when a year after he dies, and I am eight, I discover it in a dress-up box and mistake it for costume jewellery. My Pa has large hands which he spreads over his knees on the couch at Mirls Street. My father says my Pa's hands were full of metal pieces and sometimes he showed the children. The metal is from the mill, where he sharpens the stone, when he hardly sleeps – this is one artifact from Jerusalem that is never stolen or taken away, and which he is buried with and which is now metal beside bone in his plot at the cemetery.

When Dad speaks of Pa's hands he recalls his generosity, and hands, I suppose, inspire those memories. Pa was a loving father and he would allow first Dad, then Irene, to dip their pieces of bread in his finjan of coffee. Such was the grace of this man, when things he had hoped for were denied, that he never complained that what was left in the cup, after the dipping, was what we call 'mud', and scant coffee to drink. The mud is undrinkable, good only for fortunes, and once it has settled you tip the cup upside down. It is something Juju does ironically now as an old woman. She laughs when she tells me that to her grandson's friend she said she could see a cat and he said, 'That must be *my* cat', and to another, 'Well, there's a building there', to which he replied, 'I'm thinking to study architecture'. Pa's hands are spread over his knees in the picture where Dad is holding me on his shoulders, big hands around my tiny baby waist, and I am towering over their heads.

Pa is good with his hands, he's a carpenter and also a mechanic. In Australia the immigration application says he will be self-employed, but in fact he finds work as a fitter and turner at a factory. There is a photograph of Pa with a machine at one of these factories, wearing a trademark beret he acquires (and which lingers in the house after his death, something he is not buried with) that is published in a newspaper, which he dutifully clips out and files among his records in the green and rust box, stored underneath his side of the bed. It is the 1950s and Pa is in his fifties but he looks older, sitting beside some machine that is probably not used any more at a job that is later made obsolete. And there is a story that Pa is not paid what he's owed in one of these workplaces (but really I am scratching around here to bundle up straws for a story, my memories were never composed of the dull monotony of what it was like to be a refugee in Melbourne, but of the days these people spent in the iridescent city where they once lived).

Pa was always an industrious person, and while he viewed work as a necessity, he viewed survivance as something grandly essential. He deployed his fitting and turning prowess to the crafting of domestic tools, often seen in the Palestinian kitchen, but not obtainable for money or anything else at the grocers in Newport in that decade or even the next. Pa works at the McKenzie Holland factory and later at the State Electricity Commission on the Strand, and he and his brother apparently try and cycle to work although Dad says his uncle's lack of balance soon ended that. It is an unexpected image of Pa on a bicycle, which delights me (incongruent with my memory of him). When he starts at the SEC they tell him he will never make long service leave, too close to retirement age, but in the end it's a heart attack that does it, the heart attack he has before the grand trip to Syria and America. Dad says in those days men would say to their wives, 'If I have a heart attack during the night just put me out over the front gate and then we can claim employment benefits' (but that's a fil mish mish too, I suppose there are too many heart attacks and travel to work is no longer covered by the agreement).

Pa makes manakra out of metal, things that live in a jar in our kitchen my whole life in my memory (although perhaps not in reality), and these are tools for coring the squat pale Arabic zucchinis that we stuff and simmer in broth, and for which the dark green zucchini will simply not do (and I have heard stories of new wives cooking these by mistake and the flesh of the vegetable has fallen to pieces while the stuffing remains tough and uncooked). If you buy these today in the shops, the handle is plastic, or sometimes wood, and the coring part can be smooth or serrated. But Pa's is all metal, and he elegantly uses the one piece, which is folded shut at the top, and halfway down opens out into the scooping shape of the corer. This is how I learn to core kousa for mahshi and what I can say is Pa's manakra is treacherous, my fingers are blistered and stiff and I can't fold them down for hours after we core some forty-six kousas for stuffing. My father is doing a Taata, he wanders off once he's shown me the trick of it, and when I've hollowed the vegetables he rinses them in warm salt water and stacks them, hole down, in the drying rack saying, 'It's the one who collects them that matters'.

Pa, Dad says, comes up with a range of ingenious solutions both in the home and at work. It is reported that at the SEC they used to take apart valves and then put them together again, and one day Pa, who is Albert there, does this work in a day, and the foreman takes him aside and tells him that valves take a week and he'll have to slow down. There is a similar story of Ellen, finding work in a North Williamstown cottage industry where they assembled wicks for kerosene heaters. The work was by piece, seven pounds and four shillings, and the woman who refers her predicts that since she is fat she is quite probably lazy, and it will take her a week to do it. But Ellen works from six until six, eating lunch while she works (just as I have done all my life, and I see that I get it from Ellen) and the wick is assembled, like Pa's valve, in a single day.

And what we learn here in these stories is that Pa was a good employee and Ellen a clever piece worker, and that there is rarely any truth in tropes whether you're fat or an Arab. But when it comes to tropes, there is one often heard in Australia when Palestinians enjoy the implications of the rednecked epithet. Someone yells from a car with the windows rolled down and music blaring, 'Go back to where you came from!', and the dear Palestinians nod to their interlocutor like he's on their side and they say, 'Inshallah, God willing!'.

My father's first professional job is at the United Friendly Society's dispensary in Newport. I imagine the interior of this pharmacy – the mortars and pestles in ceramic and glass; the large glass plates and bone-handled knives, flat on both edges, for mixing preparations; the small brass scales; the weights, big to small, in hard wooden cases with velvet interiors. When Dad is first working at Newport, his mum is keen to lose weight (because Arab is not something you change) and the doctor prescribes her amphetamines, common diet pills of the era, and Dad likes to tell the story that he made up speed for Ellen in the dispensary, which was at that time not only legal but common.

Back then, any pharmacy was a compounding one, and Dad has a very straight hand. When he comes home, Ellen asks him to decant the olive oil into smaller containers, and even without a funnel, Dad is so steady that no drop is wasted. Ellen takes much pride in my father's execution of this task, an incontestable proof that pharmacy school has been worth all the trouble.

I don't think about Ellen's hands very often as a child. By then she is shrunken and sore, though she never complains, and when we arrive at Mirls Street, through the back door, we measure ourselves against her. And it is something when we reach the milestone of standing higher than she does. One year Ellen says she will mind our pet fish while we are on holiday, so we take the poor creature to Newport and I am showing her how to filter the water and net out the fish and then she does it to practise. And I see for the first time that on one of her hands she is missing half of her littlest finger. This comes as a shock, the fish almost flops into the sink on my watch, and I start to cry, and maybe she is surprised that I have never noticed and she says she lost it at work in the BIC biro factory. She is given a payout of maybe six pounds, along with the foreman's apology in which he acknowledges he knew the machine was faulty.

Ellen learns that observant though I am, I am also a child. This works in her favour while we are away; a young Arabic visitor feeds the fish hundreds of flakes and the next morning it's dead in the bowl, so Ellen freezes my fish and takes it down to the pet shop and chooses another. On return I stare at this fish for a very long time and finally pronounce that it has done remarkably well in my absence, and she heaves out a big sigh of relief. I am astonished to learn this story which people are laughing about at her wake, and she keeps that secret from me all her life, and it is hardly her fault if others betray it.

I inherit Pa's hands although they are scaled down to my size; I can spread my fingers out wide and also flat, reaching ten notes on the piano. 'An impressive stretch', Trazel, my lovely piano teacher, says, when as a small girl I fan out my hands on her walnut-coloured grand. Hands are comforting things, I have found, unless they are hands attempting to perform in public on the piano when they betray me always, slippery and shaking, and I say to them, *this is not the performance you were born to,* but they win and we stop performing when I am seventeen. Now I play alone in an empty room, most days if not every, and apart from Best Cake and coring kousa for mahshi, it is the one thing my unscarred hands can do that I'm proud of.

40. AN EXCEPTION CANNOT BE COMPARED

We all grow in the light of exceptionalisms that could not truly be said to be them. Each parent convinced they have given birth to a genius when their baby reaches a developmental milestone (*clever thing, your first tooth!*). There is always someone in a parents' group narcissistically obsessed with the marvellous progression of their child, and behind their backs, all the other parents confer about the ordinariness of this progeny and perhaps harbour secretly their own unshakeable belief in the magnitude of what their own baby will one day accomplish. I am struck when a builder comes to repair a crater in the ceiling of my rental property with a dear old black dog and he says, 'You know, my kids are nothing special but what they are is really good people'. Here in my mid-thirties it hits me that this is a goal not only achievable but one that truly has something to offer humanity, the event of good people. I tuck this wisdom away with me and eschew the idea that a person should strive on their own or another's behalf towards the 'exceptional'.

The exceptional is something I blame for crowding us Palestinians out of our homes and our history. I think, for example, of Larkin when I say this, in 'Afternoons', which concludes: *Something is pushing them / To the side of their own lives.* Larkin is thinking of mothers and also of youth when he writes this. I feel this often as a young student, waiting for life to arrive, and later when writing my doctoral thesis, which sucks parasitically away at me until I'm so thin that my skirts no longer sit on my hips but fall away like badly spun hula hoops. In the Australian curriculum we are painted out entirely, my sympathetic history teacher warns against the option of Middle Eastern politics. 'It's just too complex', she says, 'and no-one does well, I've marked those papers'. We collectively choose the Cold War, a topic for which I have no talent, and she suggests I prepare a different one, exceptionalising my great giftedness as a history student and fostering my capacity to excel. I select Dictators, specialising in Cuba and Italy (little of which I remember now in a sea of contemporary dictators, but their hallmarks hit me on the jaw when I'm reading the newspaper). I will recall these lessons years later at the Milanese train station, the fascist architecture a great project of Il Duce's, the vaulted steel and glass, the vast marble, once described as an *incongruous envelope of stone* – awesome and grotesque in equal measures. But what I remember best from that day is finding a ten euro note caught between the seat and the door of my taxi.

When you live in the exceptional what you find is that quite often there is no room for you and no room for your story. On a beach in Langkawi I am reading, and in the deckchair beside me is an elderly man who says, 'What do you do?'. And when I tell him he cuts me off quickly, 'Well, I really can't think about that, I'm Dutch you know, and our history is with the Holocaust'.

For a time, I make it my work to investigate the ways in which the Holocaust is used to explain the negation of Palestine, delving deep into the origins of Zionism and Israeli exceptionalism. Herzl, national hero in what becomes the state that he dreams of, is writing in the late nineteenth century and in his key work, *The Jewish State*, he outlines in remarkably generic terms a blueprint for settler-colonial management (perhaps he is looking to Australia when he writes this):

> If we wish to found a State today, we shall not do it in the way which would have been the only possible one a thousand years ago ... We should not take spear and lance and go about singly in pursuit of bears; we should organise a large and active hunting party, drive the animals together, and throw a melinite bomb in their midst (you can find this online at the Gutenberg project).

And what we learn from Herzl is that a state is founded on violence and also on modern technology, and that terrorism is a key ingredient in the rounding, and afterwards, blowing up of bears, who could in truth be bears from anywhere because Herzl never does say that the bears are Palestinian.

So here we have bears, an analogy quite transparently for unwanted people, but no place specifically. Early Zionist councils contemplated – this is common knowledge – four destinations for their future state: where they got, Argentina, Uganda (this is presented by Herzl but conceived at the turn of the century, after *The Jewish State* has been published) and finally the Kimberley Plan, which proposed that the north of Western Australia combined with parts of the Northern Territory would become a new homeland for Jews (and, you probably note, would instigate a second displacement for First Nations People, the Miriuwung and Gajerrong people particularly, already displaced by British settlement). The idea of Australia pre-dates Balfour, and post-dates it in the specific form of the Kimberley Plan, which is shot down in parliament. This is a casualty of the White Australia policy still a quarter of a century away from abolition. Prime Minister Curtin, with bi-partisan support, cites concerns that Jewish settlers will drift out of their designated areas and form a raft of unwanted migration to cities where, he is adamant, they are not welcomed. You'll recall that on Mr Andoni A Sahhar's application for immigration, it states that he is a Jordanian (truer to say a man displaced) *and is not Jewish* (true enough).

It is clear that the Zionists do not care in any specific sense for my homeland, other than to say that they want one, and as it turns out, Palestine is good enough and has a satisfying narrative arc that they start to build into the project. This movement is a modernist one, rolling like a snowball downhill, captured in what is called *aliyah* (in Hebrew, ascension, and also, as a Jewish friend tells me, anti-Semitic, this idea that you cannot live your best life as a Jew outside of a Jewish state). *Aliyah* is not as successful as the Zionists had imagined. European Jews, it transpires, are not the ideologues the Zionists hoped, whatever their suffering, and also, as Europeans, are not particularly tempted by a far-off place that is regarded in biblical imagery as Holy, but in European imagery as a wasteland. The Zionists are good at lessons and they learn from this one too. I read in Uri Davis that deals were ultimately made to block Jewish flight to their desired destinations, in an effort to bolster the *Yishuv* population in Palestine.

This is the beginning of a numbers game, numbers which are still unconvincing at the time of the United Nations Resolution 181, which sets out the partition of Palestine in a division most favourable to the minority population. Take Benny Morris in a conversation with Joseph Massad, who says *these facts are not in contention. The fact that the Israeli side accepted, and the Zionist leadership accepted formally the United*

Nations partition resolution, and the Palestinian leadership rejected it. Massad answers:

> the standard Zionist line has always been: 'we are a peace loving movement, we have tried to make peace with these people ...' What of course goes unmentioned is that the Jewish population of Palestine at the time of the resolution was a third of the total population ... According to Jewish sources, Jews owned a mere 6.5 or 6.6 percent of the total amount of the land, yet they were given a majority of the land, almost 55 percent of the land of Palestine, by the Partition Plan. This to the Palestinians, of course, seemed utterly unjust and unfair (*The Persistence of the Palestinian Question*, 2006, p. 158).

This discussion lapses into an aporia common to Palestinian–Israeli dialogues. Morris says, *I do believe that there is such a thing as historical truth ... everything is [not] one big hodgepodge of equal value.* And Massad insists, *Palestinians need not change their mind about the very injustice of their situation.* Of our expulsion he says, *given race relations in the West, and who is believable and who is not, Professor Morris's version of events had much more credibility to Western audiences.*

The first film my father sees at the cinema is Disney's *Old Yeller*, a story about a dog who in the film's devastating climax contracts rabies while protecting his beloved family and has to be put down. Dad says that they are not often allowed to go to the cinema, and it depends on who is taking you more than the film, but he's allowed to go with Mrs Livermore and Mrs Lindsay from Mirls Street. Disney films have a tendency to the mawkish and at the studio someone concludes that the only way to salvage the death of a rabid dog is to produce its pup, Young Yeller, to rehabilitate the hearts of the family and the audience with it. A few years later, Dad and Irene go with their sister-in-law to see *Exodus*, Paul Newman starring. It's a big run of years for the Israelis, *Exodus* followed by the trial of Adolf Eichmann, and then the Six-Day War, and in my mind's eye I always substitute an image of a blond soldier at the wailing wall for the face of Paul Newman. All told, the 1960s are a decade in which the Euro-Jewish story is finally acknowledged, and a decade in which Israel's apologists have said it steers off-course, because the 1967 war offers Israel a taste of omnipotence (and after the apotheosis, decline is inevitable, and there is nothing omnipotent that surrenders its power gracefully so far as I know).

In my study of how the Holocaust is appropriated, I fix for a time on the idea that it happens to other people, for instance the pink triangles a lesbian with German heritage tells me about, or the Austrian princess in our lounge room once who refers to the Catholics. And if you make a survey there are more, the mentally ill and the feeble, the Romani people. Something we grow up with as children, that we see at the Oscars, in book prizes, in the *never agains* in radio interviews, is that the Holocaust happens to Jewish people. 'Where are the others?' I ask in a year ten history class, 'All these people excluded from their own executions, where is the cultural production on this?'.

Some things do not bear comparison, I will learn three years later in a university class, and some things do not bear speaking of. There is an aura cultivated around the Holocaust, and when others *are* included I learn a new word, *Shoa*, and this is a word for Jews only. In those years I read a great deal about testimony, utterances and also the unspeakable. *This is not yours to speak of*, I think, but it is pushed down our Palestinian throats at every turning. I read Norman G Finkelstein, who writes about the commercialisation of the Holocaust in the West, and Idith Zertal, who writes about the manipulation of the Holocaust in Israel. And what I can say is I learn a lot from these scholars, chasing this thread, trying to unpick the reasons why people believe that our Nakba was a reasonable exchange for the catastrophe of Jewish suffering.

It is satisfying to me when I read the remarks of a man my supervisor is interviewing who says:

> [w]hat we end up having [in Palestine] is the most unusual situation. The Israelis monopolize everything ... We say: 'Hey, you're hurting us', and they say, 'Don't you know how hurt we are? Haven't you heard of the Holocaust!' They are suffocating us, and when we try to push them away a little bit so we can breathe, they say: 'We're being victimized. You don't recognize we exist'. How on earth you can not recognize the existence of someone as fat as Sharon sitting on top of you suffocating you, I don't know! (quoted in Hage, *Against Paranoid Nationalism*, 2003, p. 133)

When I read this, it takes a great weight off my chest, and I photocopy the page and highlight the quote, and it is pinned on my wall until the highlighter has faded off the page and it is curled at the edges. Once I have learnt this principle as intimately as the state of my photocopy suggests, I am ready for the conversation I have with a friend in London. He says, 'Why do people expect that Jews or Israelis could learn something from the Holocaust? It is a nadir of education – of everything – and there is nothing at all valuable to be made of it'.

At a conference on Jewish culture where I am asked to speak, I bring in a single picture, of Yousra and Issa in the gardens of Asa Street. At the end someone asks me a question, 'You there, the pretty one', she says, 'why do you think we care? We had houses in Poland, in Austria, in Romania, we had beautiful things too and nobody cared'.

Perhaps my father will remember a biblical parable to aid me in answering to the human paradox of why one tragedy is a commonplace, another exceptional. I do not remember what I say to this woman but what I say now is that grief is manipulative, it makes the unremarkable exceptional, it diminishes the remarkable. It makes reasonable people resent others bitterly for the rest of their days, like Jean Améry. How sorry I am for the pain of the woman who could not acknowledge our suffering. How sorry I am to know now that destruction is the only sure friend to exceptionalism, as any Palestinian in Gaza will tell you.

Stereograph I have seen, 1916, Year of the Locust. A strange and arresting application of the medium. All manner of catastrophes now captured with modern technology.

41. MY DIASPORA

Abdullah and Ellen take a tentative step into the diaspora in 1948, and my father is one of the first diaspora babies (although to my knowledge the list of diaspora babies is nowhere recorded). And later they take a definitive one, when they step onto *The Roma*, shutting the door on displacement within a homeland or hometown, and choosing to the extent they can choose a different story. Dad and Irene are 'naturalised' on Pa's citizenship certificate, too young for their own. What does this mean, to be naturalised, in a settler-colonial state? Same thing for the Israelis, who see no shadow of irony in their identity on the whole, except for one or two pre-state Jews, conscientious objectors to what has just happened and who, born before Nakba, maintain the name 'Palestinian Jew' to describe themselves.

In Australia, naturalisation works a mischief in two places: to overwrite the First Nations People and to undercut who we are (Palestinians). This overwriting and undercutting leads me to the following propositions:

> *One*: on the subject of Jewish-Israeli identity it is true, as Massad and Morris both acknowledge, that there are pre-state Jews: some of whom arrive in the waves of *aliyah* and some of whom have been there a very long time – Palestine, great land of intersections, including routes from East to West and back again, land of crusades, part of Empires

that span from Rome to the Ottomans, place of important ports such as Jaffa and Gaza – in the days before hard borders who really chose where people could stay or where they would go or with whom they might love or make lives together? So it is certainly true that there is a diversity among these people, and most obviously our patron of persecution, Jesus, is one such Palestinian Jew, and there are Jews who precede him.

Two: there is no analogy between the people who may or may not be local to the region of Palestine and the question of who is and is not local to Australia. Australia, new word in itself, has primarily two categories of people, First Nations and other, and although some people have raised the question in settler-colonial contexts of *when is a settler a local?*, I would say when the horizontal axis denoting years is casually and even conservatively estimated at 60 000, then two hundred years is notable only for its staggering insignificance on any scale graph.

Three: comparisons can perform important work but are not symmetrical. For example, in Palestine it is said that Palestinians didn't exist or if they did they no longer exist in that place (see: spatio-side; see also: ethnic cleansing). In Australia it is not contested that Aboriginal people existed but rather claimed that they have now been extinguished (see: genocide). Palestine: *a land without a people for a people without a land*. Australia: *terra nullius* (see: similar meaning). Yuval Rotem (one-time ambassador for Israel to Australia) says, *we are both relatively young countries who have made our deserts bloom* (see: Harold Pinter, *the big pricks*

> *are out*). See: originary violence, see: structural instability, see: settler-colonial criminality, see: land grab, see: national hyperbole, see: Indigenous erasure, see: *watch your back*. See.

What do we say when we are children? We who even as children will not undercut to overwrite. We say – I say – *I'm Palestinian.* I say this in the portable classrooms to my music teacher in the year of the First Intifada, when I refuse to present this as a past, in the language of heritage. Question: is a six-year-old a terrorist? Answer: yes, if a six-year-old is throwing rocks in Palestine. Answer: no, if a six-year-old wears neat pigtails and knee-high socks in Melbourne. Around the same time Juju stops saying she's Middle Eastern. Juju now says, 'I'm Palestinian'.

Question: if the Greek Colony is no longer demarked as Palestine, how can a West Jerusalemite Palestinian be born in Palestine (this is a narrow example of a broader issue). Diasporas are sometimes self-cultivated, economic migrants for instance, and diasporas are sometimes enforced because their origin is literally eviscerated out of language, documentation or recognition. Labadi writes: *the term 'diaspora' is neither politically nor epistemologically neutral.* Let me remark on this. There is a Palestinian diaspora inside Palestine (see for example: Absentee Property Law, 1950) and some of these people are called Present Absentees (see: *terra nullius* anthropomorphised to apply to people). There are Palestinians in neighbouring countries. There are Palestinians in South America and North America, in Europe, in Britain, in Australia and New Zealand. It is difficult to get a figure on the numbers that comprise this diaspora. Do you count the dakhel (inside), do you count only who is UNRWA registered, patrilineal lines, whom? All I can say is the figures available are a gross underestimate of the situation.

UNRWA has a registry, but even this list has its limits, it excludes some diaspora Palestinians until we are the diaspora of the diaspora, the outside of the outside, the kharej of the kharej. It is, like much else, a political decision. A woman I know is outraged to find that she cannot register with UNRWA. Matrilineal and patrilineal diaspora are not the same they tell her. 'Who', she asks and I think quite pertinently, 'who is giving birth to all these boys?' (see: *Salt of This Sea*). On this I will say: no-one gets to decide with a piece of paper whether we are or are not Palestinian, not when we are standing up to be counted, and we will count ourselves if we have to.

What is the relationship between the diaspora and those who remain? I watched a documentary once about a Palestinian man who returns to his house after Oslo and there is a spider in the centre of a web in the doorframe and he says, *I was so ashamed, I couldn't look that spider in the eye because I left and she stayed*. In other words, I have nothing I can rightly say to Palestinians whose families remained.

I learn this when I am writing a paper for a conference at Bir Zeit. I have written the first half of it sitting in Tony Issa's flat on the Upper West Side of Manhattan, and later I am sitting in East Jerusalem when I see this work deserves to be put in the bin. Instead, I write a paper about paranoia, about diaspora, about how surveillance works at borders and how it works in the minds of diaspora at the moment they are crossing a border. How effective is a surveillance of which I am so convinced that I surveil myself? And frankly, I'm not interested in your Benthams or your Foucaults here, just in the raw atrocity of power whose omnipresence shadows us always (outside, *Mossad*, inside, *Shin Bet*). It is a memorable experience, talking about kharej and dakhel, an outsider looking in; I become quite lightheaded and the words start to swim and I imagine I've missed some central chunk of my thesis, like it doesn't make sense to be a Palestinian all your life when you are kharej and to be less than Palestinian now you are dakhel (a woman who is quite well known in certain philosophical circles congratulates me at the end, and also gives me half a sandwich, perhaps because I look as lightheaded as I am feeling).

I hear from Ahmad that a colleague in Melbourne once invited him to share in a birthday cake and then stopped herself. 'Do you know what that is?' she said. And Ahmad says with his beautiful conspiratorial snicker when he tells me that he answers, 'My father had a hotel in Cairo with a French patisserie chef and we helped ourselves to the cake in the fridge. Is that the sort of cake you were meaning?'.

Diasporas can be split and split again, split by class, split by religion, split by where you went and how you fared there. This is not in any way to contradict or discredit diaspora. Diaspora is at its essence fragmented. Do you get to answer the question of whether my diaspora exists and if I'm included in it?

The question of why some people need to control other people is a heavy one. I am watching a film with Ahmad called *The Law in These Parts* and an Israeli judge says at point blank, as he relativises the legitimacy of torture which the filmmaker shows us in photos more shocking than Abu Ghraib (and we feel the ricochet in our skulls when he says it): 'There are people whose job is to protect your life. So you can sit across from me now and go to a movie this evening. And you won't be blown up or killed or shot at in the street ... First of all I do believe people, that is my point of departure ...' The filmmaker interjects. Who is the judge referring to? He asks, 'The detainee or the interrogator?'.

'So. I believe ... when a detainee tells me what they did to him. I'm pretty suspicious. Because he has his interests.'

Answer: don't ask a person in the diaspora how it is that they are a person in the diaspora. Like Nina Simone says, *that's it!*

42. THE SEAMSTRESS OF JERUSALEM

There is a tidiness to the life of a woman without children. They are surely a boon to a family, this aunt or that sister, around whom a family might orientate itself, no toys to trip over, no school runs, dinners at reliable hours, bath time, *I've just put the kids down*. I have spoken before of Badia, Ellen's sister, third daughter and also third child, a woman who, I think, was just like me. Badia was a resourceful person who led a quiet but full life of creative things. I hear she makes Hilbe, and writes poetry like me. She takes an interest in family history (me again) and quite late in her life meets Luigi, a Neapolitan man who insists on marrying her. By then, Badia, at least, is long past children and past marriage also, but Luigi insists. I like that Badia is similarly disinterested in the institution of marriage (or children).

Here, again, I refer to the portrait I have of all Hanna's children. Ellen, the eldest, and soon to be married. Her hair is long and dark and in pigtails. Badia is there, and if you press me to guess her age, I'll say fourteen (but there's little I know about children nor the date of her birth). She has short light hair like Alice, it covers her ears but is clear of her neck. Badia is slightly infantilised here, her dress is quite smart but the collar of it is trussed up with a tie, like a sailor's suit (strange thing to dress children in mock-military dress, but people still do it). Perhaps through her childhood she immensely dislikes the way she is dressed by her parents, perhaps these are dresses handed down from Alice or Ellen, perhaps Badia thinks she would like to make choices herself about what she is wearing. Perhaps the third daughter is uniquely positioned to take up a needle the way Badia takes up a needle as a young woman, who is not pressured by Hanna to marry after watching the way arranged marriage wears with Ellen (not well, at least in its beginning).

Badia is in fewer photos than anyone else, or at least there are fewer photos I have of her. I think that like me, Badia does not enjoy being the person in front of the camera. In the glimpses I have, beginning and end of a life, her face remains quite unchanged from fourteen to old lady, and at fourteen she has an old face and I suppose she grows into it and then out of it again. It is a face quite like mine in this respect, adult face on a young child, old soul at the start, young soul at the end.

At Juju's eightieth birthday she gives her guests a poem about autumn that she writes when she already feels she is old, but is in her late fifties. Juju is describing a tree, the glowing halo of gold and red cheeks and she says that now they are missing: *Is this what age is all about / Or is there more beauty / At another stage?* We are left with this question. Sometimes, Juju says, she gets a shock when she looks in the mirror. She says, 'I see Mum looking back at me'. Neither she nor the love of her life, who she spends his whole life with, from the time that they meet until the time he dies recently, is impressed by old age, as she says.

In the archives of Yousra's images from Jerusalem, it is clear that this is a beautifully dressed family. More than one source has informed me that their clothes are made by Badia. Industrious woman with a needle, she is seldom in portraits but often the costumier for the shots that are taken of Yousra, of Ellen, and a portrait of Juju dressed in an elegant white dress with a neat fitted bodice to show off her gorgeous young figure. Under the belt, Badia's design gives way to a fuller skirt with simple but masterful tiers of detail, three bands of four pintucked rows to create a ripple when Juju walks ('Look at this bombshell!' her son says, one day, when we are looking with Juju at pictures together, and her face melts into the face of a teenager to hear it). Juju remembers this dress was for her graduation and you can see she is holding in her left hand the certificate. The dress is so beautiful that people ask Juju where it is from, and Juju says that Badia offered to make it for others and Juju says 'don't!' because she wants to be the only one to have it (and she has always been a confident individual, has Juju, who sees most of all the beauty in difference).

Badia makes gorgeous things for Yousra, more photos of Yousra than anyone, and she does not follow patterns, I think. There are dresses dropping out of her fingers like magic, she must see them fully formed in her mind, or maybe the fabric tells her what is to be done with it when she lays her hands over its warp and its weft (and such are the miracles attributed to our town, that this miracle would be quite a minor one seen from that angle). I assume the female form is her muse since I hear nothing of clothes sewn for brothers, and maybe she is the best dressed of all through these years, a walking advertisement of her own patterning, cutting and stitching, but there is almost nothing to go on between the school picture and the photo I never have seen at the pier, where she is stricken with Nakba and farewelling Ellen.

For a time in the 1940s, Badia teaches at a school where Alice is the principal, in Akka or maybe Tarshiha, and there she taught dressmaking to girls, one imagines, since few men of the era seemed to have known a great deal about needles. Juju writes that these two unmarried women came home together one year in a taxi (snow on the windowsill for Christmas) *laden with food supplies* like labany in tins of olive oil, dried fruit and mlukhiyeh. Is there no work in Jerusalem, I wonder, though these places in the past were not far (certainly). Do they make a fair bundle in Tarshiha, evinced in the extravagance of their transport (taxi), or is life just cheaper in this gone time (likely)?

Does she learn at the Friends School how to stitch like a master and does she place advertisements in the Mandate's papers; or perhaps her trade is something more exclusive, travelling by word of mouth or on the models of her family whose bodies she knows so intimately. Badia steps through my memory quite singularly, although I have no memories of my own of Badia and she keeps her proud surname for more than half of her lifetime. What does she do in America and how does she get there? She must emigrate after Fouad becomes a doctor; Fouad, the youngest, who sponsors, like Nicola in Australia, most of the family's arrival once he is there and established. She lives in Orange County, and when I am there with my dad, our cousin drives us to the neighbourhood where she once lived to collect an elderly Palestinian, whom we drive to a party in Palos Verdes, held at a new mansion with a steep flight of steps (and I regret the treacherous heel on the boots I am wearing).

Badia comes of age in Jerusalem during the Mandate period. Since I picture her most clearly in Palestine, she is a glimpse of what is lost when we leave our beautiful homes. Palestinians leave gramophones behind and hand-made lace, these markers of civility which even a European idiom might recognise. That we wore lace and listened to gramophones does, in no way, prioritise our claims over the claims of the vast dispossessed that straddle the globe. But that we had these machines, that we tatted and crocheted curtains and collars and tablecloths – these skills of quiet refinement that inhered in Badia – illustrate at least that the national narratives used to negate us are hollow fabrications. Whose word is the word that the West will accept? Not, it would seem, as Massad later says, the account of the Palestinians.

Does Badia concern herself with the rewriting of a national identity, with her industrious hands, her poetry, her trays of Jerusalemite Hilbe? I like to think that she glides, serene, through her displacement, and that she is not importuned (and I am certain she is not importuned by Luigi) by the tedium of explaining at too frequent intervals, who she had been in Jerusalem as pitted against the mono-reality of imperial politics. In the absence of children I imagine Badia remained above all as she was, in each of the any places that exile forced upon her. What trace remains of Hanna's third daughter, of a woman with no direct descendants? In our family legends Badia Sahhar will always be the seamstress of Jerusalem.

43. GOD'S RICHEST BLESSINGS

I hear Ellen's voice on the answering machine saying this, never one to waste an opportunity to say what she feels for each of us, even when nobody has answered the phone. Ellen's hands are crooked and arthritic and my father brings her thick pens from the pharmacy and rubber triangles to put around them, and she writes in her shaky large handwriting, *God's Richest Blessings*, on all of our cards, one of her trademark phrases, these physical impressions of her passage through the world. The last book she reads before she dies is the *Diving Bell and the Butterfly*, and I still have her copy which she lent to everyone including my father and me, where it was when she passed, and several nights after she does, I notice the dust jacket contains the impressions of her handwriting where she spread her paper to write something I cannot rightly make out. This palimpsest, which evinces her and whose content is also effaced, means I reify this book and I do not lend it to anyone, and it is filed under B on my literature bookshelf.

Ellen crochets for all of us blankets, which are haphazard but also planned. The centre begins with wool colours carefully selected and ends with the wool that is left (see: technicolour dream vest). These have been keeping us warm for decades, since before my childhood, and now numbering two more since her death. She is more particular about babies' clothes, beautiful two-toned jackets and capes that she knits (and Irene saves some and now her grandchildren wear them). Not understanding much of yarn, how a whole long string can be knotted and hooked into patterns and shapes, it always seemed miraculous when we would bring her something with a loose thread in it, and she would repair it with her crochet hook, quick and deft.

English is not an example of a faithful language, but Arabic is, so many daily expressions laden with God in them – *inshallah*, we all say it, whatever our faith or denomination, and whether we are of faith or not, it is embedded in the language. *Allah*, God in Arabic, the God to whom Ellen is born, although she is always Christian (mother tongue Arabic). Does it make you more faithful, Allah all around you? I am a child in the years of a great secular wave in Australia, and my father is Christian when he answers the census but lapsed, or non-practising, as an adult.

At Mirls Street, regardless of season, there's a side table by the place where my Pa sits, beneath the old Kelvinator and a portrait of his parents-in-law, stacked with several Bibles in English and Arabic. This is how Abdullah A Sahhar (his own Christian name an illustration of faith, meaning servant of Allah) learns English. He speaks a beautiful tongue, comparing the passages he knows in each language (and these stories are always a kind of miracle, the willing of knowledge) until the English untangles into the language he will speak with all of his grandchildren for whom Arabic has yet to untangle even all these years later. We do not visit Ellen on the evenings when she holds Bible meetings, which she does weekly until almost the end of her life. Four of the children do not much like these devotions, a dislike borne out at Ellen's funeral when after the service a neighbour says to my father, 'You broke your mother's heart', and my mother, a Catholic, says, 'What absolute nonsense!'. And I think now, *imagine saying that to someone on the day that they are lowering a mother into the ground.*

Despite the strictures of their religious practice, the Bible meetings, the services at the Williamstown Gospel Mission, the Allah that my grandparents adhered to was, I think, a forgiving one. I do not believe they believed, as some Protestants do, in an idea of the elect or the chosen; what mischief an idea of the chosen worked in their lifetime so starkly apparent, it is impossible to estimate. During Ellen's last week in hospital (before she dies of nothing particular, but the death certificate is crammed with the registrar's itemisation of organ failures, which occur concurrently when life leaves a body with finality), she apparently says to her daughters, 'I hope I will see you again'. This is something the religious chapter who attends her house will interpret as an expression of faith and an invective that both these daughters should *Repent!* But I very much doubt that Ellen saw heaven as something exclusive, this generous woman; I think she referred only to the temporal realm she was just hanging onto, like *come back to see me*. During this last week of her life, my father mislays his sunglasses, which are later found upon Ellen's head, the light of this world too brilliant for a person at peace with passing out of it.

Not long ago, Juju gives me a small pocket Bible, leather bound with black endpapers, red edging on all of the pages: *New Testament*, in Arabic (a book that has worked no magic on my acquisition of language). Year of publication, 1948, maybe Ellen's book, her name is written in English at the top of it. It is presented to Juju sometime in the 1980s with a handwritten note at the start, from my Pa to his dearest firstborn, and perhaps she doesn't think to open this good book for some years. She translates the note for me and also records that she finds the inscription in 2007. Juju brings this gift to a christening and entrusts it to my father, who gives it to me with a card that says: *Please accept your Grandpa Sahbar's gift to us – now to you.* Then later: *I am not religious and am not intending to convert you. My dad Abdullah I am sure will be happy with my decision.* I have often pondered this last line, *Abdullah I am sure will be happy with my decision*, juxtaposed with the one before it, *I am not religious.* This Bible is not a Bible that holds any power of conversion; Pa knew, I suppose, that conversion does not inhere in the physical objects around us but something inside us.

It is something I have lacked all my life, this imperative to faith, although my mother works hard to make me a Catholic, and perhaps it doesn't help that the despicable Pell confirms me into the church community (much good does it do me, or him for that matter). At age twelve I am given a black velvet jacket with interior pockets which conceals a black Walkman, and I listen in Mass (quite religiously) to Jon Stevens, bawling out his recriminations at Jesus, which is the emotional core of Lloyd Webber's *Jesus Christ Superstar* (and it instils in me a great love, in my own secular way, for Easter, the Passion story, set to an electric instrumentation). I spend many hours of my youth staring at the foreboding cross, this fearful object meant to compel us to faith, with Jesus impaled and bleeding, INRI in the scroll at the top above the crown of thorns used to mock him (and I think, *why do the Catholics celebrate this, give the man some peace, take it off!*). This Christogram or initialism is an odd one, Iesus Nazarenus Rex Iudaeorum, like Herod and Pilate call him, and the riled-up crowd, *King of the Jews but not ours*, the unbearable persecution they level at this Nazarene (a great smuggler's work, to emblazon his identity like this, in the N of the INRI, in all the cathedrals). My mother says to me when I'm an adult, 'I did my best but you were never convinced'. I remain unconvinced, but this in no way impedes my great if irreverent love for Jesus, and Sary and I have long played a game where we send each other pictures of men who look like regional variants of the man, who Western Christianity has quite erroneously given blond hair and blue eyes (awful Aryan spectre, and possibly the worst of the persecutions he endures, living or dead).

For my Pa, the Bible is a work of truth, he believes I suppose the stories in it, but more than that, the good book works to document the spatial relations of Jerusalem, the mounts on the left (or the right), Gethsemane, the tombs, the Via Dolorosa in the Old City. Pa baptises my father in the Jordan, same as John before him, a river so narrow in places an old man could spring over it (and which, as Ilan Pappé says, makes the Israeli claims to the Jordan on grounds of defence and security unsupportable, these tendentious jokes with their sinister punchlines that illustrate the narrow grasp outsiders have had on our geography). When I read Christos Tsiolkas's *Loaded*, it is a kind of revelation, the first book I remember reading about Melbourne, and in walking the streets between Richmond and Collingwood, the young Greek–gay Ari negotiates too the complexity of multiple identities. As the protagonist walks, his walk is punctuated by the tunes in his Walkman, and *Loaded* in this sense is quite like the Bible, describing to me something I knew, like the Bible described, to my Pa and to Ellen, their home.

I am no more inclined to faith now than I ever have been, although I always say I am a Christian Palestinian, a relevant marker, if not an expression of faith, in locating oneself in the terrain of the Palestinian diaspora. I am no more inclined to faith than I ever have been, although I am sometimes surprised to learn of the insults flung by various sects, the ones filled with hysteria and speaking in tongues, who tell you that heaven does not await you, unless you repent. Some of the best people I have met are the faithful, and some of the worst, and what I can say is that faith on its own is no guarantee of who you will be. But if there is a god (and I am fascinated by the mathematicians and scientists who believe in one), then it is my belief that his blessings are non-denominational, like Allah in Arabic, and that believer or no, the light of God's richest blessings will surely rain down on us all.

44. WHO ARE THE PALESTINIANS?

An easy question to answer.

But often you do not accept the answer.

If you ask me, 'Where are you from?' I will tell you (see: My diaspora). Emily Jacir says: *this is the hardest question to answer because our answers never satisfy you.* She says: *in extreme cases we are simply told that that in fact is not where we are from.*

The extreme case is not an exception. It doesn't occur to me for a long time that the contestation of my identity is a proof of what has happened.

Jerusalem, I have mentioned it previously, Jerusalem is divided and then it undergoes a *re-unification* as the Israelis call it (and we call it Naksa). Naksa understands linear chronology and also the teleology of ownership. This is a word that means setback. Naksa is a sub-section of Nakba, rightly understood. I attend a lecture called 'Why the Arabs are not free', and the speaker contends that we peak too soon, our Renaissance occurs while the Europeans are still crawling around in muddy quagmires and building structures out of sticks (first thesis). His second thesis pertains to the vernacular, and hinges on the first. He says the Arab Renaissance is just too early. What sends the English-speaking world flying ahead when it arrives in the sun? Apparently writers like Mark Twain and Norman Lindsay, spruiking vernacular dialects.

I cast about for the exception to such a withering critique, where I find the Syrian poet Nizar Qabbani, but as he is eighty-eight years later than Twain, what this comparison avails us of is not strictly relevant, though Qabbani is strictly anti-colonial and to many Palestinians a hero. I know several Palestinian men who are all named Nizar in honour of this poet, all born in the year following the December in which his second wife is murdered as an incidental casualty to the bombing of the Iraqi Embassy in Beirut. Of this, Qabbani writes in one poetic eulogy: *She was not afraid that the homeland would kill her / but she was afraid that the homeland / would kill itself.*

This is an apt reminder of the imprudence of attaching your hope to politics – though a homeland may still command worship. Do the Arabs also colonise? They do (they trade in slaves too). Although I am not aware of Palestinian colonisation so this depends how much *pan* you can put in the *Arab.* But I say this because I want you to know that I know, people on the receiving end of persecution are not saints. Nor is a sainthood the prerequisite for demanding your rights, nor having them enforced.

Some people have said that Palestinians do not exist and for a people who do not exist we are discussed frequently, perhaps more frequently than unicorns. Palestinians are not to blame for this, but this blindness is one of the burdens we carry and may not lay down.

Who knows we exist? Funnily enough, the early Zionists. These are a cruel but comparatively honest people.

Jabotinsky says, for example: *[some] attempt to convince us that the Arabs are some kind of fools who can be tricked ... [and] who will abandon their birth right to Palestine ... I flatly reject this assessment of the Palestinian Arabs.*

The first prime minister of Israel, Ben-Gurion, is also patently aware of us: *If I was an Arab leader, I would never make terms with Israel. That is natural; we have taken their country. Sure, God promised it to us, but what does it matter to them?* He has quite a lot of insight for a victor; he says, *they only see one thing: we have come and stolen their country. Why should they accept that?*

Sometimes when we are looking for traces of our existence it is a balm to read the early Zionist writings. Later the state conceals us so well that it is argued in the *Knesset* today that all Palestinians in the area of Gaza should be transferred, and what is that to an Arab?

My father, for instance, maintains that the coffee with hel was not something they drank but a thing Ellen would offer when Lebanese guests came calling, although they all like the sugar. My father, for instance, maintains that at the Mirimar nut shop on Lygon Street he cannot make sense of the Lebanese grocer's Arabic, Dad dropping the k of the ahwe like all good Jerusalemites. The old grocer signals to me from across the counter, handing me a piece of soft nougat, leaning in to confirm my father's order for a kilo of kahwe. A Palestinian man and a Lebanese one who both turn to a girl learning Fusha and declaim, 'I don't know what he's saying!', and if to my unpractised ear it all sounds the same, I delight in the way these two regional neighbours emphasise their differences for decades. I will go on loving these antagonisms, as does my dad and the grocer who greets us 'Ahlaaaan!', and we talk about the days when he fought alongside the Palestinians, which is celebrated in a photograph he hangs high on the wall and commands all of his customers to admire. And then one day the grocer will no longer be sitting there, and I still miss that man who would recognise my face and let me take groceries even when I had no money to pay for them.

It is true we have had some incompetent statesmen and also some fine ones (the latter of whom are systematically assassinated and imprisoned by agents of the state, both inside and outside its undeclared perimeters). In a democratic vote, the Israelis and Americans do not accept our decision (we elect Hamas, a party I will not defend and a party I will not criticise – they have some faults and some merits, same as any elected body chosen by the people, same as any choice when there is little to choose from).

An Israeli analyst of Palestinian affairs states that following this election and Israel's official statement regarding its view of that outcome, Hamas seizes control of the entirety of the Gaza area, due to *the fact that Fatah has refused to fully share the Palestinian Authority's mechanism of power with its rival Hamas, despite Hamas's decisive victory in the January 2006 general election* (Erlanger and El-Khodary, *New York Times*, June 14, 2007). Following which, Israel throws some energy into 'building up Fatah' as it says and besieging Gaza, economically and militarily.

It is hard to envisage the current state of Gaza, which has been described by multiple onlookers with concern as 'the world's largest open-air prison' (though the use of carceral logic has little to say of Palestinians but offers a window onto linguisitc and literal cages). Yet whatever its value, this description is now superseded by a tundra that the equivalent of more than six nuclear bombs once dropped on Hiroshima has made of it. An editor I have been writing to in Gaza says simply in one of his emails, *remember us*. I spend close to a decade writing about Gaza's bombardment and I think my doctoral supervisor captures something essential when he says, *Gaza itself is a permanent state of criminality*, to which he adds that it is not what *happens* in Gaza that makes it so. But I am kharej and it is shameful to say more here about the dahkel, other than that *I remember you*.

What I can say is this is not the first time Zionists have imprisoned the Palestinians (1948 in Jerusalem is front of mind, always). What I can say is I admire every last Palestinian whose family remained.

I am not interested in the function of law or in the operation of our unelected representatives. I am in Jerusalem and there is an expert in international law giving a talk on the possibility of mounting another case in the International Court of Justice. Two things to say: we always win these cases; and second, so what? What good does it do us – take a court that says 'stop the genocide', from whom we do not learn that a genocide is a genocide, but that the utterances of international law are non-binding.

'Why waste your time?' I ask in the question part of the talk; the speaker says, 'Perhaps you don't understand the operation of law?'.

'I agree', I say, 'I don't understand why we invest, in inherently oppressive laws, any legitimacy'.

When I am a young student my family prevails on me to study law; there is a saying that you can become a doctor, a lawyer, an engineer, or a failure – I laugh now to think of it. But I will remember the lessons most especially from property law, which is a powerful tool in colonial hands, the methodologies of thinking about land that is granulated through settlement and exceptions and the planting of flags.

Fundamentally I have no faith in a law that can make us disappear although we are present. Fundamentally, law is a tool of colonial power. Law, fundamentally, as it takes me the span of a law degree to discover, is not about justice but ritual. Law performs, law makes *your* hurt *my* fact, law legitimises your criminality, law is made illegitimately all the time. Law is force, is brutal, is ignorant of who I am. Khalas!

I make a statement one Nakba and I will make it again. I say: *this is not a debate.*

It is 2019 when I write this, year of Eurovision in Israel and questions of cultural boycott abound. I say: *I'm not going to reason with anyone. Because this is not a debate.*

False debates are not worth your time or mine. There are too many of them in the twenty-first century, like, *do gay people deserve equality? Have migrants stolen my job? Why are Aboriginal people so angry? If there are, in fact, Palestinians, to what extent are they culpable or implicated in their own catastrophe?* These are all disingenuous questions, and I will not answer them. Dad says to his sisters when they tease him for being born in Amman, 'Micaela knows who I am'.

What I will say is this: a Palestinian is a person who says, *I'm Palestinian*. When is a Palestinian a Palestinian? When we tell you we are (Palestinian).

Palestinians are frankly unconcerned by your opinion.

Welcome Stranger refers to the large gold nugget found on Dja Dja Wurrung Country in 1869 at Moliagul near Bendigo. It is reported the nugget was hardly buried, sitting in the roots of a tree. Gold, we are instructed by Moore and in this story, is ascribed no value in utopia.

45. PORTRAITURE

Perhaps I have already picked the bones clean of some of these images: Ellen with all of her siblings, dear Najla, ill-humoured, and Lily wearing the necklace they fought over. I have mentioned my Pa, at twenty or so, in a collarless shirt and suit jacket, tarboosh on his head, splayed so gloriously over his first new car (the Dodge). The ABC women who journey around the Mediterranean; Taata Barbara smiling in snow. And later Dad says the last picture of Taata is taken after she dies, when they send an image of her laid in her coffin, to provide some sense of closure to Yousra and Issa in America.

What do we learn from these pictures? We learn that Palestinians love the new art of photography, but we know that this love runs parallel to the plans of the would-be colonial powers (and some real ones) that come to survey in aerial images our land. In a photo I've mentioned before at the Fast (Australian Soldiers Club), which shows Robert Menzies, you can see that there is a shop on the ground floor, Matson Photo Service, and I suppose George M Sahhar, our travel guide writer, passes this business each day on his way into work. The Matson Photograph Collection is a significant one, over 22000 glass and film negatives from the late nineteenth century which ends, somewhat abruptly, in 1946. This is the year of the King David Hotel bombing, and although one cannot always tether the facts to grand narratives, it is the arc of destruction that prompts the Matsons' departure from Jerusalem to California. Today this collection is associated with the American Colony, a complex which remains in Jerusalem, and which was established by Swedes and Americans as a utopian and independent Christian sect. But this alliance collapses, which is a partial explanation at least for how, decades later, the Matsons come to donate the vast bulk of the collection's photographic materials to the Library of Congress. And though the colony remains it is without this vital archive (although neither is this the Elgin Marbles nor the Shelal Mosaic for that matter).

The Library of Congress maintains a large holding of Palestine images through the last years of the Ottoman Empire, the First World War and the British Mandate. So too, the Palestine Exploration Fund which was housed on Wigmore Street in Marylebone but is now relocated to Dreadnought Walk, Greenwich, London.

There are itinerant travellers who photograph Palestine. Freya Stark is one, who favours fig sandwiches, which she carries cross-country when exploring *Druse territory* (an anecdote I read in a 1973 list of essential pantry items for the Arab kitchen) and some of her photos are itemised in the collection of St Anthony's, Oxford, but few digitised. Stark writes sympathetically about Palestinians in *East Is West*; for example:

> ... I have no wish to enter the Palestine arena or to take up any position beyond the very simple and fundamental one that it must be wrong to make a country accept immigration *by force.* The people of Palestine, after two thousand years or indeed longer, are attached – like all the Middle Eastern peoples – to their soil; and they have already admitted close upon half a million Jewish immigrants within the last twenty-five years ...

> in proportion of populations the Jewish immigration would correspond to sixty-five millions in the United States. If America *had* admitted sixty-five million Jews, or Gentiles, or indeed Angels, all in one lump in less than thirty years, and it were proposed still *to coerce her to keep her door open*, it is easy to imagine what her reaction would be. The Palestinian reaction is exactly the same (1945, p. 99–100).

Stark concludes, *why a reasonable recognition of these facts should brand one as an anti-Semite I do not know*, and I hear that after this book she says little else of political import for the rest of her life.

It is unlikely to surprise a reader to learn that Stark's work in this area is regarded as her most controversial. This is notwithstanding the Peel Commission, first written in a requisitioned premises that began as the Palace Hotel and was built by the Supreme Muslim Council, but which is now the Waldorf Astoria. The commission is engaged to reflect on the causes of the 1936 Arab General Strike, which bleeds as you might know, and before the commission's eyes, into the Arab Revolt. During my stay in East Jerusalem I find a copy of the report, replete with marginalia and discarded notes interleaved in its pages; for example, a loose note tucked into page twenty-eight reads:

> *We should not assume*
> *that Jewish and Arab interests*
> *will not conflict.*

I find this double negative to be a quiet scream in the archive, waiting for someone these eighty-three or so years later to read it. Or again on a loose sheet between pages sixty-eight and sixty-nine:

> *On the contrary, the longer the*
> *mandate operated, the stronger*
> *and more bitter Arab antagonism*
> *to it became.*

One of the effects, incidental perhaps, to all this photography, colonial surveys, pictures of pilgrimage, biblification is that Palestinians take to the documentation of who they are, and quite frankly the fabric of their lives, with the well known fervour of any new convert. Sary restores a photograph of what might be the employees of Abdullah at the carpentry workshop on Mamillah, or perhaps at a job site, constructing the frame of a shed or a stable (which might have once housed a donkey, Dad speculates while he looks at the picture, telling me how one of his cousins envied the donkey when he was toilet training, *if I was a donkey no-one would care*, he apparently said; and of course, Dad says, nobody minded a bit what the Donkey did).

I have told you of Juju in the white graduation dress, stitched by Badia, of the small, bevelled pictures in Amman with Juju, with Rose, and with Lily (of whom little is known). There are pictures of Pa with his clients, right through I suppose to the 1940s, in Baalbek, in Jericho and in the Haram Al-Sharif complex in our own Old City with soldiers in hats that were nicknamed lemon squeezers (something I now know fixes them as the NZ part of ANZAC). There are photographs of children on a camel, the camel so pale in the flesh that in the photograph it is almost not there, handsome men in Edwardian bathing costumes at the beach with handlebar moustaches and stylish tortoiseshell spectacles. There is a sequence of people dipping their legs in an irrigation system, smoking a shisha, dishdash robed and mysterious. There are some men on a stage at a local scout hall, holding rifles and masbahas between their thumbs and index fingers. Many intriguing images of people who were known to some of my family but which can offer me only ambient views of Ottoman or Mandate Palestine and considerable opacity. There's a picture of Taata with some of her children and a woman in a glowing white wimple, a nurse or a sister, perhaps our relative, but no-one remembers and perhaps this is because nuns passing into new orders leave their familial connections behind them.

Photography is so commonplace in Palestine that it has time to be playful, and there is a picture my friend recounts to me of a great-aunt (quite certainly a lesbian) dressed in men's wear; in this vein there is also a picture of Sary's jiddo and a mate, one formal, the other adoring, and who knows if this is a comic artifice that comes over them, or whether in costume they express in a photography studio their truest of feelings? Palestinian families know many things they don't talk about.

The ordinariness of photography, its common place in our lives, means also that many of the sitters (or standers) are smiling, often to one another, instead of the camera. There stands Yousra with Issa in the gardens of 8 Asa Street, Yousra, beautifully dressed in a tailored frock with a belt, left hand in her pocket, Issa leaning his arm on her shoulder. They are turned slightly towards one another, and they smile in opposite directions, winter perhaps, though the sun shines down and they stand just behind the central water fountain (filled, I believe, with large red goldfish, a fact I learn in Pa's account of the house). Yousra is, I suppose, unmarried, the cinched-in waist suggests she has not yet had children, and there is a laugh in her squinting eyes like the photographer or Issa has said something funny. This is one of my most prized images, an image of my great-aunt and uncle as two young people who stand in the blissful joy of Jerusalem, and in the blissful ignorance of what is not far away, that will cleave them apart from this fountain, from each other, the photographer, their mother, my Pa, this city and Palestine. Behind them there is a garden seat, painted white, set to the side of a low stone balcony.

This seat is pictured a second time on a very hot day since what it records is six people with their feet in the fountain (four known) and one at the back near the half-moon-shaped carving over the door of the house. This figure at the back who does not cool his feet in the fountain might be an image of Andoni (Pa's father, who we hear speaks good French). Yousra looks pregnant in this one and there is Taata, flanked by two of her sons, one Nicola, a fact that places this picture sometime before Nicola's departure from Jerusalem.

There are fewer photographs of the house after Yousra departs to her husband's Old City quarters, although I have often wondered why there are no photos here of Ellen at Asa Street, who has already given birth to Pa's dearest firstborn, and Juju recalls Yousra's marriage to her handsome groom. They are friends, I believe, Yousra and Ellen, and one day with Ajia they arrange, perhaps by appointment, to visit a rather upmarket photography studio where a series of portraits are taken of these three women in traditional costumes.

Ajia is standing at the left and Yousra the right and Ellen sits between them, her mother and cousin, and also her sister-in-law (as Yousra becomes). Ajia and Yousra both wear intricate headpieces, threaded with coins, and light-coloured dresses, embroidered with tatreez, and if I had to guess I would say that the stitching is red, they are fellah costumes based on the Ramallah style, although the photos are black and white. Everyone's arms are half-bare and Yousra holds to the right of her head (the photo's centre) a terracotta water jug. She is the tallest of the figures, a look on her face that is dreamy, not quite a smile, and if you can recall to mind the Mona Lisa then this is the look one finds here in Yousra. Ellen wears black, unlike the others, a Bedouin dress and perhaps a judicious suggestion made by the photographer to bring out a contrast. And you can see the hint of Ellen's dark hair beneath the fabric that swathes her, and brightens the ivory gloss of her skin. She clutches a woven basket filled with straw to her knee, suggesting, perhaps, a woman who collects eggs with the dawn, and the three of them are wearing necklaces of shells or bone pieces, which stands out the best on Ellen's plainer dress.

I do not know if there are more portraits from this sequence, although Ellen is extracted from this image into a solo portrait of which I have a photocopy, ribbed with the fading lines of the scanner, and in which I can see her wedding ring now and the subtle embroidery around the collar of her dress (a portrait on many a table in the rooms of those who loved her, like Najla in Phoenix and Irene in Melbourne). The backdrop used by the studio is quite incongruent with the costumes these women have chosen for photos, something middle-class women, and men for that matter, do (classist thing to do, I suppose, to impersonate the rural people from whom they must feel quite remote, living their cosmopolitan lives in Jerusalem). Behind Ajia is a large old tree, perhaps an oak, and behind Ellen's head, a neglected white picket gate. What place does this backdrop have then, or ever, among these women, evoking a nostalgia for an old country, no older than theirs, and one they neither see nor particularly care to?

Whatever the folly of portraiture might be I have no doubt that pictures we left behind were misunderstood by those who incidentally acquired them along with our houses (the many armfuls of photographs that didn't fit in our arms, and were pawed over perhaps and afterwards burnt, by the settlers who stole our homes). Perhaps it confirmed to these settlers, with all the ignorance of their foreignness, that the Palestinians were a backward people. And it is true enough that culture even without catastrophe struggles to travel. It is clear from the collection I have – and from the photographs I've seen and from the prints that various descendants of photographers still sell in the Old City of Jerusalem – that for the Palestinians who lived through the last days of their homeland, portraiture was a matter of fun, and at a studio perhaps a matter of occasion also. With their obvious love for fancy dress and the art of the costumier, this taste is not so dissimilar to contemporaneous people elsewhere when rightly considered.

The portrait of Ellen, of her dear friend and relative Yousra, of her mother Ajia, is a testament then to a trend that swept through the mercantile Jerusalemite Christians, a fashion for portraiture in Bedouin dress. I do not know if this portrait was once a glass plate or on cellulose, since all I have known is the image of the image which is infinitely reproducible. Yet nor does it trouble the point of what such an image illuminates. That these women are a part of their times, no more and no less, who relish the city in which their families have lived for centuries. Women with little idea on the day that they visit the studio that these joyous keepsakes will become, overnight, one decade hence, the records instead of a gone life, with only this portrait to show for it.

46. THE SEMIRAMIS HOTEL

Recently this has become unbearable, the date, like a spear, comes stabbing at night. I might be casually making a tea or in the bath when it grips me.

I must have known about the Semiramis Hotel for many years already. It is in Qatamon, a chic suburb in the New Jerusalem, a ten-minute walk from our home.

How does a deep-sea diver like me miss a vital clue? (Maybe I do not miss it, maybe it is *repressed*.)

There are some famous points in the chain of a national history's demise which links to a family. Mine. The bombing of the King David and of course, Deir Yassin. This happens in April, and Juju says, 'I remember it, we were still in Jerusalem. I turned off the radio in disgust' (part of this is not true, they are not in Jerusalem by April, they are in Amman, of this I am certain. But there is nothing to gain in contradicting a precious aunt while she is trying to find me her memories). I may be open to correction here, but I am not aware that the Semiramis Hotel is one of these points, though it has local significance in Jerusalem.

I am reading about how news reporters failed in their duty to make the news – News.

Krystall, a man who serves a prison term for refusing to participate in the project of a Jewish State, will write later:

> ... on 4 January 1948 the Haganah blew up the Semiramis Hotel in the prosperous Arab neighbourhood of Qatamon

> claiming to have suspected that the hotel served as a headquarters to local irregulars. In fact, 26 civilians, most from two Christian Arab families of Jerusalem, were killed, causing major panic and triggering the exodus of Arab residents ...

This is an extract from a paper called 'The de-Arabization of West Jerusalem 1947–1950'. This un-sensational title is a portrait of my family.

I am speaking to Juju on the phone. She says, 'I'm glad you've got the date, I've been looking for it everywhere' (although not on the internet, which she conscientiously objects to).

January 4 will always arrive two days before the Epiphany.

I am starting to wonder how many dates there are on the calendar that are not burdened by commemorations of loss, dispossession and massacre.

Once I was in a relationship with someone born on May 15. *This won't work*, I thought, one day is not big enough for you and a whole catastrophe. It was probably always clear to us both which one I would choose.

January 4 has been waking me up at odd hours with a subterranean beat of alarm. It is making me palpitate even now.

I ask Juju what she remembers. Here's what she says:

We all got out of bed

We crawled around the floor of the house

Was it the next day we left (I don't know) the hospitals were overflowing. Joey arrives eleven days later.

Pa will say little of how this specific event, after which he leaves

Jerusalem, contributes to their leaving. But he fears that the Jerusalem hospitals, to say nothing of the maternity wards, are in crisis. *That the weapons held by the Arab fighters were antiquated and in short supply* may have affected this decision and one old fighter recounts, 'You could press the trigger one hundred times, and the gun would only fire once, with a burst of flames so bright that I could not use it at night'.

Hala Sakakini, daughter of the famous Khalil, describes Qatamon after this bombing:

> The rumor spread that leaflets had been dropped by the Jews saying that they would make out of Qatamon one heap of rubble. Whenever we saw people moving away we tried to encourage them to stay. We would tell them: 'You ought to be ashamed to leave ...'

'I used to write diaries', Juju tells me. 'It made sense' (and again when she says it) 'because I was thinking that we would go home'. This is a crucial document, now destroyed, of a fourteen-year-old's impression of what was in train. What happens to it? Her brother finds it one day and is reading it aloud in the house (in Amman, I suppose) and she says:

> *I was that mad; I tore it up—*
> *And that was the end of that.*

At eighty-seven she has a laugh in her voice and sounds resigned, with respect to the diary at least.

Juju says to my father on the phone quite recently, 'It was a good thing you needed to be born, if we'd stayed I suppose they would have shot us all'.

Does she mean it? My dad repeats it several times, so at the least it does the work of making him feel better after all these years (how a baby might carry the blame of a Nakba inside him, ridiculous and also unbearable).

There is a noose around Jerusalem, narrowing around the necks of the Palestinians. This is quite an unbearable thing to write. There are not many left at the end of this period, some keep diaries, some lie on the floor, some are shot at as they wave improvised white flags of personal surrender. They are starving. A note from Husein al-Khalidi in the week that Joey is born confirms this, *There are no people, no discipline, no arms, and no ammunition. Over and above this, there is no tinned food and no foodstuffs*. The Jerusalemites who stay are surrounded by barbed wire. An exception cannot be compared but Jerusalem is in a terrible state at this time.

No travellers are welcomed.

No travellers (just journalists, like ravens, who somehow miss our Nakba, which is a spectacular omission even for these narcissists).

There are no fellaheen from villages with baskets of fruit on their heads who arrive to the front door of Asa Street. Now Tony is dead perhaps only Juju is left to remember what the fellaheen brought, and what excitement there once was at their knock.

The fellaheen, some thousands a day, are on the roads with their clothes, and not saleable wares, on their heads. They too are in exodus. Feet on the road, one in front of another, like words this is how you begin and continue (and I say nothing of endings, there isn't an ending to speak of).

What becomes of a man Juju says that she sees in Ramallah, who is working a loom with his toes? (Perhaps he remains, Ramallah falls to Jordanian hands.)

I have wondered for some time whether saying this name would have the effect of striking a match and holding it to the tail of a leech: the Semiramis Hotel, Semiramis Hotel, Semiramis! Third time the charm, now I breathe out more calmly. How long will it stay on the page, I wonder? Can I lay these things down like a burden, or must I always hold onto them? If I lay down my burden will it be where I left it if I should ever want to find it again? Answer: not if you are a Jerusalemite Palestinian in the year of our Nakba.

Haganah: Jewish terrorist group that does it. Is this the source of my anger – the leech that has gorged itself on our blood? (Am I trying to shed the event or the perpetrator? Psychic scarring walks sideways and in truth I cannot say.)

I teach courses on terrorism for more than half a decade and I could give you some elegant theory here. But instead I will give you the title of a lecture I delivered: *White People's Ideas About Terrorism*.

This is the second reason why I have some passing time for the early Zionists, they not only acknowledge that they *perform* terrorism, they also call themselves *Terrorists*.

Irgun (this is not their bombing, but a group reportedly more barbaric than the *Haganah*, and proud of it).

It is not a person or a group who takes a country. It is an ideology (and the force of arms, and the complicity of every single Nation State who looks on in 1948 and Does Nothing).

Scholars, Krystall writes, *have waged endless debate on whether [what happens is] attributable to a conscious Zionist plan*. The test, he concludes, is simple: *To this day, not one Palestinian Arab refugee has returned to his or her home in West Jerusalem*.

There are lots of ideas that emerge after the Second World War that make people feel they have recovered something of their humanity. Like international organisations, collaborations, coalitions, like humanitarian aid, like human rights, like international humanitarian law, like the Nuremberg trials, like Geneva Conventions one to four, like covenants on a series of soft-core rights that only some people ever get a sniff of, like disaster tourism, like the scales have fallen from your eyes, like save the children or – god help me, after more aerial bombardments on Gaza – the inane *we are all Palestinians*!

Does naming the Semiramis Hotel quicken your heart? Deir Yassin? The incineration of villages, the burning tyres rolled down from the mountains in Haifa, are you still breathing when you hear these things, does this happen to you or the people whom you resemble (like a baby on the television during the massacres at Sabra and Shatila, a sobering sight to my mother who says, *she looked just like you*)? Does my story bear any resemblance to your experience? As exact as a resemblance? Can you relate to this?

Is it possible to wrestle the spear off a date and expertly work its tip through the armoury? Can you poke a date in the eye and hope to vanquish it? I am reminded of the Bayeux Tapestry, stray arrow that pierces King Harold, determining the outcome of Hastings. If I had a spear and a chance, or even an arrow, I would choose this way to slaughter my demon date and its haunting, a certain way to death to be sure, but I hope not too swift: January 4 deserves to feel it.

Sometimes, there is nothing else for it but to be an angry Palestinian. I take up no arms, but in the privacy of my mind it's a blood bath. And I want to watch. I am thinking about Hasib Hourani's thesis in *rock flight* when I write this, Hourani who lays out instructions for 'how to make a box', 'how to make a sling', 'how to make a rock' (please find a piece of paper, as above, as above). He is thinking about the enclosures of a state that suffocates; he is thinking about divestments, that are cultural and economic. And he is thinking about boycotts (that are cultural and economic). He is thinking about many forms of suffocation when he writes this and the tools we have to hand (see: paper). He is thinking about all these things when he writes, *suffocate settler annette*.

47. 8 ASA STREET

In 1987, my Pa records a narrative about his life, and I see how incomplete it is when I listen to his voice, now. I wish, how many decades too late, that I might have put my own questions to Pa, and seen for myself how he drew in the air at Mirls Street with the end of his key, our house at Asa Street.

The neighbourhood of the Greek Colony was sold off throughout the nineteenth century and into the twentieth. Pa says that as a young man, Abdullah 'saved enough money and then I bought a piece of land in the Greek Colony. I bought it from the Vice-Consul of the Greek Council in Jerusalem, for I think, one hundred and twenty pounds' (what precision; a man of eighty-seven recalls what he paid for a plot in Jerusalem in the 1920s, Pa the same age as the year, or very nearly).

From the Greek Colony one might walk to a showroom on Mamillah displaying a wide beautiful bed in the window, or to the meeting point at the Jaffa Gate where all the tourist guides once stood and from where Pa could visit his father-in-law, Hanna, at a restaurant the old Jerusalemites who were young then recall as Abou Petro's. The Greek Colony today is an expensive neighbourhood. When people rent there, advertisements say (I've told you) *Arab style* – an adjective to describe the houses and sometimes their interiors, which is at best a half-truth, since what these houses are is Palestinian.

Sometime in the 1980s, an aunt goes to visit 8 Asa Street. I am quite small at the time and I see that the house is not dissimilar to the one my parents live in. Later when I see the photos again I discover that this is a lie, something a small girl's mind does to make the strange familiar, superimposing one image onto another. For instance, my recollection of those photos is that Asa Street is a pink building, much like the house we are living in when I am six. But, as far as I know, Asa Street was never pink, although there is a Jerusalem stone which is famous for its reddish hue and perhaps I combine these disparate facts in my mind.

This is the house my Pa built and here's how he does it, he says: 'I asked people to start bringing the stones to prepare the cement, and everything. And one time, I took the passengers over to Baghdad, to Babylon, and all these places, and then asked the builders to build it. So the stones were there – and Emile would stand over there' (you can see at this time Pa has built a house in his mind and positioned his brother who he gestures towards with the key, just so in the Mirls Street lounge room). A query that arises from this account is the provenance of the stones at Asa Street, why intersperse this story about Baghdad? Does he transport Iraqi stones back to Jerusalem for building?

I have told you before that my Pa was a generous man, and he says, 'When I bought the land I didn't write it in my own name, I wrote it in all the names that is to say' and he states all the brothers' names, and then his sister's too, to whom he would give a share (and he would have too, if there had been a share that remained on the other side of a Nakba). This property is mentioned on an inventory sample compiled by Frank Jarvis for the UN Conciliation Commission for Palestine in 1964. Dr Salman Abu-Sitta suggests that these records should be used not to secure compensation but to repossess property, and that we might follow the work of the World Jewish Restitution

Organisation as a model. Dr Salman concludes, *the right of return is both legal and possible.*

Perhaps my aunt's pictures of Asa Street are taken after Pa dies. You can hear in this account, where he describes the house, that he is uncertain about the details of what has survived. Pa says, and here he passes again into the present tense:

> We've got a pool with water and red ... red fish and a fountain in the middle of it. And this pool it was sort of like a garden all around it, that is to say on the edge of the pool, flowers ... And the length of the pool is about two metres or something of that sort all around. Maybe still there now under the Israelites.

I think it is very likely that the fountain remains, Pa. About the red fish I could not say.

Vera remembers that the house is two stories with five apartments, one of these rented. She remembers playing on the roof. Juju remembers reading on the balcony.

Pa says:

> We became two stories because we became a big family because my brother Issa was married. And then I was married after that. Issa and I we lived in the upper part of the house. And Emile with my mother and sister they lived in the lower part.

One of Issa's children is a daughter called Grace. Grace might be the age of Vera or thereabouts. I asked Grace once what she remembered from the house. She says she recalls a terracotta water jug, shooting out water from its spout, and then smashing into little pieces, the water bursting all at once and together out of it. Grace says she cannot find more memories of her life in Jerusalem than this, although half a childhood had passed before she left it.

My Pa collapses an era of his life into just a few lines, it is prefaced by the imminent arrival of Joey, my father. He says:

> So what happened, Elleni was pregnant with Joey. And the British took over from the Turks, this is at the end of 1917, almost 18. And the British Mandate was terminated and they wanted to go. And there was some fighting between the British and the Arabs and the Jews. Because the Jews want to take our country by the help of their people.

There is no need, I suppose, for Pa to dwell on this happening. You already know what happens and it keeps happening each time we return to these years, all the archival work that documents our erasure, and the contemporary work that disappears a genocide in Gaza, and the supercilious diplomacy between that first erasure and a disappearing genocide that with words and force for decades has sought to vanish Palestinian life. And the rejoinder to all of this, quite simply, is sumud.

Quite recently, Vera returns to Jerusalem and bold as you like, she knocks on the door of our house. Who answers? A man who says he has been waiting for her to arrive for as long as he has lived there. He is living upstairs, in Pa's apartment at the front, where the smoke from the bombing of the King David Hotel may once have been visible. The man in our house is so moved by Vera that he writes to us all to extend a virtual key to Asa Street for as long as he lives there, a man who has made *aliyah* and yet who cannot ignore that there is a past to redress, and who cannot ignore his subterranean sense of what Evan has said: *we own that house in a way that no-one can ever take away.*

Perhaps one day Sary and I might execute a project among my Pa's gardens, dressed like Yousra and Issa, on a bright winter's day behind the fountain. Some old Jerusalemites observed in their memoirs that a great source of pain was how their beautifully tended gardens were abandoned. I think of the passionfruit vine Juju asks after, and I speak of the bougainvillea that still swathes the fence.

My Pa will narrate the Nakba in less than a hundred words when he is speaking to the tape at Juju's request, and he tells us all of the time when my little father was born: 'So what I did. I asked my father-in-law, he said take her to Amman' (Elleni he calls her, such love in his voice):

> We crossed the Jordan with my shevro-lett, 1947 model.
> And took the four children, which there were, with us, they were little ones. We slept in the church that night and so on.
>
> I went back to Jerusalem to look for the rest of the family.
>
> We were there in Jordan because the Jews took all our property, our money, our cars and the carpentry shop and the showroom, our tourist offices.
>
> *It's all gone.*

I would like to say to my Pa and to Ellen that nothing is truly gone if you know how to look, to say, *look here, I have built our beautiful home out of words,* a house Pa built twice in his life already, first in Jerusalem and then with the shape of his key in the eye of his mind. One day I will echo the father of Mahmoud Darwish, I will shout as his father shouted, *I am I. And I am here.* And when I do, I know that Ellen and Pa will be with me too.

I will shout this at the intersection of Mamillah, and on the balcony of the house my Pa built, and I will give what voice I have to the most joyous euphonia of the Palestinians returning to our once and future home, with the dead on our shoulders and the living in our arms. We will burst through the gates of the Old City and roam the New Jerusalem from the Greek Colony to Talbiyeh, from Qatamon to Baq'a, sweeping south to Gaza and north to the Galilee, and to all the places we are indivisibly from and that are ours. And as I cross the threshold of my grandfather's house, I will lay my burden down.

And if it should not be me, then it will be another, when I will be an ancestor and those that I have loved will all be stars.

48. NAKBA

Well, what can I say? You have read it all here in these pages:
(Not an event, but a structure).

I have visited Palestine twice, but in truth
it is with me each day of my life.

And also (and always)
Too far away.

NOTES AND REFERENCES BY ENTRY

Where references are not noted in the body of the text but a direct quote has been used, or a specific paraphrase has been made, page numbers are given here alongside the reference.

Origin

The term 'survivance', coined in the Native American context by Anishinaabe writer Gerald Vizenor, is gaining wider recognition in related fields as a vital concept (and not a typographic error).

- Abu-Manneh, Bashir (2016). *The Palestinian Novel: From 1948 to the present.* Cambridge: Cambridge University Press. See in particular chapter 3, 'Emile Habiby: Capture and cultural escape in the Pessoptimist (1974)', pp. 96–115.

Freemasons

Some consternation has ensued about what exactly Ellen threw that day at Pa. It must have been substantial enough that the event was recalled, which rules out such ordinary objects to hand in a kitchen as tea-towels. But it is possible that a chopping board was thrown and not a knife, weighty enough to remember but also less shocking.

Though Hanna was Ellen's father, the matrilineal grandfather which in Arabic is denoted as Jiddo, for reasons not wholly available other than the wealth of obscure curiosities in the business of family naming, Hanna was known as Sedo by Ellen's children.

Palestine Restaurants

- '1st Palestine Restaurants for Jerusalem' (1943). *The Palestine Post*, November 10, p. 3.
- Advertisement (1944). *The Palestine Post*, March 9, p. 4.
- 'Govt. no longer financing restaurants' (1945). *The Palestine Post*, July 19, p. 2.
- Hintlian, George (2004). 'An attempt to reconstruct the pre-48 Arab commercial center of Jerusalem'. In *Between the Archival Forest and the Anecdotal Trees: A multidisciplinary approach to Palestinian social history*. Birzeit: Ibrahim Abu-Lughod Institute of International Studies, pp. 25–33.

- 'Hope deferred' (1943). *The Palestine Post*, December 16, p. 4.
- Seikaly, Sherene (2015). *Men of Capital: Scarcity and economy in Mandate Palestine*. Stanford: Stanford University Press, p. 216.
- 'Shilling Restaurants for Palestine' (1943). *The Palestine Post*, October 22, p. 3.

Bethlehem

The walking through walls thesis is presented by Eyal Weizman (2006), 'Walking through walls: Soldiers as architects in the Israeli-Palestinian conflict,' *Radical Philosophy* 136: pp. 8–22. The paper outlines the use of theory as a military 'tool' employed by the IDF (as is their official title though IOF is more accurate) and deployed specifically in *Operation Defensive Shield* (2002). The title of the strategy is quite illustrative since walking through walls is not a metaphor; to which I will add the remarks of a Palestinian woman interviewed for this study, Aisha, who pointing to a wall that had once housed a built-in custom bookcase, said, 'And this is where they left. They blew up the wall and continued to our neighbour's house', p. 10.

Jerusalem Railway Station

- Sahhar, Micaela (2024). 'Where is Palestine in the Anzacs' Palestine Campaign? Israel and the struggle for Indigeneity in commemorative state practice'. *Middle East Critique* 33 (2): pp. 245-261.

East/West

- *Persona Non Grata* (2003). Directed by Oliver Stone. [Feature Documentary Film]. HBO America Undercover.

Intifada

- Kifner, John (1987). 'Israel bears down to stop protests in occupied areas'. *New York Times*, December 24, p. 1.
- Sahhar, Micaela (2015). 'Occupied Narrative: On Western media collusion with Israel's "wars" and recovering the Palestinian story'. PhD thesis, University of Melbourne, p. 41.

Cars

At some stage it is said that Pa said that he had the number plate J5 and that J1–J4 were held by the British. There are many pictures of Pa with vehicles from across the Mandate era, though none I have yet found with this plate. The verbal testimony I have does not speak of J5 on this occasion.

- *Arabic for a Shilling: Specially Prepared for H.M. Forces in Middle East* (undated). Jerusalem: Steimatzky Publishing Co. Ltd.

ABC women

I could not entirely verify the circumstances in which the conjoined naming of the *Fr. Vester & Co., The American Colony Store* happened. In 1923 the matriarch of the colony's first generation, Anna Spafford, dies. At this time the store, the American Colony's single most valuable commercial asset, is registered in the names of her daughters' two husbands, one of these being a Frederick Vester. However, the name is already used as is illustrated in the business's letterhead from as early as 1909, an example of which is to be found in a Harvard digital collection. I have also read that the conjoining of names occurs after the American Colony purchases a curio store from the father of Anna Spafford's son-in-law, Frederick, and that this is how the name comes to pass.

- Lesk, Alexandra L (2004). 'A diachronic examination of the Erechtheion and its reception'. PhD thesis, University of Cincinnati, pp. 545–546.

The Roma

- Wolfe, Patrick (2006). 'Settler colonialism and the elimination of the native'. *Journal of Genocide Research* 8 (4): pp. 387–409; p. 388.

Italian Hospital

The curly-haired Palestinian noted on page 98 in the chapter, 'Revenge', also has an eagle eye for detail. In the first printing of the book, at page 93, I spoke of the Jordan running through Amman. This claim, he told me, was one of the factual errors that led to the deceptions of Norma Khouri's hoax memoir, *Forbidden Love*, being exposed. I have since confirmed that what Ali was speaking of was the Seil Amman, a stream or rivulet, that ran through the downtown area, and was concreted over in the 1960s. The Seil joined with the larger Zarqa River which in turn flows into the Jordan. I credit my own linguistic deficiencies, which stretched Ali's accommodations to me in English, for this error.

Revenge

Dad is quite breathless after this entry, he just says, *that was an epic!*

- Ali, Taha Muhamad (2007). 'Revenge'. In *Two Lines XIV: World writing in translation*. Translated by Peter Cole, Yahya Hijaza and Gabriel Levin. San Francisco: Centre for the Art of Translation, pp. 4–11.
- *Divine Intervention: A chronicle of love and pain* (2002). Directed by Elia Suleiman. [Feature Film]. USA: Avatar Films.
- *Salt of This Sea* (2008). Directed by Annemarie Jacir. [Feature Film]. France: Pyramide Distribution.
- *Taha* (2018) by Amer Hlehel. Directed by Amir Zizar Zubai [Arts Centre, Melbourne, July 13].

It is to my regret that an earlier parenthetical narrative in this chapter was not retained. It detailed a 2014 theatre piece, *Wael Zuaiter: Unknown*, made by radio documentarian Jesse Cox. The show portrayed the life and assassination of the Palestinian intellectual Wael Zuaiter, the first of a series of prominent Palestinians to be murdered disgracefully by *Mossad* following the 1972 Summer Olympic Games in Munich. Zuaiter's partner was the Australian artist Janet Venn-Brown who, being Jesse's great aunt, had led him to this story. Four years later, when I attended *Taha* with my father, I heard from the former director of Theatre Works who had programmed Jesse's piece, that he had died very suddenly not many months earlier. All this I wove into the opening of 'Revenge', but later removed again.

Several months after publication of this book, the Powerful Stories Network invited me to participate in a conversation for their collective. After the talk, a slight and energetic woman introduced herself to me as Louise. She said she had missed the talk entirely, but wanted to speak with me all the same. I learnt only later that this was Wael and Janet's niece, and Jesse's mother. There was something about Louise that made me instantly regret this earlier editing decision; and such has been the genuine feeling and depth of our subsequent exchanges, that it became a matter of importance to restore all three of these loved names to a future printing, alongside Louise's, so that they too might dwell here together on my page.

Fil mish mish

On the subject of drive-sides, I later learn that garages offered conversion services. The process is expensive and not widely adopted. The Mandate moment is too late to gain control of vehicular order. The only response left is the liberal display of warning signs regarding drive sides, which become, during this period, ubiquitous.

- Adil, Alev (2004). *Venus Infers.* London: NE Publications, pp. 66–67; p. 66.
- *Divine Intervention: A chronicle of love and pain* (2002). Directed by Elia Suleiman. [Feature Film]. USA: Avatar Films.
- Said, Edward W (1984). 'Permission to narrate'. *Journal of Palestine Studies* 13 (3): pp. 27–48; p. 30.

Mr Settler-Colonialism

The song from which the title of the infamous *Operation Cast Lead* was derived – which in its time (2008–9) represented an unprecedented bombardment on Gaza with an appalling human cost for Palestinian people, though it was not the first of its kind – is taken from the lyrics of a poem by H N Bialik. The poem is for Hanukkah, but its recent composition makes it a piece of Zionist cultural heritage rather than a matter of longstanding tradition. It is noted further by my friend that the name of the operation was an efficient propaganda in its evocation of childhood memories. The lyrics of the poem, should you seek them out, hardly convey what the legacy of that massacre now evokes.

Road trip

In their early years in Newport, Irene recounts the family would forage for artichokes which grew wild near the quarry on Johnstone Street, and which Ellen would afterwards stuff. Irene recounts also the mortification of this task, for fear an acquaintance would spy their car stopping to pick up such weeds.

- *Extreme Rambling (walking the wall)* (2012) by Mark Thomas. [Trades Hall, Melbourne, April 20].
- Hanafi, Sari (2013). 'Explaining spacio-cide in the Palestinian territory: Colonization, separation, and state of exception'. *Current Sociology* 61(2): pp. 190–205.

Mamillah

- Advertisement (1944). *The Palestine Post*, April 12, p. 2.
- Advertisement (1935). *The Palestine Post*, June 4, p. 4.

- Nesnas, Antoine D (2022). 'Childhood Memories'. *This Week in Palestine* 289, May: pp. 20–27; p. 25.
- Pappé, Ilan (2006). *The Ethnic Cleansing of Palestine*. Oxford: Oneworld, p. 226.
- Vilnay, Zev (1941). *Steimatzky's Palestine Guide*. Jerusalem: Steimatzky Publishing Co.
- Zananiri, Sary (2015). *Unpicking Jerusalem: A re-examination of the archives*. [Exhibition Notes]. Collingwood: Little Woods.

Visit Palestine

In quite a nice story I meet Issam by chance and learn that he is a relative of mine, and that we know intimate things about each other's pasts though nothing of one another's lives. Later I find an original studio portrait of his mother's wedding at Juju's house. This is a tangible iteration of Nakba.

- Green, David B (2016). '1905: The Man who would design the "Visit Palestine" poster is born'. *Haaretz*, May 13.
- Nassar, Issam (2005). 'Jerusalem in nineteenth-century English travel narratives'. In *Pilgrims, Lepers and Stuffed Cabbages*, edited by Issam Nassar and Salim Tamari. Jerusalem: Institute of Jerusaelm Studies, pp. 38–63; p. 53. Quote from Karl Baedeker (1876) cited in Nassar.
- Newby, Eric (1985). *A Book of Travellers' Tales*. London: Picador, p. 280.

Fruits of the Loom

Dad says of this entry, *have you heard the story about the new priest and the bishop? The priest says, how was the sermon, and the bishop says, it's a good start but there's room for improvement, for example there were ten commandments, not twelve, and Jesus had twelve disciples not ten.* So I have changed the weight of the freekeh that Najla sends with us to reflect this remark.

- Johnson, Penny and Raja Shehadeh, eds (2013). *Seeking Palestine: New Palestinian writing on exile and home*. Massachusetts: Olive Branch Press.
- Manning, Peter (2018). *Representing Palestine: Media and journalism in Australia since World War I*. London: I.B. Tauris, p. 138.

Pa and the Turks (in Palestine)

The reference to St George and the Dragon Church comes from Juju's memories of a story Taata Barbara must have told her. I found this in some handwritten annotations she made while reading the edited collection *Seeking Palestine* (though my edition does not correlate to the page numbers Juju has written). This is likely referring to the St George Monastery and Church, in Al-Khader, a town named after the saint for which the monastery is also named.

- Aaronsohn, Alexander (2017). *With the Turks in Palestine*. Edited by Robert Pascoe. Redland Bay: Connor Court Publishing, p. 56.

Snow fight

- Beinart, Peter (2021). 'A Jewish case for Palestinian refugee return'. *Guardian*, May 18.

- El-Asmar, Fouzi (1978). *To be an Arab in Israel.* Beirut: The Institute for Palestine Studies, pp. 60–61.
- Morris, Benny (2002). 'Arafat didn't negotiate – he just kept saying no'. *Guardian*, May 23.

(Not Running), in Ramallah

This references the title of an artist book, Guy Mannes-Abbott (2012) *In Ramallah, Running*, London: Black Dog Publishing.

Skeletons

- *The Palestine Gazette: Extraordinary issue* (1937). No. 733. October 28.

This way to the bomb shelter

- Pappé, Ilan (2014). *The Idea of Israel: A history of power and knowledge.* London: Verso, p. 177.
- *To See If I'm Smiling* (2007). Directed by Tamar Yarom [Feature Documentary Film]. Ruth Diskin Films.

Traveller, welcome!

- Afif, P and G M Sahhar (1931). *Travellers' Note-Book for Palestine.* Jerusalem: The Commercial Press.
- 'More Aids to Tourists' (1935). *The Palestine Post*, February 3, p. 7.
- Sahhar, George M and Morcos Essa (1935). *The Traveller's Companion to the Holy Land: Being a concise and accurate guide and easy reference when travelling through Palestine, Syria and Transjordania.* Jerusalem: The Modern Press.

Jerusalem syndrome

The quote from George Barker is apparently a thing he confessed to his biographer, Robert Fraser, and which is used in the various blurbs to describe the 2002 publication of *The Chameleon Poet: A life of George Barker.* London: Pimlico.

- Said, Edward W (2000). 'On lost causes'. In *Reflections on Exile and Other Literary and Cultural Essays.* London: Granta, pp. 527–553, p. 553.
- Saner, Emine (2018). 'What is Jerusalem syndrome?'. *Guardian*, January 17.
- Sherwood, Harriet (2018). 'British tourist missing in Israel may have Jerusalem syndrome'. *Guardian*, January 17.

Our local parish

- Timmer, Jaap (2015). 'Building Jerusalem in North Malaita, Solomon Islands'. *Oceania*, 85 (3): pp. 299–314; p. 304.
- Newby, Eric (1985). *A Book of Travellers' Tales.* London: Picador, p. 282.

Hands

The nerves in Ellen's damaged finger became desensitised. It had been this finger with which she would test the temperature of milk when making yoghurt, and for a period after the accident, her yoghurt refused to set. Finally, at the urging of Andoni, she employed a different finger for yoghurt making.

An exception cannot be compared

- Améry, Jean (1980). *At the Mind's Limits: Contemplations by a survivor on Auschwitz and its realities.* Trans. Sidney Rosenfeld & Stella P Rosenfeld. Bloomington: Indiana University Press. See particularly 'Resentments', pp. 62–81.
- Davis, Uri (2003). *Apartheid Israel: Possibilities for the struggle within.* London: Zed Books.
- Finkelstein, Norman G (2000). *The Holocaust Industry: Reflections on the exploitation of Jewish suffering.* 2nd Edition. London: Verso.
- Hage, Ghassan (2003). *Against Paranoid Nationalism: Searching for hope in a shrinking society.* Sydney: Pluto Press.
- Herzl, Theodore (1988). *The Jewish State.* New York: Dover Publications Inc (based on the first English language edition, *A Jewish State* (1896) trans. Sylvie d'Avigdor).
- Larkin, Philip (1964). 'Afternoons'. In *The Whitsun Weddings.* London: Faber and Faber, p. 44.
- Massad, Joseph (2006). *The Persistence of the Palestinian Question: Essays on Zionism and the Palestinians.* London: Routledge, pp. 156–159; p. 161.
- Zertal, Idith (2005). *Israel's Holocaust and the Politics of Nationhood.* Trans. Chaya Galai. Cambridge: Cambridge University Press.

My diaspora

On more than one live recording of 'Mississippi Goddamn', Nina Simone can be heard to exclaim this at the end of the rendition.

- Labadi, Taher (2018). 'The Palestinian diaspora and the state-building process'. *Arab Reform Initiative*, December 5.
- Pinter, Harold (2005). *Death etc.* New York: Grove Press, p. 3.
- *The Law in These Parts* (2011). Directed by Ra'anan Alexandrowicz. [Feature Documentary Film]. Roco Films International.

Who are the Palestinians?

- Vladimir Jabotinsky in 1923, quoted in Brenner, Lenni (1984). *The Iron Wall: Zionist revisionism from Jabotinsky to Shamir.* London: Zed Books, p. 74.
- Erlanger, Steve and Taghreed El-Khodary (2007). 'Hamas seizes broad control in Gaza Strip'. *New York Times*, June 14.
- David Ben-Gurion quoted by Goldmann, Nahum (1978). *The Jewish Paradox.* New York: Fred Jordan Books, p. 99.
- Hage, Ghassan (2010). 'On Narcissistic Victimhood'. In *Gaza: Morality, law and politics*, edited by Raimond Gaita. Crawley: UWA Publishing, pp. 101–126; pp. 106–107.
- Jacir, Emily (2008). 'Some things I probably should not say and some things I should have said (fragments of a diary)'. In

Guy Mannes-Abbott (2012). *In Ramallah, Running.* London: Black Dog Publishing, pp. 141–151; p. 150.

- Qabbani, Nizar (2006). 'Twelve roses in Balqis's hair'. In *On Entering the Sea: The erotic and other poetry of Nizar Qabbani.* Translated by Lena Jayyusi and WS Merwin. North Hampton: Interlink Books, pp. 64–66; p. 65.

Portraiture

- Shaheer, Jameela (1973). *Arab World Cook Book.* Saudi Arabia: The International Bookshops, p. 38.
- Stark, Freya (1945). *East Is West.* London: John Murray.

The Semiramis Hotel

- Hourani, Hasib (2024). *rock flight.* Artarmon: Giramondo, p. 75.
- Krystall, Nathan (1998). 'The de-Arabization of West Jerusalem 1947–1950'. *Journal of Palestine Studies* 27 (2): pp. 5–22; p. 7.
- Krystall, Nathan (1999). 'The Fall of the New City 1947–1950'. In *Jerusalem 1948: The Arab neighbourhoods and their fate in the war,* edited by Salim Tamari. Jerusalem & Bethlehem: Institute of Jerusalem Studies & Badil Resource Centre, pp. 92–153; p. 97; p. 102; pp. 134–135.
- Sakakini, Hala (1990). *Jerusalem and I: A personal record.* Jordan: Economic Press Co, p. 111.

8 Asa Street

- Abu-Sitta, Salman (1999). 'Documenting Arab property in West Jerusalem: B. Notes on the Landowners record of the UN Conciliation Commission for Palestine for Urban West Jerusalem in 1948'. In *Jerusalem 1948: The Arab neighbourhoods and their fate in the war,* edited by Salim Tamari. Jerusalem & Bethlehem: Institute of Jerusalem Studies & Badil Resource Centre, pp. 240–257; p. 244.
- Darwish, Mahmoud (2009). 'Take care of the stags, Father'. In *If I Were Another.* Translated by Fady Joudah. New York: Farrar Straus and Giroux, pp. 9–15; p. 12.

A PARTIAL FAMILY TREE

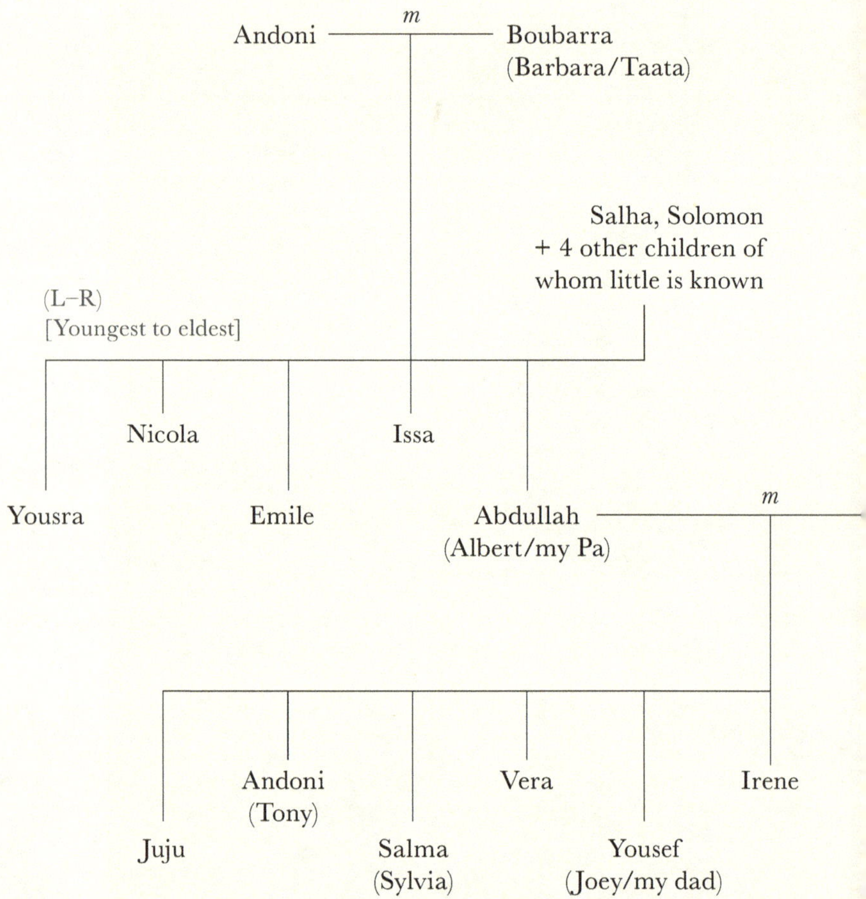

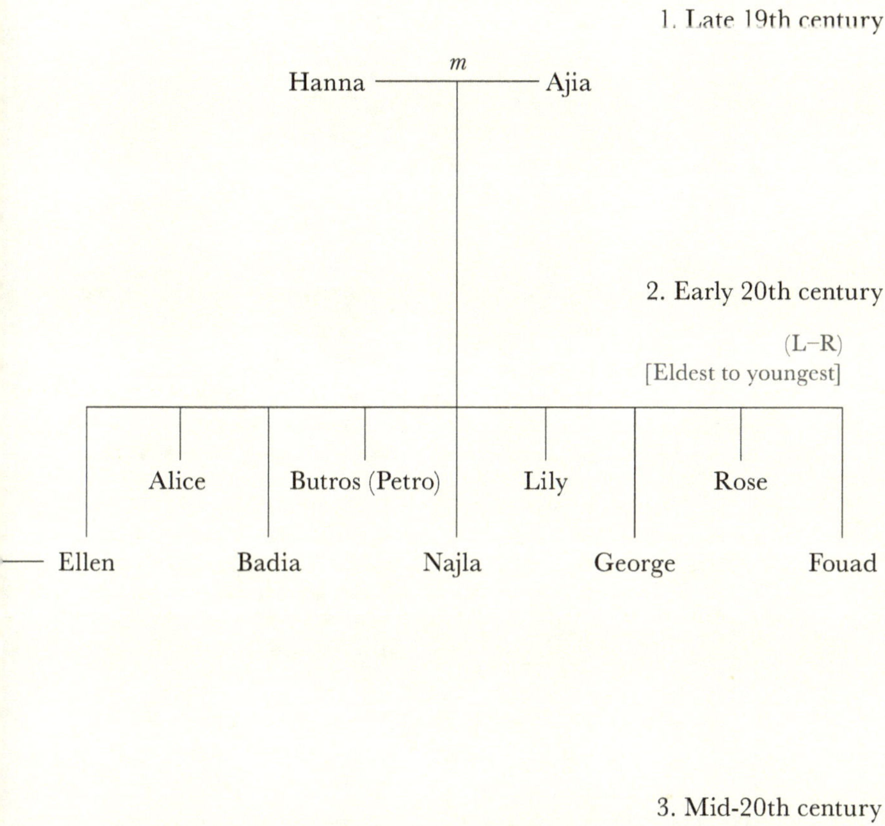
1. Late 19th century
m
Hanna
Ajia
2. Early 20th century
(L–R)
[Eldest to youngest]
Alice
Butros (Petro)
Lily
Rose
Ellen
Badia
Najla
George
Fouad
3. Mid-20th century

LIST OF IMAGES

ACKNOWLEDGMENTS

As a Palestinian writer in diaspora, I am acutely aware that I have spent my life on the unceded lands of the Wurundjeri people; I can only remain acutely aware of this fact, so entwined with my own writing practice and person. What is to be done with a settler? I have no conclusive answer to that question, but I am certain that a settler must cede space of all kinds. I will always be in the debt of First Nations people who have made space and platforms for Palestinian voices. Thank you to all my First Nations friends and colleagues for the immense solidarity you have shown me, and us, particularly during the genocide in Gaza. Yours is an ongoing lesson in humility, and the power and necessity of intersectional struggle. In solidarity always, and until liberation.

The first draft of this book was written in a frenzy, the structure for telling the story of diaspora, in ferment for many years in my mind, suddenly arrived as if by something divine, the framework on which to hang the ephemera of diaspora and of a diaspora whose history has been occluded and negated. As I started to understand what I was creating I would ring my father each time I completed a chapter – or entry as I referred to them. Separated by lockdown restrictions and following the death of my grandmother Ellen's last sister, Aunty Najla, Dad and I shared in another reality beyond either the domestic world of a pandemic or the imposition of an Occupation on every Palestinian, wherever they now are. For this, my deepest and most heartfelt thanks to my father, Joseph Sahhar, who offered me memories and stories while I wrote, and sometimes learnt things from me too. It is one of the best things we have done together. Thank you, Dad.

To all my family, particularly to my mother, Maxine, my brother, Julian, my aunts – Juju, Salma, Vera and Irene (who read a late version of the work and to whom and for which special thanks is owed). To those who are no longer with us – Abdullah and Ellen, my grandparents, their firstborn son Tony, my great-aunt Najla, and all the other great-aunts and -uncles, most of whom I never met, but of whom I have thought often. To my vast network of cousins, particularly Carey, Christoph, Di, Evan, George, Issam, Paul, Raja, Rasha, Rhema, Robert and Sophia.

To my first writing mentor, Marion May Campbell, who read with such electric enthusiasm the first draft of this book and spurred me on immeasurably. I am extraordinarily fortunate to have met you: first as a teacher, when you helped me find my voice; and then as a friend, when you performed this already immense service a second time. Above all, you have made writing a reality for me.

To Randa Abdel-Fattah and Arnold Zable, two early and equally encouraging readers who believed in what this book could be. To other vital friends who have read, advocated for or encouraged me in this process: Michael Mohammed Ahmad, Jumana Bayeh, Tamar Blickstein, Michael Griffiths, Zoe Holman, Keren Rubinstein and Shannon Woodcock – thank you each for these extraordinary gifts.

To Maeve Wolfe, who might have been included above, but who unexpectedly did not get to see the book in its finished form. I am pleased to have shared an earlier version of

'Mr Settler-Colonialism' with Maeve, who wrote with her simple and generous appreciation, *that brought a tear to my eye.* Thank you, Maeve. You will always now bring a tear to mine.

To my incredible diaspora community of Palestinian warriors and friends, far too many to name but especially to Ahmad Al-Mousa and Nader Ruhayel, who have let me sift instances from our lives; and to Hasib Hourani and Sara Saleh, who inspired me to write creatively again. To Sary Zananiri for all these things, and for engaging with the book as a reader. You have all sustained me, in ways I can hardly put words to.

To the literary havens who have encouraged my return to creative practice, particularly Evelyn Araluen and Jonathan Dunk at *Overland*, Kent MacCarter at *Cordite*, Jessica Wilkinson at *Rabbit*, and my friends at Sweatshop Literacy Movement. I should note that an earlier version of 'Ma'amoul' was published in *Griffith Review* as 'Easter cakes', and my thanks to Carody Culver in particular for this vote of confidence in my then unsigned manuscript.

To my Next Chapter mentor, Jeanine Leane, who worked through several revisions with me and in whom I could not have asked for a more committed mentor nor a greater friend to have in my corner. Thank you also to my Next Chapter cohort, particularly Tristen Harwood, Brooke Maddison, Mykaela Saunders and Anne-Marie Te Whiu, who have in so many ways enriched my life and creative practice.

To all those who have agreed to support the book with your generous endorsements, some named already, and also to Ghassan Hage and Antony Loewenstein. With great thanks.

To the NewSouth team, particularly Joumana Awad, my thoughtful and patient copyeditor, Jocelyn Hungerford, and especially Harriet McInerney. There was not a more sensitive and astute editor to be found for this project, who shared in my vision, understood immediately what I was doing and sometimes articulated it better than I could, and advised me so well.

Support for writing development is a crucial part of the literary ecology and I was fortunate to receive several avenues of development funding for this book. With thanks to the Wheeler Centre for a Next Chapter Fellowship and to all the lovely staff there for their ongoing support of my work, and to the Neilma Sidney Literary Travel Fund that supported a trip to Jerusalem in 2023.

Thank you to the Palestinian staff at the Kenyon Institute, particularly Sami who has welcomed me more than once, and to the many interesting people I have met there in the kitchen or on the beautiful front terrace. To the generosity also of two vital Palestinian institutions – the Khazaaen Archive and the Palestinian Museum – for permission to use two of the images that appear in these pages.

To my keffiyeh-coloured cat, Omar Mittens, who though not yet born when the first draft was written, encouraged me with his cheer and discipline, in equal measures, through the long process of bringing a draft manuscript to publication.

And above all, words can hardly convey either my love or the thanks that are owed to Justin Tighe, my greatest ally and dearest friend. You have been with me each step of the way and sometimes walked for us both when I could do no other than Palestine. If you have flagged, I have never once known it. There is no greater generosity than that which you have given me, nor any greater love than what I will always offer you in return.

Underwood & Underwood, Publishers.
(10) The Jaffa Gate—from outside—Jerusalem, Palestine.

FSC
www.fsc.org
MIX
Papier | Fördert
gute Waldnutzung
FSC® C083411

Zeitfracht Medien GmbH
Ferdinand-Jühlke-Straße 7
99095 Erfurt, Deutschland
produktsicherheit@kolibri360.de